RESURRECTION

RESURRECTION

The Power of God for Christians and Jews

Kevin J. Madigan and Jon D. Levenson

Yale University Press
New Haven & London

Published with assistance from the Kingsley Trust Association Publication
Fund established by the Scroll and Key Society of Yale College.

Set in Postscript Electra and Trajan types by The Composing Room of Michigan, Inc.
Printed in the United States of America.

Library of Congress Cataloging-in-Publication Data

Madigan, Kevin, 1960–
Resurrection : the power of God for Christians and Jews / Kevin J. Madigan and
Jon D. Levenson.
p. cm.
Includes bibliographical references and indexes.
ISBN 978-0-300-12277-0 (cloth : alk. paper)
1. Resurrection.   2. Christianity and other religions—Judaism.   3. Judaism—
Relations—Christianity.   I. Levenson, Jon Douglas.   II. Title.
BL505.M33 2008
236′.8—dc22
2007040498

10 9 8 7 6 5 4 3 2 1

Uxoribus Nostris Excellentibus Eminentibusque
Stephanie Paulsell et Beverly Levenson
Hunc Librum Magno Cum Amore
Dedicamus.

CONTENTS

Preface xi

Acknowledgments xv

Abbreviations xvii

ONE Christian Hope and Its Jewish Roots 1
"He is risen!" 1,   Restoring Israel 5,   Jesus of Nazareth,
Apocalyptic Prophet 9,   New Heaven, New Earth, and New
Temple 17,   An Eschatological Sign to the People 20,
Resurrection Life and the Body 21

TWO The First Fruits of Those Who Have Died 24
Jesus as the First of Many 24,   Imminence 27,   The Church
as Israel 29,   Participation in Christ 36,   What Kind
of Resurrected Body? 39

THREE A Journey to Sheol (and Back) 42
Did Jesus and Paul Find Resurrection in the Bible? 42,
The Land of No Return 42,   Existing without Living 45,
"When my life was ebbing away, I called the LORD to mind" 48,
Communicating with the Dead 54,   The Passages That
Aren't There (and What They Tell Us) 62,   Returning
from the Land of No Return 66

FOUR Who Goes to Sheol—and Who Does Not 69
When and Why Sheol Is Mentioned 69,   Sheol Is Not Hell 75,
Death Defanged 80

FIVE Heaven on Earth 81
The Temple as the Garden of Eden 81,   Immortality
in the House of the LORD 89,   Adam Foresees the Destruction
of the Temple 96,   "You will receive me with glory" 98,
Confidence in the Face of Death 104

SIX How Birth Reverses Death 107
Individual and Family in Biblical Israel 107,   The Functional
Equivalent of Resurrection 111,   The Name Survives Death 117,
A Foretaste of Resurrection 119

SEVEN The Death and Resurrection of the Promised Son 121
"Pick up your son" 121,   Four Little Stories with One
Big Message 126,   A Look Ahead, 130

EIGHT Revival in Two Modes 132
Zion's Children Return to Their Mother 132,   The Widow
Re-Wed (and to the Same Husband) 143,   Israel's Exodus from
the Grave 146,   Mortal Israelites and Immortal Israel 152

NINE "I deal death and give life" 156
Inevitable Death and the Promise of Life 156,   "He shall turn
back from his ways and live" 165,   From Death to Life 168

TEN The Great Awakening 171
The Reversal 171,   Why Resurrection? A False Answer 180,
"Oh, let Your dead revive!" 185,   The Deeper Roots of
Resurrection 188,   The Victory of the Divine Warrior 192,
Summary: Old and New in Resurrection 196

ELEVEN The Least Known Teaching in Judaism 201
"Powerful to save" 201, An Obligation, Not an Option 206,
Doubts and Reforms 213

TWELVE What Was Wrong with the Gnostic Gospel? 221
Skeptics and Heretics 221, Dualism 222, Dry Bones,
Restoration, and Resurrection 227, Resurrection
and the Power of God 229, The Flesh 231, Resurrection,
Truth, and Power 234

THIRTEEN The Redeemed Life—in the Here and Now 235
Christians and Jews 235, The New Life of the Christian 237,
The Eucharist 243, The Lord's Prayer 245, Torah and
Eternal Life 246, Resurrection at Sinai 254,
Christians and Jews—Again 256

Notes 259

Index of Primary Sources 269

General Index 280

PREFACE

This is a book by a Christian and a Jew, written for religious and nonreligious people alike, about a teaching central to both our traditions: the teaching that at the end of time God will cause the dead to live again. Although this expectation, known as the resurrection of the dead, has been a part of Christianity from its beginnings nearly two thousand years ago, and a part of Judaism even longer, it is widely misunderstood by both believers and nonbelievers. We intend this book to clear up some of the confusion by telling the fascinating but little-known story of the origins of the belief in resurrection, exploring why in ancient times some Christians and Jews actually opposed the teaching, and showing why others insisted that the belief was essential to their faith and must never be surrendered or reinterpreted out of existence. Along the way, we explore a neglected continuity between Christianity and Judaism, and in our last chapter, we discuss ways in which these two religious traditions relate their respective practices in the here-and-now to the new life that they believe will follow upon the anticipated resurrection.

For whom have we written this book? We have not had our fellow scholars primarily in mind, but rather the layperson who may have an interest in the Bible and in ancient Christianity and Judaism but lacks specialized training in those highly technical and often frustrating subjects, with all their foreign terms and complex histories. Our goal is to communicate to a larger readership some of the rich insights into the resurrection of the dead that have emerged among scholars of antiquity in recent decades and yet mostly remain, unfortunately, unknown to the general public.

One of the most common misunderstandings of resurrection is that it is the same thing as immortality, that is, life after death. Many people think that "resurrection" is just an old-fashioned religious word for the survival of our souls after the inevitable deaths of our bodies. In fact, however, resurrection envisions the return of the *whole* person, body and soul together, not simply the continuing survival of his or her "spiritual" dimension. It is thus not at all a natural event—what could be more natural than death?—but rather a reversal of death brought about by the God who is the creator of nature and thus the sole master over it. Indeed, for ancient Christians and for their contemporaries, the early Talmudic rabbis, the resurrection of the dead was the prime example of the incomparable power of God.

The hope that the dead would rise from the grave thus rested not on an analysis of human nature but on the conviction that God would prove faithful to his promises. It was a matter of faith in the classical biblical understanding of the word: unwavering trust in God. It did not, in the first instance, speak to the self-interested question, "Will I have life after death?" but to the more encompassing—and vastly more profound—question, "Will God prove faithful to his promises?"

Because Christians associate "the Resurrection" (with a capital R) with the reports in the gospels of Jesus' rising from his grave, they are often surprised to find that Jews had believed in resurrection long before Christianity emerged. And Christians and Jews alike who think that Judaism is defined by the plain sense of the Hebrew Bible (or Old Testament, as Christians eventually came to call it) may for that reason, too, think that resurrection was a Christian innovation with no parallel in Judaism. For the Hebrew Bible rarely speaks of the reversal of death. But in this book we show that things were actually quite different. The Hebrew Bible occasionally attests to God's power over death and even tells a few stories of how he raised dead individuals. But, more centrally, it speaks with great frequency of God's everlasting promise to Israel, the Jewish people, a promise that they would recover from even the most deadly adversity. In that promise, we show, lay the seeds of the belief in a future resurrection of the dead, brought about by the faithfulness of the God of Israel to the people Israel. About the time that the Christian church was emerging, rabbis found the promise of resurrection even in the five books of Moses—or the Pentateuch—and they made the belief in resurrection an obligatory aspect of Judaism. Although both Christians and Jews often think otherwise, one cannot understand Jesus or the early church apart from ancient Judaism in general and the question of how the Jews read their scriptures in particular.

This is the story we tell. Let it begin.

Acknowledgments

The idea for this volume originally came from our editor at Yale University Press, Christopher Rogers, to whom abundant thanks are obviously due, both for the suggestion itself and for all his help during the time the book was being written and produced. We are also indebted to his assistant, Laura Davulis, and to our copy editor, Jessie Dolch, for their assistance. Kevin Madigan researched some and wrote all of his chapters for this volume while a Henry R. Luce III Senior Fellow in Theology in 2006–07. We would like to thank the Henry Luce Foundation and the Association of Theological Schools for their support and generosity.

Mark A. Nussberger and Jonathan Kaplan served us admirably with their expert proofreading and stylistic suggestions, not to mention some keen and helpful remarks about more substantive matters. They deserve our gratitude. Both they and Zach Matus cheerfully supplied us with books and articles. Sarah Lefebvre, one of our fine faculty assistants at Harvard Divinity School, was also of important assistance to us and we thank her. Dr. Suzanne Smith offered us sage advice on each chapter. We owe a debt of gratitude as well to the anonymous reviewers whom Yale University Press engaged to evaluate our manuscript, many of whose suggestions for improvement we have implemented. The errors that remain are, of course, the sole responsibility of the authors.

Quotations from the Hebrew Bible are taken from *Tanakh* (Philadelphia: Jewish Publication Society, 5746/1985), unless otherwise indicated. In the notes, we refer to this translation as the NJPS (for the New Jewish Publication Society version). As in the NJPS, the enumeration of chapters and verses follows the Hebrew, not the English, where there is a divergence. Citations from the New Testament and the Apocrypha are taken from the New Revised Standard Version (NRSV). The sources of nonbiblical quotations are given in the notes.

We have rendered the four-letter proper name of the God of Israel without vowels in this volume, even when quoting authors who inserted the vowels, and we have indicated the difference by putting the term in brackets: [Yʜwʜ]. Most of the time, following ancient and modern convention, we simply translate the term as Lᴏʀᴅ, as does the NJPS.

ABBREVIATIONS

Hebrew Bible

1 Chr	1 Chronicles
Dan	Daniel
Deut	Deuteronomy
Exod	Exodus
Ezek	Ezekiel
Gen	Genesis
Hos	Hosea
Isa	Isaiah
Jer	Jeremiah
Jon	Jonah
Josh	Joshua
Judg	Judges
1 Kgs	1 Kings
2 Kgs	2 Kings
Lam	Lamentations
Lev	Leviticus
Mal	Malachi
Mic	Micah
Num	Numbers
Prov	Proverbs
Ps	Psalms
Qoh	Qohelet (Ecclesiastes)
1 Sam	1 Samuel

2 Sam	2 Samuel
Song	Song of Songs (Song of Solomon, Canticles)
Zech	Zechariah

Rabbinic Literature

Avod. Zara	*Avodah Zarah*
b.	*Babylonian Talmud*
B. Bat.	*Bava Batra*
Ber.	*Berakhot*
Gen. Rab.	*Genesis Rabbah*
m.	*Mishnah*
Meg.	*Megillah*
Num. Rab.	*Numbers Rabbah*
Qidd.	*Qiddushin*
Sanh.	*Sanhedrin*
Shab.	*Shabbat*
Suk.	*Sukkah*
Tam.	*Tamid*

Other Ancient Jewish Literature

Jub	Jubilees
2 Macc	2 Maccabees
Sir	Wisdom of Joshua ben Sira (Ecclesiasticus)
Tob	Tobit

New Testament

Acts	Acts of the Apostles
1 Cor	1 Corinthians
2 Cor	2 Corinthians
Eph	Ephesians
Gal	Galatians
Matt	Gospel of Matthew
Phil	Philippians
Rom	Romans
1 Thess	1 Thessalonians

CHRISTIAN HOPE AND
ITS JEWISH ROOTS

"HE IS RISEN!"

Darkness prevailed early that spring morning in Jerusalem. It was the middle of the Jewish month of Nisan, just at the start of the feast of Passover, perhaps around the year 30 C.E. Shortly after Jesus of Nazareth's grisly execution by crucifixion, his friends and followers gathered, in fidelity to long practice and the prescription of the Torah, or "the Law," to observe the Sabbath. We can only imagine their feelings; presumably they were crushed with shock and despair.

Within a day or so of Jesus' death, several of his female followers, including those who had witnessed his death and burial, walked to his tomb. Perhaps they went to anoint his body, perhaps merely to view his place of burial. Arriving at the sepulcher, they were startled at what they saw: a stone slab covering the entryway had somehow been moved from the tomb. They went in. To their astonishment, the dead prophet's body, the body of their lord and leader—their "king"—was gone and his tomb empty. They became convinced that he who had died had been restored to life. He had been "raised." The saga that had begun with Jesus' humiliating death and his languishing, lifeless, in a criminal's tomb concludes, amazingly—miraculously—with his victorious exodus from the grave.

"He is risen!" These three words are, needless to say, familiar to Christians. Hardly any sentence in their Bible, or any acclamation in the history of Christian worship, is better known or more precious to Christian believers. Proclaimed with jubilation annually at Easter, this affirmation expresses (among other things) the Christian conviction that in raising Jesus, God had forever broken the power of death itself; in so doing, he had, Christians believe, consummated the drama of divine salvation. These words also form the bedrock of the faith that God will raise all humankind at the end of time. On that claim, the larger truth of all Christian belief— expressed in its creeds and confessions of faith, in its preaching, and in its education of adults and children alike—has historically rested. As the apostle Paul first observed to the Corinthians, "If Christ has not been raised, then our proclamation has been in vain and your faith has been in vain" (1 Cor 15:14). One of the oldest extant Christian statements of faith, the so-called Apostles' Creed, written around 200 C.E., unambiguously declares that Jesus "rose from the dead on the third day." Similarly, the fourth-century Nicene Creed states that Jesus rose, significantly, "in fulfillment of the Scriptures." Both creeds explicitly look forward to the general resurrection of the dead. Christians around the world, or those who are members of "creedal" churches, are at one with the apostles when they recite these words and reaffirm their resurrection faith weekly on Sunday. We know, then, that these creedal words, familiar from the New Testament and the classic Christian statements of faith, and the belief in the resurrection they have inspired and authenticated, are of cardinal significance to Christian faith. Even more, resurrection is (or so many Christians have been taught to believe) not only central to Christian faith but *unique* to it. It is an article of the church's faith, the anchor of *Christian* hope.

And it *is* that. Yet Christian understandings of resurrection, along with the church's appreciation of its religious depth, its historical richness, and its reverberations, would be much impoverished if Christians thought that the expectation of resurrection were merely theirs. In particular, and what is most crucial, they would lose sight of the extent to which resurrection is rooted in the belief and practice of Judaism. Indeed, it occurs already in the Old Testament, the only scriptures the church knew at the time of Jesus (when it wasn't yet called the "Old Testament"). In fact, not only the notion of the resurrection of the dead, but the expression of God's vindication of Jesus in the language of resurrection, owes its origins to its parent religion, Judaism—or, to be more precise, to Judaism as it stood late in the Second Temple period (about 515 B.C.E., when the Temple was rebuilt after its destruction in 586 B.C.E. by the Babylonians, to 70 C.E., when the Romans destroyed it). This was the world of thought and practice of which Jesus and his followers partook and by which their piety was essentially formed.

To be sure, not every Jew or Christian in the ancient world believed in bodily resurrection. According to multiple sources, the "Sadducees," the priestly elite of Judea in the late Second Temple period, denied it. The Pharisees, another group that emerged during the same period, affirmed it, and it is with the Pharisees that Jesus has the most in common. Nor does every Jew or Christian believe it today—think, for example, of those for whom Christianity is summed up by this-worldly political and social action. Still, the affirmation that God would raise all from the dead remains a key normative claim in both historic traditions. Though Judaism and Christianity do not share belief in the messiahship of Jesus of Nazareth, nor in the reading of the Hebrew scriptures through the lens of the New Testament, many Jews and Christians have shared and do today affirm belief in the resurrection of the dead.

This may come as a surprise to Christian readers. But for Christians, not only is it important to realize that this shared belief links Christianity historically and theologically with the form of Judaism out of which it grew; understanding the Jewish matrix of Christian belief in the resurrection is imperative for at least two additional reasons. First, it enriches and deepens the Christian view of the significance of Jesus' resurrection and the general resurrection for which the church hopes and that it expects will happen at the end of history. More importantly, it helps to define the ancient and classical understanding of resurrection. Many ancient Jews and Christians held, unshakably, that resurrection was a bodily and communal event. They understood the classic scriptural sources and heritages of both traditions to maintain that God would raise the dead in their full humanity, or as we should say today, as a physico-psycho-social unity. The authoritative sources of the ongoing traditions in both Judaism and Christianity spoke of a resurrection of the whole person—body and soul, we might put it—and not simply the survival of some indestructible personal core or some divine dimension deep within ourselves. Many Christian writers throughout history—beginning with the author of the Apostles' Creed—have spoken of the resurrection simply as the *resurrectio carnis*, the resurrection of the flesh or body. Though they coexist with resurrection, categories like the "immortality of the soul" and the survival of the spirit or (much later) the posthumous endurance of individual consciousness do not express the richness or reality of classical Jewish and Christian views of resurrection, which are inevitably and self-consciously bodily and communal. When examined against the religious background out of which Christianity arose, the continuities between Christian views of resurrection and those of Judaism are quite striking—and for good reason!

In order to appreciate ancient Christian views of Jesus' resurrection in all their richness and historical complexity, we need to relate the Christian sources affirming resurrection specifically to the context of late Second Temple Judaism. From a political point of view, Judaism in Palestine was set and, in complex ways, shaped by eight or so centuries of almost continuous conquest, occupation, and domination by foreign powers. It is important neither to underestimate nor to exaggerate this fact, nor to simplify a picture that, not surprisingly, changed over time, even under conditions of nearly unbroken subjugation. It would also be a gross overstatement to suggest that Jewish religiousness during this period was molded *only*, or even primarily, by the grim realities of subjugation and submission. Jewish piety was, rather, primarily shaped by well-established internal norms and the long, deeply cherished memory of past communal experience, especially the conviction that God had chosen the people Israel, made a covenant with them, liberated them from bondage in Egypt, given them the Land of Israel, and bestowed upon them the Torah to instruct and guide them in right and God-pleasing worship and service. These caveats having been registered, however, the piety prevalent in the Judaism of Jesus' time and place was given a distinctive cast by the political matrix of foreign rule.

In the century before Jesus' birth and in the decades during and succeeding his career, Rome ruled Palestine (as the Romans were later to call it). In his campaign throughout the Near East, the brilliant tactician Pompey (106–48 B.C.E.), son-in-law and sometime ally of Julius Caesar, established Roman dominion in Jewish Palestine in 63 B.C.E. It is certainly possible to overstress the negative or oppressive effect of Roman overlordship. For one thing, precise geography means a great deal: living in Judea to the south and living in Galilee to the north, even at the same moment in history, were not quite the same experience. The degree of Roman presence was never so high in Galilee as in Judea. Precise chronology is also important. It would be wrong to suggest that Palestine was seething with resentment, or ready for revolt, throughout the period of Roman rule from Pompey through the emperor Hadrian (63 B.C.E.–135 C.E.) — though insurrectionist movements were afoot, and major revolts would occur at least twice during those two centuries. Rome had little desire to "Romanize" Palestine culturally; mainly, it was interested in the financial benefits that would flow to the homeland if the province remained stable. Again, it is important not to speculate from the known particular to the unknown general, especially in a case like this, where our sources are few and fragmentary. That many longed for freedom from Roman (or all foreign) rule is likely; that some violent (and more nonviolent) protest occurred is sure; that some expected God to establish his final reign on earth and restore Israel is true; that Rome was wary of uprising is certain. That *all* Jews were ready for violent revolt, or expected a Davidic messiah to free them, vanquish the Romans, and establish the final kingdom of God, while colorful material for movies, does not fit the literary and archaeological evidence.

RESTORING ISRAEL

The general fact of long domination by foreign powers surely helped shape one kind of Jewish piety: what E. P. Sanders and others have called "restoration eschatology." *Eschatology* refers to the events that Jews (and later Christians) believed God had ordained to occur at the end of history. *Restoration eschatology* arose in large part out of prophetic reaction to the Jewish experience of exile in Babylonia in the sixth century B.C.E., as well as out of reflection during the postexilic period on the experience of domination by outsiders. The experience of exile and subjugation, fused with the abiding conviction that God would remain true to his covenant, gave rise to the hope, expressed classically by the prophets, that God would "restore" Israel, the Jewish people. Despite present circumstances of exile or subjugation, the prophets affirmed, God would eventually establish his reign or kingdom. The forces dominating, frustrating, often even polluting and provoking Israel would ultimately and definitively be overthrown. The God of Israel would reclaim his throne, his capital city Jerusalem would be restored, and his palace, the Temple, rebuilt. The lost tribes would also be "gathered back in." The dead would rise and all would be judged by God. Consider the following text from Isa 26:19:

Oh, let Your dead revive!
Let corpses arise!
Awake and shout for joy,
For Your dew is like the dew on fresh growth;
You make the land of shades come to life.

Or this text from Dan 12:2–3:

[2]Many of those that sleep in the dust of the earth will awake, some to eternal life, others to reproaches, to everlasting abhorrence. [3]And the wise will be radiant like the bright expanse of sky, and those who lead the many to righteousness will be like the stars forever and ever

For the visionaries who authored these two texts, sleep is, of course, a metaphor for death. Both passages (whose views on resurrection would become widespread during the late Second Temple period) suggest that the righteous will be rewarded. God would, in the end, vindicate those who had suffered for him and raise them to glory. According to the book of Daniel, the wicked, too, will be raised to a new kind of existence; they will be forever disgraced and dishonored—and forever overthrown or displaced as leaders in this world. In the eyes of both books, Isaiah and Daniel, the God of life and of creation has the power, finally, to overcome death and the forces of this world that deal in death. In short, the God who had chosen the people Israel and had bound himself to guide and protect them would, in the last days, honor his unbreakable covenant and deliver them from oppression at the hands of the pagans and even from the reach of death. This ancient conviction, based in early Israelite tradition, could grow in strength among the people even if, or rather because, circumstances seemed particularly bleak or rulers especially iniquitous at the moment. Prophecies of the end times were cherished throughout the postexilic period. They may be said to have become "apocalyptic" when it was believed that the eschatological events they foretold were about to occur.

For our purposes, it is essential to remember that belief in resurrection was linked during this period to expectation of the dawning new age, to the belief that God was about to make a new creation and to vindicate his loyal people. The new creation is not to be identified with belief in an otherwordly "heaven," but with the regeneration of the present world, with the rectification of wrongs and the vindication of the righteous. Varied as the texts regarding resurrection are during the late Second Temple period, they do agree that it takes place in the context of divine judgment. As such, faith in the resurrection to come depended theologically on the prior conviction of the goodness, sovereignty, and above all justice of the God of Israel. Such faith was also linked to belief in the goodness of the created world, a point on which Jewish writings of this period would emphatically insist. Finally, resurrection was, as many scholars have pointed out, a potentially revolutionary doctrine, precisely because it is inevitably linked with the conviction that the God of justice would soon intervene to bring an end to the present age and inaugurate the age to come, an event that seemed to demand the exaltation of the righteous and the punishment of the wicked. Resurrection, in other words, was allied to the reversal both of death and of injustice. More specifically, it was linked with ending foreign oppression and the reversal of national misfortune. Jewish belief in resurrection was not, thus, only or even primarily about the ultimate destiny of mortal human beings. It was about God's righteousness, the vindication of those loyal to him, and the establishment of justice. The earth would give up its dead only in the context of the righting of Israel's wrongs, the punishment of the wicked, the restoration of the lost, the reconstruction of the holy city and the Temple, and the universal recognition of the LORD as the faithful God of justice.

Strong evidence suggests that restoration eschatology, involving many or most of these elements of expectant hope, was widespread during both the century before Jesus' death and the century in which he grew to maturity. Many (including Jesus) came to believe that the hopes of the prophetic tradition were about to be realized in God's last act in history

We know from the writings of the historian Josephus (who lived about 37–100 C.E.), the principal source for knowledge of Palestinian Judaism in the first century, that some of the prophetic books that contained eschatological material, above all the book of Daniel, were particularly popular during this period. In addition, we have to account for much literature that has not been incorporated into the Bible, written in the later centuries of the Second Temple period, texts such as the *First Book of Enoch*, the *Testament of Moses*, the *Second Book of Baruch*, a number of the so-called Jewish Sibylline oracles (prophetic writings), and the aptly named *Apoca-*

lypse of Abraham. Many of these expressed the classical hopes of restoration eschatology: that God was about to establish a new order; that all of Israel, especially the dispersed tribes, would be restored; that Israel would finally be freed from foreign dominion; and that Jerusalem and the Temple would be rebuilt—indeed that nature itself would be restored and renewed.

This, too, was the age in which the sectarian scrolls discovered at Qumran, on the edge of the Dead Sea, mostly took shape. These documents, first discovered in 1947 and known at the Dead Sea Scrolls, attest to a vivid expectation of the imminent end. Many of them are, in fact, shot through with apocalyptic expectation. Though we cannot be certain about every element of their religious regimen, the sect reflected in the Dead Sea Scrolls seems to have encouraged a rigorously separatist life. Dedicated to personal and communal purity, they followed a strict ascetical regime, and not only in matters of sexuality. Interestingly, John the Baptizer may have been one who eventually split off from the community to launch his own career as an apocalyptic preacher of repentance. In any case, a document found at Qumran that scholars often call the *War Rule* prophesies an apocalyptic battle that pits the "Sons of Darkness" against the "Sons of Light." One obscure fragment of this text, relying on Isa 11:4, reads:

> [The thickets of the forest] will be cut down with an ax, and Lebanon by a majestic one will fall. And there shall come a shoot from the Branch of David, and they will enter into judgment . . . and the Prince of the Congregation, the Branch [of David] will kill him by strokes and wounds.

The translation of this text is difficult, and some passages have provoked warm debate. What is clear is the expectation in the text of a Davidic messiah, judgment, and the punishment of the wicked—staples of the apocalyptic worldview of the late Second Temple period. In any event, the group that authored the Qumran findings was almost certainly devastated by the forces of the emperor Vespasian sometime during the Jewish-Roman war (66–73 C.E.). With the approach of the Roman army, the members of the group probably hid their scrolls in caves near the Dead Sea. Whatever the precise scenario, they left a vivid record of apocalyptic expectation in late Second Temple Judaism.

Another sign of widespread eschatological expectation was that a number of apocalyptic prophets also appeared in Roman Palestine in the first century, sometimes in direct response to Roman provocation. One of the few but infamous examples of gross Roman insensitivity to Jewish piety was the emperor Caligula's proposal that a statue of himself be placed in the Temple. His death in 41 C.E. prevented this from occurring, but such a shocking proposal could easily be read—and was read—as an apocalyptic sign. A Jewish prophet named Theudas emerged in the wake of Caligula's astonishing suggestion. Around him, a following of some size formed. Theudas' followers expected their leader to part the water of the Jordan, recalling the biblical account of the miraculous parting of the sea at the exodus from Egypt (Exod 14:21–23). Nonetheless, Theudas and his followers were mowed down by Roman cavalry. Around the same time (according to Josephus), a man named Judah the Galilean and his two sons, again motivated by hopes for the restoration of Israel, began fomenting rebellion. The Roman authorities crucified Judah's two sons. Another Jew, known only as "the Egyptian," gathered an enormous following or force in the desert. Not only does Josephus mention him, suggesting he had thirty thousand soldiers, but the New Testament book of Acts also refers to him, though with a much smaller force of only four thousand (Acts 21:38). According to Josephus, the Egyptian planned to march on Jerusalem. He expected that, at his command, the walls of the city would collapse—another miracle with deep resonance in Jewish history, this one harking back to the taking of the land under Joshua. The Egyptian and his followers were also thwarted before the promised restoration could be attempted. These are the apocalyptic prophets about which we know; there could well have been more.

JESUS OF NAZARETH, APOCALYPTIC PROPHET

For about a century now, many New Testament scholars, following the lead of Albert Schweitzer (1875–1965), have seen both Jesus and John the Baptizer as Jewish eschatological prophets who, like Judah and his sons, Theudas, the Egyptian, and presumably others, inhabited the cultural world of Jewish apocalyptic expectation and dwelt in the imaginative cosmos of Jewish apocalyptic literature. Naturally, not all scholars agree with Schweitzer's groundbreaking book, *The Quest of the Historical Jesus* (1906), in which the theologian and New Testament scholar (later an illustrious musician and humanitarian) argued his bold thesis. But scholars like E. P. Sanders and, more recently, Dale Allison have, to our minds, persuasively fortified the case Schweitzer presented, situating Jesus convincingly in his own first-century Palestinian Jewish context. The evidence for the Schweitzer thesis in its general contours is now extraordinarily strong.

We can begin to review this evidence by recalling that Jesus appears first to have allied himself with another Jewish apocalyptic prophet. John the Baptizer was himself a preacher of restoration eschatology. He preached hauntingly about the "coming wrath" of God, which was so close, he announced metaphorically, "Even now the ax is lying at the root of the trees" (Luke 3:9). God would punish those who did not produce good fruit and would reward the good—and do so very soon: "His winnowing fork is in his hand, to clear his threshing floor and to gather the wheat into his granary; but the chaff he will burn with unquenchable fire" (Luke 3:17). This fearsome apocalyptic prophet baptized Jesus. (Baptism, which derives from the Jewish practice of immersion in a special pool of water known as a *mikveh*, is ultimately rooted in the laws of ritual purity of the Hebrew Bible. At some point, such immersion came to be required for those converting to Judaism, and this may be the connection between John's practice and his announcement of the imminent arrival of the kingdom of God.) Jesus must have accepted John's basic message and initially been a member of the movement that gathered around the Baptizer. Why else would he have submitted to baptism at his hand?

When Jesus came to form his own movement after the Baptizer's death, his apocalyptic view of history did not change. Like the Baptizer, he felt the cosmos to be in the control of evil forces. God would soon overthrow these principalities and powers and establish his kingdom to replace the evil kingdoms of this world. Each of these things he felt to be imminent. Like John, Jesus may have seen it as his mission to proclaim that the eschatological events foretold by the prophets were about to transpire.

Actually, it seems ever more likely that Jesus was seen, and probably saw himself, as an apocalyptic prophet in the style of John the Baptizer. Our earliest sources appear to agree that some of his contemporaries acknowledged Jesus as such. Mark, the earliest gospel (written probably around 70 C.E.), reports that some identified him with John the Baptizer: "Some were saying, 'John the baptizer has been raised from the dead; and for this reason these powers are at work in him'" (Mark 6:14). A text from Matthew suggests that Jesus compared himself with the Baptizer: "[18]For John came neither eating nor drinking, and they say, 'He has a demon'; [19]the Son of Man came eating and drinking, and they say, 'Look, a glutton and a drunkard, a friend of tax collectors and sinners!' Yet wisdom is vindicated by her deeds" (Matt 11:18–19). Mark also announces that Jesus' contemporaries identified him as a "prophet, like one of the prophets of old" (Mark 6:15), as does Matthew: "This is the prophet Jesus from Nazareth in Galilee" (Matt 21:11). When, in Luke, Jesus raises the widow's son (Luke 7:11–17), the crowd responds, "A great prophet has risen among us!" and "God has looked favorably on his people!" In Acts 5:35–39, Gamaliel, while advising his fellow Jews how to treat Jesus' followers, likens them and their leader to Theudas and Judah the Galilean and their followers:

> [35]Then he said to them, "Fellow Israelites, consider carefully what you propose to do to these men. [36]For some time ago Theudas rose up, claiming to be somebody, and a number of men, about four hundred, joined him; but he was killed, and all who followed him were dispersed and disappeared. [37]After him Judas the Galilean rose up at the time of the census and got people to follow him; he also perished, and all who followed him were scattered. [38]So in the present case, I tell you, keep away from these men and let them alone; because if this plan or this undertaking is of human origin, it will fail; [39]but if it is of God, you will not be able to overthrow them — in that case you may even be found fighting against God!"

Here, Gamaliel clearly sees Jesus as an eschatological prophet.

For many Jews of the Second Temple period, prophets like Judah the Galilean were regarded as potential or real revolutionaries. Josephus, for example, regarded some of the prophets we have discussed in precisely this way, and he even bitterly lays the blame for the Jewish-Roman war at their feet. We must, however, hesitate to classify Jesus purely and simply as a revolutionary. It is essential to remember that politics in the Jewish world in which Jesus lived was deeply involved in religion; there was no purely secular political action for a Jewish revolutionary of those times. What should not be reasonably doubted is that others saw Jesus as an eschatological prophet whose work would set in motion that which God would bring to completion. In addition, *anyone* preaching the coming resurrection, with its allied notions of total transformation, punishment of the wicked, and vindication of the righteous, could be regarded as having revolutionary potential.

The Beatitudes present additional evidence that Jesus saw himself as a prophet of the last days. Consider Matt 5:3–10:

[3]Blessed are the poor in spirit, for theirs is the kingdom of heaven.
[4]Blessed are those who mourn, for they will be comforted.
[5]Blessed are the meek, for they will inherit the earth.
[6]Blessed are those who hunger and thirst for righteousness, for they will be filled.
[7]Blessed are the merciful, for they will receive mercy.
[8]Blessed are the pure in heart, for they will see God.
[9]Blessed are the peacemakers, for they will be called children of God.
[10]Blessed are those who are persecuted for righteousness' sake, for theirs is the kingdom of heaven.

Here Jesus seems to identify himself with the eschatological figure in Isaiah 61, who is anointed by God to bring good news to the poor. This is the oracle to which Jesus refers:

> [1]The spirit of the Lord GOD is upon me,
> Because the LORD has anointed me;
> He has sent me as a herald of joy to the humble,
> To bind up the wounded of heart,
> To proclaim release to the captives,
> Liberation to the imprisoned;
> [2]To proclaim a year of the LORD's favor
> And a day of vindication by our God;
> To comfort all who mourn —
> [3]To provide for the mourners in Zion —
> To give them a turban instead of ashes,
> The festive ointment instead of mourning,
> A garment of splendor instead of a drooping spirit.
> They shall be called terebinths of victory,
> Planted by the LORD for His glory. (Isa 61:1–3)

Jesus appears to have seen himself in terms of this passage from Isaiah. That is, he understood himself as a medium of God's message, charged with proclaiming the imminent reversal for which Israel has longed. Jesus' response to John the Baptizer reveals a similar self-understanding. In Matthew 11, John inquires from prison of Jesus, "Are you the one who is to come, or are we to wait for another?"

> [4]Jesus answered them, "Go and tell John what you hear and see: [5]the blind receive their sight, the lame walk, the lepers are cleansed, the deaf hear, the dead are raised, and the poor have good news brought to them. [6]And blessed is anyone who takes no offense at me." (Matt 11:4–6)

Jesus' response again harkens back to Isaiah 61 and the cosmic reversals promised there, as well as to other texts from the same scriptural book (for example, Isa 35:5–6). He seems to understand himself in the terms laid out there: a prophet appointed by God to announce and even bring the final liberation of Israel. In short, he was seen and saw himself, as Dale Allison has helpfully put it, as "the last prophet in the cosmic drama," whose mission it was "to prepare his people for the eschatological finale."

Accordingly, a major theme of Jesus' preaching was the closeness of this eschatological finale and the impending arrival of the kingdom of God. In Mark, Jesus announces, "Truly I tell you, there are some standing here who will not taste death until they see that the kingdom of God has come with power" (Mark 9:1). In Mark 13:30, Jesus proclaims that the present generation will not perish before the end of the present order. In Matthew, when commissioning the disciples, Jesus assures them, "Truly I tell you, you will not have gone through all the towns of Israel before the Son of Man comes" (Matt 10:23). He urged his contemporaries to be ready and to repent. The time "was fulfilled," the kingdom of God was near, and the Son of Man would soon come: "You know that he is near, at the very gates" (Mark 13:29).

As Sanders and Allison have demonstrated, one of the most important elements of Jewish restoration eschatology in late Second Temple Judaism was not only imminence but the expectation that the ten lost tribes should return or be restored in the end. (The Assyrian Empire had exiled the so-called lost tribes in the eight century B.C.E.) Consider, for example, these verses from Isaiah 11:

> [11]In that day, my Lord will apply His hand again to redeeming the other part of His people from Assyria—as also from Egypt, Pathros, Nubia, Elam, Shinar, Hamath, and the coastlands.

> [12]He will hold up a signal to the nations
> And assemble the banished of Israel,
> And gather the dispersed of Judah
> From the four corners of the earth. (Isa 11:11–12)

Many passages in the Jewish Bible indicate that this expectation — the anticipation that God would reassemble his people, all twelve tribes — was widespread in the centuries before Jesus' career; it was a major part of Jewish expectation of God's redemption. This almost surely explains why Jesus chose twelve disciples. The choice was doubtlessly symbolic. The point? That all of Israel would soon be restored: "Many will come from east and west and will eat with Abraham and Isaac and Jacob in the kingdom of heaven" (Matt 8:11–12; Luke 13:28–29). Here the kingdom is imagined as an eschatological banquet over which the fathers of the Jewish nation help to preside and to which the lost tribes will journey from the ends of the earth.

This, too, was a prophetic or *eschatological* point. Jesus chose twelve as a way of symbolizing the imminent restoration of the lost tribes, the apocalyptic ingathering of all Israel. In prophesying this ingathering, Jesus was expressing again the conviction, found in the prophetic books of Isaiah, Ezekiel, Hosea, and Micah and in other ancient Jewish literature, that the Jewish people would in the end return to their God-given land and attain sovereignty in it. As Sanders has concluded, "in the first century Jewish hopes for the future would have included the restoration of the twelve tribes of Israel. It is . . . against this background that we are to understand the motif of the twelve disciples in the Gospels."

Certain of Jesus' teachings in which he invokes the idea of resurrection are also capable of being read as metaphors for the coming restoration of Israel. The Prodigal Son (Luke 15:11–32) can certainly be read in many ways, and one way is as an allegory of the restoration of Israel.

> [11]Then Jesus said, "There was a man who had two sons. [12]The younger of them said to his father, 'Father, give me the share of the property that will belong to me.' So he divided his property between them. [13]A few days later the younger son gathered all he had and traveled to a distant country, and there he squandered his property in dissolute living. [14]When he had spent everything, a severe famine took place throughout that country, and he began to be in need. [15]So he went and hired himself out to one of the citizens of that

country, who sent him to his fields to feed the pigs. [16]He would gladly have filled himself with the pods that the pigs were eating; and no one gave him anything. [17]But when he came to himself he said, 'How many of my father's hired hands have bread enough and to spare, but here I am dying of hunger! [18]I will get up and go to my father, and I will say to him, "Father, I have sinned against heaven and before you; [19]I am no longer worthy to be called your son; treat me like one of your hired hands."' [20]So he set off and went to his father. But while he was still far off, his father saw him and was filled with compassion; he ran and put his arms around him and kissed him. [21]Then the son said to him, 'Father, I have sinned against heaven and before you; I am no longer worthy to be called your son.' [22]But the father said to his slaves, 'Quickly, bring out a robe—the best one—and put it on him; put a ring on his finger and sandals on his feet. [23]And get the fatted calf and kill it, and let us eat and celebrate; [24]for this son of mine was dead and is alive again; he was lost and is found!' And they began to celebrate.

[25]"Now his elder son was in the field; and when he came and approached the house, he heard music and dancing. [26]He called one of the slaves and asked what was going on. [27]He replied, 'Your brother has come, and your father has killed the fatted calf, because he has got him back safe and sound.' [28]Then he became angry and refused to go in. His father came out and began to plead with him. [29]But he answered his father, 'Listen! For all these years I have been working like a slave for you, and I have never disobeyed your command; yet you have never given me even a young goat so that I might celebrate with my friends. [30]But when this son of yours came back, who has devoured your property with prostitutes, you killed the fatted calf for him!' [31]Then the father said to him, 'Son, you are always with me, and all that is mine is yours. [32]But we had to celebrate and rejoice, because this brother of yours was dead and has come to life; he was lost and has been found.'"

Read allegorically, the lost son becomes a symbol of Israel in exile in a distant country, his poverty a metaphor for the bitterness of displacement, alien rule, and general injustice, and his return represents the restoration of Israel by the action of the forgiving, loving God of the covenant. Twice in this parable, the son's return is explicitly celebrated in terms of resurrection from the dead: "This son of mine," the father proclaims, "was dead and is alive again; he was lost and is found" (v 24); to the elder brother, the father announces, "this brother of yours was dead and has come to life; he was lost and has been found" (v 32). Here individual return and restoration are connected explicitly to resurrection, and individual restoration stands symbolically for the way in which all Israel will be restored at the end of days.

Some evidence suggests that Jesus came into conflict with others over his belief in the resurrection to come. In Mark 12:18–27, the Sadducees (who, as we have already mentioned, did not believe in the resurrection) challenge Jesus (and, implicitly, the Pharisees) to explain his views. Jesus grounds his defense in the testimony of the scriptures and on the power of the God of life. He rebukes the Sadducees about their understanding of God and their disbelief in the resurrection of the dead. God, Jesus says, "is God not of the dead, but of the living; you are quite wrong" (Mark 12:27). Buried in this rebuke is an allusion to Exod 3:6 and 3:15–16 and to Israel's God as the God of deliverance, victory, and life. Jesus' belief in the resurrection to come, then, is grounded theologically in faith in the God of creation to bring life out of death, in the power of God as the creator of the cosmos. This belief is also grounded scripturally in the conviction that the doctrine of resurrection is given in the Pentateuch—the only grounds on which the Sadducees could be persuaded. The same God who was God of Abraham, Isaac, and Jacob would raise up his people at the end of time. The patriarchs experienced a God capable of vanquishing death. In the end, all of Israel would experience that same power in the final victory of God over death, a victory that mirrored his defeat of the primordial chaos in the act of creation.

Another example of Jesus' eschatological symbolism appears in the way in which he entered Jerusalem—on an ass (Matt 21:1–5). In the Jewish world of Jesus' time, a world pervaded with scripture, the detail could not but call to mind a prophecy in Zechariah:

> Rejoice greatly, Fair Zion;
> Raise a shout, Fair Jerusalem!
> Lo, your king is coming to you.
> He is victorious, triumphant,
> Yet humble, riding on an ass,
> On a donkey foaled by a she-ass. (Zech 9:9)

The evangelist Matthew inserts the prophecy right into the gospel, lest the point be missed (Matt 21:4–8). But Jesus' followers would have gotten it. Jesus was announcing himself to be the king promised in Zechariah. That Jesus' followers understood the point he was making symbolically is proven when his followers proclaim him king: "Blessed is the king who comes in the name of the Lord!" (Luke 19:38).

NEW HEAVEN, NEW EARTH, AND NEW TEMPLE

A similar point can be made about the event that unfortunately has come to be called "the cleansing of the Temple." Sanders has gone to some pains to demonstrate that this, too, was a symbolic act, one that fit well with Jesus' overall outlook, that of Jewish restoration theology. The story is told in Mark 11 (and Matt 21:12–17; Luke 19:45–48; John 2:13–22):

> [15]Then they came to Jerusalem. And he entered the temple and began to drive out those who were selling and those who were buying in the temple, and he overturned the tables of the money-changers and the seats of those who sold doves; [16]and he would not allow anyone to carry anything through the temple. [17]He was teaching and saying, "Is it not written,
>
> > 'My house shall be called a house of prayer for all the nations'?
> > But you have made it a den of robbers."
>
> [18]And when the chief priests and the scribes heard it, they kept looking for a way to kill him; for they were afraid of him, because the whole crowd was spellbound by his teaching. (Mark 11:15–18, quoting Isa 56:7 and Jer 7:11)

Contrary to popular belief, the point of Jesus' action here had nothing to do with purification of divine worship. Now, it is certainly true that the accounts of the Temple action in the gospels make it appear, as it is often called, an act of "cleansing." But there are good reasons for doubting that Jesus thought the Temple needed to be reformed. For one, there is no indication in the gospel accounts, other than this one episode, that Jesus thought the Temple needed to be purified. Nor is there any evidence in the New Testament that Jesus opposed the system of sacrifice or the sacrificial theology that underlay it. As Sanders has reminded us, "the Temple was central to Palestinian Judaism and important to all Jews everywhere. To be against it would be to oppose Judaism as a religion. It would also be an attack on the main unifying symbol of the Jewish people." Jesus himself accepted the Temple, and, after his death and resurrection, his followers

continued to worship there. Had he been opposed to it, they surely would
not have done so. The gospel accounts in which Jesus denounces the
money changers were written long after his death. *By that time*, perhaps
forty or so years after the crucifixion, Christians came to regard Jesus' death
as an atonement for sin, and thus many of them came to regard the Temple
as superfluous. But, as Sanders has observed, Jesus, like "all Jews everywhere," regarded the Temple as central to his religion. It is simply implau-
sible, because it is anachronistic, to regard Jesus, a pious Jew, as "oppose[d]
to Judaism as a religion."

Rather, Jesus' action at the Temple was symbolic; he was enacting his
message and signifying that the Temple would be destroyed. This action in
turn was related to his expectation of a new kingdom. In the coming new
age, with the twelve tribes once again assembled, Israel would worship its
God and thank him for his saving action in a new and more perfect Temple. The current Temple would be destroyed as a sign that the evil present
order would soon be shattered and a new Temple given by God. Here Jesus
was very likely following the biblical prophets again. Consider this passage
from Isaiah:

> The majesty of Lebanon shall come to you —
> Cypress and pine and box —
> To adorn the site of My Sanctuary,
> To glorify the place where My feet rest. (Isa 60:13)

("My Sanctuary" is a reference to the Temple, as is "where My feet rest.")
Nonbiblical Jewish texts, from roughly the same period as Jesus, make the
same general point:

> [28]And I stood up to see till they folded up that old house; and carried off all
> the pillars, and all the beams and ornaments of the house were at the same
> time folded up with it, and they carried it off. . . . [29]And I saw till the Lord . . .
> brought a new house greater and loftier than the first, and set it in the place
> of the first . . . and its pillars were new, and its ornaments were new and
> larger than those of the first. (1 Enoch 90: 28–29)

The author of the book of Tobit (written perhaps 150 years or so before Jesus' death and now part of the Roman Catholic and Eastern Orthodox
Bibles) has a similar prophecy:

[T]hey will rebuild the temple of God, but not like the first one until the period when the times of fulfillment shall come. After this they all will return
from their exile and will rebuild Jerusalem in splendor; and in it the temple
of God will be rebuilt, just as the prophets of Israel have said concerning it.
(Tob 14:5).

Thus Jesus thought, not that the Temple would be permanently destroyed,
but, as these texts suggest, that it would be replaced and renewed by God in
the coming kingdom. In other words, the action by Jesus at the Temple and
his prediction that it would be rebuilt are not criticisms of the forms of worship in the Temple, nor a protest against sacrificial theology, which he almost certainly accepted. They are characteristically symbolic predictions
of the imminence of God's kingdom and signs of Jesus' confidence in the
power and nearness of God's merciful, just, and final intervention in the
world.

Both Jesus and his earliest followers did indeed dwell in a world of *imminent*, or apocalyptic, eschatological expectation. We have already seen
that Jesus preached that the end was near. After his death, so did his followers. In Luke, we are told that they "supposed that the kingdom of God
was to appear immediately" (Luke 19:11). That is, the earliest Christian
movement shared in the belief rooted in the apocalyptic perspective
preached by Jesus. Like Jesus, they expected the restoration of Israel by an
act of God. That this is so is reflected in Mark 9:12 (and its parallel in Matt
17:11): "Elijah," Jesus is reported as observing to his followers, "is indeed
coming to restore all things." And in Acts 1:6, written perhaps between 80
and 90 C.E., the resurrected Jesus' followers ask him, "Lord, is this the time
when you will restore the kingdom to Israel?" Like Jesus, his followers expected the kingdom to come in the near future. They regarded Jesus as he
likely regarded himself: namely, as a prophet of the restoration of Israel. It
is quite possible that they thought that they, like Jesus, would play some
sort of role in the kingdom: "Truly I tell you, at the renewal of all things,
when the Son of Man is seated on the throne of his glory, you who have followed me will also sit on twelve thrones, judging the twelve tribes of Israel"
(Matt 19:28). (By "judging" Jesus means to suggest that they will be governing, not criticizing.) As Sanders has summarized the matter, "that his followers worked within the framework of Jewish eschatological expectation

is indisputable." Like Jesus, the earliest Christians expected God to restore Israel, to renew or rebuild the Temple, and to regather the lost tribes.

AN ESCHATOLOGICAL SIGN TO THE PEOPLE

This shared theological perspective helps to explain why several of Jesus' followers announced that God had raised Jesus from the dead (Mark 16:6; Acts 2:24). Like Jesus, they were influenced by apocalyptic thinking and looked forward to the restoration of Israel. Before his death, Jesus had, as we have seen, proclaimed that there would be a resurrection of the dead at the end, one followed by a judgment of the good and the evil. When dining at a Pharisee's house, Jesus admonishes his host to invite the poor and the lame to his banquets, for then he would be blessed: "And you will be blessed, because they cannot repay you, for you will be repaid at the resurrection of the righteous" (Luke 14:12–14). In Matthew and Luke, Jesus is depicted urging his followers not to "fear those who kill the body" (Matt 10:28; compare Luke 12:4). He says this, of course, because he presumes that there will be a life to come beyond the death of his present body. Again, speaking of Jonah in the belly of the large fish for three days, Jesus prophesied, "The people of Nineveh will rise up at the judgment" (Matt 12:41; Luke 11:32). Just as Jonah was a sign to the people of Nineveh, so Jesus would be to this generation, when he would emerge, like Jonah, from the place of no return.

On at least three occasions, Jesus predicts his own resurrection. In Mark 8:31, he proclaims that he will "be killed, and after three days rise again." In the following chapter of the same gospel, he foresees that the Son of Man will be betrayed and killed, "and three days after being killed, he will rise again" (Mark 9:31). The same sort of sequence—betrayal, condemnation, death, and resurrection after three days—is predicted once again in Mark 10:33–34. The expectation of resurrection on the third day again harkens back to the Hebrew scriptures. We read in Hosea, for example:

> In two days He will make us whole again;
> On the third day He will raise us up,
> And we shall be whole by His favor. (Hos 6:2)

And in the book of Jonah, of course, Jonah rests within the great fish for three days (Jon 2:1). Many scholars regard these predictions as prophesies formulated by the evangelist, Mark, rather than by Jesus. Nonetheless, it is possible that the basic expectation of betrayal, death, and final vindication does, in fact, go back to Jesus, in which case these verses represent Jesus' own understanding of how his life would end and his message and career be redeemed.

Convinced that the end was near, Jesus' first followers explained his vindication in terms with which they were familiar: as a resurrection. Jesus' own resurrection they interpreted, in turn, as an eschatological sign: namely, that the end promised by Jesus and foretold by the prophets had begun. As the apostle Paul put it, Jesus was "the first fruits of those who have died" (1 Cor 15:20). This statement assumes both that the end times had begun and that the general resurrection, of which Jesus' resurrection was a sign, would soon occur. Jesus had taught his followers that the resurrection of the dead was imminent. Once they became convinced that he had himself been resurrected, they regarded this stupendous event as a sign that the final gathering-in and judgment were at last at hand. They saw Jesus' resurrection as an apocalyptic sign. Or, as N. T. Wright has put it, "this event was . . . the proleptic fulfillment of Israel's great hope." Jesus' resurrection signified that the new age or kingdom, and with it the restoration of Israel, was near. Terrified, awestruck, jubilant, Jesus' followers now confidently expected that the new age had dawned.

RESURRECTION LIFE AND THE BODY

In Matt 28:9, Jesus meets the women who are rushing from the empty tomb, at once euphoric and frightened, in order to report on their astonishing discovery. In their flight, they encounter Jesus. At once, they "took hold of his feet" (Matt 28:9). This is a gesture of spontaneous affection and veneration, but it also testifies to the reality and materiality—the corporeality—of Jesus' body after the resurrection. In Luke, the resurrected Jesus shares bread with his uncomprehending followers (Luke 24:30). This, too, is an eschatological sign, for Jesus at his last meal had promised that he would not eat or drink of the vine again until the kingdom had come (Luke 22:16, 18). A few days later in Luke's narrative, Jesus consumes a piece of broiled fish. There could hardly be a more direct or simple testament to the reality of Jesus' resurrected flesh than hunger and its satisfaction.

No resurrection narrative underscores the identity of the crucified and resurrected body as forcefully as Jesus' encounter with "Doubting Thomas":

> [24]But Thomas (who was called the Twin), one of the twelve, was not with them when Jesus came. [25]So the other disciples told him, "We have seen the Lord." But he said to them, "Unless I see the mark of the nails in his hands, and put my finger in the mark of the nails and my hand in his side, I will not believe."
>
> [26]A week later his disciples were again in the house, and Thomas was with them. Although the doors were shut, Jesus came and stood among them and said, "Peace be with you." [27]Then he said to Thomas, "Put your finger here and see my hands. Reach out your hand and put it in my side. Do not doubt but believe." [28]Thomas answered him, "My Lord and my God!" (John 20: 24–28).

So plainly corporeal is Jesus' resurrected flesh that it still bears the wounds of the crucifixion.

On the other hand, the resurrection narratives make it equally clear that Jesus' resurrected body is not *exactly* the same as his preresurrected body. In Matthew, for example, he stands quite "suddenly" in the path of the women running away in terror from the empty tomb (Matt 28:9). In addition, Jesus makes equally sudden appearances to the disciples. In John 20, for example, we learn:

> When it was evening on that day, the first day of the week, and the doors of the house where the disciples had met were locked . . . Jesus came and stood among them and said, "Peace be with you." (John 20:19)

The objective of this text is to make it clear that the resurrected body of Jesus is not *merely* a resuscitated corpse. It is a *transformed* body. But it is still a body. N. T. Wright has helpfully used the term "transphysical" to describe Jesus' resurrected body. It is corporeal, but it is able also to transcend normal bodily limitations. It is clearly not the sort of "raised body" that Lazarus had (John 11:1–44). Having been raised by Jesus from the dead, Lazarus would nonetheless die again. Jesus, by contrast, had defeated death. Having risen, he would never die again. This is, to say the least, a different kind of embodiment. He had risen to immortal life.

Beyond this there is not much we can say about the nature of resurrected flesh. The character of the resurrected life is simply not a question that interested the evangelists. The notion that did deeply engage the writers of the gospels was that God had raised Jesus bodily from the dead, and that this was a sign — *the* sign — that the present aeon was ending and the age to come dawning, and that the long-promised restoration had begun. Jesus' resurrection from the dead to new, transformed embodiment was, in the eyes of his followers, a sign that, after centuries of dispossession, loss, and oppression, God, faithful to his promises to his people, had powerfully and dramatically inaugurated the new age of all Israel.

THE FIRST FRUITS OF THOSE
WHO HAVE DIED

JESUS AS THE FIRST OF MANY

An apostle who was not one of the disciples, a follower who never knew Jesus in the flesh, Paul was nonetheless transformed by the message that Jesus had been raised from the dead. In turn, Paul transformed his world—and world history—by tireless proclamation of that message. A zealot for the traditions of his fathers, he became *the* apostle to the gentiles. After what he took to be a life-transforming encounter with the risen Christ near Damascus, he soon became a champion for the good news of Christ risen. A persecutor of the "church of God" who hoped indeed to destroy it (1 Cor 15:9; Gal 1:13), it was his destiny to become, according to tradition, its preeminent martyr (along with Peter, the apostle to the Jews, and, according to legend, the first bishop of Rome).

As for Jesus' earliest followers, so for Paul. For early Christian apostles and teachers, the claim that Jesus had risen was fraught with eschatological significance. It signified that the end time had begun. It portended that the general resurrection was near. In his first letter to the Corinthians, Paul assures his readers and listeners (for Paul's letters would have been read aloud, often in small gatherings in the home of a local Christian), "Christ has been raised from the dead, the first fruits of those who have died" (1 Cor 15:20). In deploying the metaphor of "first fruits," Paul meant to suggest that Jesus was only the first of many who would be raised. Those who believed in him would, in the end, also share in the resurrection of Jesus and in the splendor of the new aeon, the glory already borne by their heavenly

Lord, King, and Christ: "if children, then heirs, heirs of God and joint heirs with Christ—if, in fact, we suffer with him so that we may also be glorified with him" (Rom 8:17). Just as the first fruits herald a good harvest, so Jesus' resurrection inaugurated and guaranteed the full ingathering of the faithful at his return. Jesus' rising therefore can be understood as a victorious initial note, a trumpet cry proclaiming the year of God's redemption; the resurrection of his faithful followers constitutes the finale in a coherent, ultimate, and exultant movement in history.

Paul insists that the entire gospel, the good news of salvation, rests on the truth of Jesus' having been raised. The gospel message that pithily states that Christ died in accordance with the scriptures and was buried and raised on the third day, he says, is "of first importance" (1 Cor 15:3). Its significance is underscored by Paul's admission, or insistence, that this good news, this gospel, was not unique to him; it was not an article of his exclusive teaching. To the contrary, Paul implies that by the time of his conversion, this proclamation was already being preached by his predecessors. Indeed, he was transmitting a young but well-established tradition: "I handed on to you . . . what I in turn had received" (1 Cor 15:3). In all probability, this gospel was already proclaimed during the decade in which Jesus died, some twenty years or so before Paul sent his letter to the Corinthians (around 55 C.E.).

This claim that Christ had been raised was so important to Paul, he believed that if it were false, every Christian's faith would be in vain. If it were false, Paul's work—any apostle's work—would be a mere exercise in futility. More importantly, had Christ not risen from the dead, the promise of salvation expressed by the gospel would be worthless and void. All would remain in thrall to sin. Even those who had died, baptized in Christ and faithful to him, would have gone to a dismal place of no return, a vast tomb, their bodies forever inert. Their faith, their willingness to repose their trust in the message of resurrection, would have merited them no reward. They would have perished for good, and so would Paul's listeners: "If the dead are not raised, 'Let us eat and drink, for tomorrow we die'" (1 Cor 15:32)—a quotation, as Paul's readers would have recognized, from Isa 22:13. Paul concludes, drearily, that if Christ were not in fact raised, it would be pointless to hope any more for the millennial transformation for which Israel had for centuries yearned: "If for this life only we have hoped in Christ, we are of all people most to be pitied" (1 Cor 15:19). Is this all?

Is *this* all there is? Sadly, yes. In Paul's mind, nothing had in that case changed; nothing would change. The powers and dominions of this world? They reigned still.

But, Paul passionately believed, Christ *had* risen. (Had he not appeared, he asks in 1 Cor 15:6–8, to more than five hundred?) In raising Jesus from the dead, God had defeated death and vanquished the principalities and powers opposed to God. The eschatological battle had been fought and won — by God. There *was* more to hope for than "this life only."

Indeed, this message of hope long antedated Paul or even, as we have seen, Jesus. The reference in that terse creed to Jesus' having been raised "on the third day" would have called to mind the miraculous revivals and acts of liberation wrought by God in the Hebrew Bible (the only Bible Paul knew) on a "third day." We have already referred to the story of Jonah. Recall, too, Hos 6:1–2. There, the prophet looks forward to the restoration of Israel:

> ¹Come, let us turn back to the LORD:
> He attacked, and He can heal us;
> He wounded, and He can bind us up.
> ²In two days He will make us whole again;
> On the third day He will raise us up.

Jesus' earliest followers took this notion of dramatic acts of God on the third day over from the Hebrew Bible and adapted it to their own new proclamation. Paul, by his own testimony a former Pharisee (Phil 3:5), would surely have known this tradition and recognized its implications when he heard the earliest Christians preach that, on the third day, God had raised Jesus from the dead. In fact, in his first letter to the Corinthians, Paul proclaims that Christ was raised on the third day "in accordance with the scriptures" (1 Cor 15:4) — words that would make it into the earliest Christian creed, as we saw in Chapter 1. While not impossible that Paul may have had a specific text in mind here (like the lines from Hosea just quoted), his use of the plural scriptures indicates that he believed that the Hebrew scriptures in general proclaimed a doctrine of resurrection. Like contemporary Pharisees, Paul believed in the general resurrection, and, like them (and like Jesus of Nazareth), he associated it with the final restoration and redemption of Israel. Again, with the Pharisees he believed that this would occur at the end of time. As N. T. Wright has observed, if you take Jesus out of Paul's picture of the resurrection, "What is being asserted—the future resurrection to salvation from wrath . . . is familiar from . . . Judaism: it is the position of the Pharisees. Whatever other beliefs Paul revised following his conversion, resurrection remained constant." For Paul after his conversion, the God of Israel had acted to redeem his people in Christ's death and resurrection. That act had triggered the dawning of the new age. All of God's people would soon be redeemed, nature recreated, and God's faithful rescued from death. The resurrection, Paul was convinced, would occur with the royal appearance of the messiah (technically called the *parousia*) at the end of time that was now at hand: "But each in his own order: Christ the first fruits, then at his coming those who belong to Christ" (1 Cor 15:23).

IMMINENCE

Expectation of a bodily resurrection, followed by judgment, is, as we have seen and shall see again in greater detail, an idea many Jews and Christians shared at the time of Paul. Steeped in Jewish apocalyptic literature himself, his mind deeply imbued, like other early Christians, with apocalyptic expectation, Paul looked for the royal return of Jesus to occur very soon. The Christian expectation of bodily resurrection at the end of time, which associates it with the return of Jesus in glory, goes back very far in the church's tradition, almost certainly to Jesus' earliest followers. So, too, does the expectation of its near occurrence, or imminence. Actually, Paul thought the return of Jesus and the resurrection would occur so soon that it caught him by surprise when some Christians died before the glorious event.

In fact, Paul assured his first listeners that they would not die before Jesus descended from heaven. This is very clear from his first letter to the Thessalonians. Written around the year 50 C.E. (and thus the earliest book in the New Testament), this letter was composed perhaps within a few months of Paul's initial visit to Thessalonica. Paul seems to have written it because the death of Christians in the community had created both a religious crisis and a severe erosion in the credibility of Paul and his message. For what Paul had expressly promised would *not* happen had now come to pass. Jesus had not returned, yet some of the faithful had perished. Just as Jesus expected that his disciples would not have time to go through all the towns of Israel before the coming of the Son of Man (Matt 10:23), so Paul declared that the end was so near that none would die before the day of the Lord. "But we do not want you to be uninformed, brothers and sisters, about those who have died," Paul assures the Thessalonians (1 Thess 4:13). Yet it was the message enunciated on his first visit to them that led to doubts and questions which, in turn, occasioned the writing of his first letter. What, the Thessalonians wondered, grief-stricken and perhaps disenchanted with Paul himself, was the fate of their dead? Would they be passed over at the return of the Lord? Would they not rise after all? Not be saved?

Paul encourages the Thessalonian Christians that they need not worry about those who had died in Christ. Writing in dramatic apocalyptic language, Paul consoles them by asserting:

> [16]For the Lord himself, with a cry of command, with the archangel's call and with the sound of God's trumpet, will descend from heaven, and the dead in Christ will rise first. [17]Then we who are alive, who are left, will be caught up in the clouds together with them to meet the Lord in the air; and so we will be with the Lord for ever. (1 Thess 4:16–17)

In Paul's language we hear a distant echo of one of the apocalyptic visions in the book of Daniel:

> As I looked on, in the night vision,
> One like a human being
> Came with the clouds of heaven. (Dan 7:13)

The coming of this quasi-human figure, ferried along by the clouds of heaven, is explicitly associated in Daniel with the redemption of all Israel after trial and the establishment of God's everlasting kingdom. Here, Paul draws on the Jewish apocalyptic tradition as a way to dramatize the nearness of the dominion of God and to reassure the Thessalonians that they will share in that everlasting kingdom.

It is clear from Paul's words "we who are alive, who are left" that he still fully anticipated being alive at the time of Jesus' return in glory. Echoing Dan 12:2, which, as we have seen, spoke of death and resurrection in the idiom of sleeping and waking, Paul, at the end of his letter, admonishes the faithful, "let us keep awake." For the "day of the Lord" is very near (1 Thess 5:2, 6). (Employing similar imagery, the author of Ephesians would later write: "Sleeper, awake! Rise from the dead. . . ." Eph 5:14.) Precisely this expectation of imminent return, one of the central elements of Paul's early preaching (and the preaching of other early Christian apostles and teachers), was disrupted by the death of the faithful in Thessalonica.

The deaths of some of the Thessalonian Christians did not dissuade Paul from believing, nor from continuing to preach, that Christ would soon return in glory. "Let your gentleness be known to everyone," Paul admonishes the Philippians. Why? Because "the Lord is near" (Phil 4:5). To the Philippian church, Paul also declares, "I am confident of this, that the one who began a good work among you will bring it to completion by the day of Jesus Christ" (Phil 1:6). Again, Paul, when referring to the "day of Jesus Christ," has in mind the royal return of the messiah. The dead would soon wake, and God would complete his plan of salvation. To the Corinthians, Paul could confidently announce, "the appointed time has grown short." It was upon them that "the ends of the ages" had come (1 Cor 7:29; 10:11). Again drawing on the antithesis of light and dark found so pervasively in Jewish apocalyptic literature, Paul pleads with the Romans, "Lay aside the works of darkness and put on the armor of light" (Rom 13:12). An urgent sense that time was growing very short drives Paul's rigorous moral instruction; the day of the Lord was drawing ever closer: "Salvation is nearer to us now than when we became believers; the night is far gone, the day is near" (Rom 13:11–12). This ingredient of Jewish restoration eschatology, along with the characteristically apocalyptic language of night and day, Paul never felt cause to relinquish.

THE CHURCH AS ISRAEL

The earliest Christian community conceived of itself as Israel. In the book of Acts, the earliest believers in Jesus' messiahship are addressed as "Israelites," the "entire house of Israel," "You Israelites," "people of Israel," or "fellow Israelites" (Acts 2:22, 36; 3:12; 4:10; 5:35). Like the members of the Jewish sect who left the Dead Sea Scrolls, the earliest Christians regarded themselves as the *true* Israel, the assembly of Israel. When Jesus reappeared to consummate the divine plan, he would, they believed, bring the travails of Jewish history to their glorious messianic conclusion. Those Jewish sectarians believed that, in the end, Israel would be saved and reformed—by conforming to the way of the sect itself. Other Israelites would join the community in the last days. Yet they would gain access to salvation only by following the practices and beliefs of the sectarian community.

Just so, the earliest followers of Jesus of Nazareth appropriated to themselves the title of "Israel." Put another way, they regarded themselves as God's elect community. Just as the Israelite covenant distinguished (as any community must) between insiders and outsiders, so members of the new Christian community made the same distinction. Again, like the Jewish sectarians who left us the Dead Sea Scrolls, so for the earliest church, salvation lay within their own community. This is not to say that the earliest Christians were a community of the predestined. To say that would be to apply to the first century a later understanding of God's plan for salvation. For one could *become* part of the elect community by professing faith, undergoing ritual induction through baptism, and thus "joining" the congregation of the saved—or, as Paul characteristically expressed it, by assimilating oneself to Christ by dying and rising with him, by becoming a member of Christ's body. As Paul put it to the Romans, "Therefore we have been buried with him by baptism into death, so that, just as Christ was raised from the dead by the glory of the Father, so we too might walk in newness of life" (Rom 6:4).

But, contrary to what one often hears, it is not true that the earliest church understood itself as a community of "universal salvation." The old dichotomy that presents the Jews as tribalistic and exclusive but the Christians as universal and inclusive does not hold water. Whether we would like him to be or not, Paul was certainly not, as some would have it, the founder of universalism. This contrast between Paul as representative of universalism and Judaism as a religion of particularism and exclusivism received classic expression in mid-nineteenth-century German scholarship on the New Testament, especially in the work of Ferdinand Christian Baur (1792–1860), doyen of the so-called Tübingen school of theology. Baur regarded Paul's letter to the Romans, especially, as the apostle's manifesto against Jewish particularism (which he pejoratively associated with Jewish law, "legalism," and righteousness earned by following Torah). Paul's letter to the church of Rome was also a manifesto, Baur argued, for the universal doctrine of salvation of the Christian church.

For Baur, Christian universalism was not merely different from Jewish particularism; rather, it represented a higher stage of development in the history of religion. In this view, Paul was the first thinker to have liberated

faith in Christ from the shackles of ancient, tribal, legal, and sacrificial religion. Without him, Christianity would not have developed into the religion of grace and pure spirit that it was its destiny to become. Paul was the
first, or so Baur argued, to have cut the ties from the ancestral, ethnocen-
tric faith that relied on good works, the particular requirements of the Law,
and the embodied, familial, ethnic exclusivity of a covenant relationship.

For all its flaws, the basic contrast Baur drew has proven remarkably flex-
ible and durable. The Baur paradigm still undergirds the structure of many
studies of Paul and has been appropriated by many well-known scholars in
the twentieth century. One can sometimes hear it taught in classrooms
and preached in churches to this day. But there are a number of problems
with this paradigm. First of all, it is not clear that Paul regarded fidelity to
his ancestral religion and faith in Christ as absolutely incompatible; one
may interpret Paul simply to mean that, with Christ, Israel has now ex-
panded as to include the gentiles. More seriously, it overlooks the extent to
which, in imagining Judaism and Christianity, Paul was not thinking of
one particularistic and one universal faith; he was imagining two religious
ways, *each* particularistic, though in different ways. Each way had its own
particular beliefs, requirements, and rituals for inclusion (for example,
one had circumcision, the other baptism); each had its normative ritual,
legal, and moral structures. Neither was "inclusive" in the modern sense of
the term in its understanding of community or of the opportunity for salvation.

For Paul, gentile Christians had to become sons, not of Adam, nor of
Noah (figures associated with the universality of God's care), but of Abraham, "the father of all of us" (Rom 4:16) — that is, of the children of Israel.
More than that, Paul thought of the new Christian community as, if not Israel or the new Israel, then (to use Yale theologian George Lindbeck's
term) an "Israel-like" body. In Paul's view, the assembly of Christians is like
the assembly of Israelites insofar as it participates in Christ as one regenerate body whose corporate character marks members off from the world.
For Paul, the church could borrow Israel's self-understanding as a single
community, one body, of the saved because neither Jews nor Christians
participate in their faith as atomized individuals.

The notion of the church as a *body* is, for our purposes, hard to exaggerate. It connects Jesus and thus the church with the physicality of the Jews,
a natural family. In Paul's mind, both assemblies *are* bodies; both are fami-

lies—one natural and biological, the other mystical, both preferred by God. (About the Jews and their continuing election, Paul rhetorically asks in Rom 11:1, "has God rejected his people? By no means!") Both communities conceive of resurrection in terms of the restoration of a community, or, in Paul's terms, a body. Neither Judaism nor Christianity associates resurrection primarily with individual survival after death. It has to do, in the first place, with the community rather than the individual. Thus when raised, the body, the congregation of the faithful in Christ, will be raised. To be sure, it will be luminescent and transformed. At the same time, its members will retain their individual and physical, corporate character. So embodiment for Paul is not merely a spiritualization or a metaphor for the Christian assembly. It is closely associated with the expectation of resurrection, an expectation shared with Pharisees and other Jewish believers in the resurrection of the dead during the late Second Temple period.

To be sure, Second Temple notions of community and Paul's view of the saved body are not identical. The key difference is simple: in Paul's thought, the saved body is not a natural or biological family. Nor is it a national community. It is not a family that is replenished across time by childbearing, as the Jewish people was in his time and is today. Rather, the congregation of the Christian faithful is a family by virtue of what it holds in common: belief in and commitment to Christ crucified and risen. It is a family insofar as the many are linked by their confidence that God has acted in the death and resurrection of Jesus Christ, inaugurating them into a new life together as members of the same body.

Another problem with the Baur paradigm is that Paul would never have recognized himself in the word "universalist." That is to say, the paradigm is anachronistic. At the end of the ages, the *faithful* would be raised. But those Paul condemns as idolaters and unfaithful, those who denied the messiahship of Jesus Christ or who lay outside the covenant established by God, were destined to be destroyed.

It is helpful to remember that, as he looked around the Mediterranean world, Paul thought in terms of three groups: Jews, pagans, and the church. For the pagans of that world, the only hope was to cease to be pagans and to become sons of Abraham: "You, my friends, are children of the promise, like Isaac," Paul tells the baptized Galatians (Gal 4:28). For Christians, Paul thought that this adoption would be effected through baptism;

for Jews, it had been accomplished through circumcision, and so Israel and the sons of Abraham would be saved:

> [25]So that you may not claim to be wiser than you are, brothers and sisters, I want you to understand this mystery: a hardening has come upon part of Israel, until the full number of the Gentiles has come in. [26]*And so all Israel will be saved;* as it is written,
>
> > "Out of Zion will come the Deliverer;
> > he will banish ungodliness from Jacob."
> > [27]"And this is my covenant with them,
> > when I take away their sins." (Rom 11:25–27,
> > quoting Isa 59:20–21; emphasis added)

The only hope for non-Jews, Paul thought, lay in joining the community of the saved, in conversion to Christianity. In Paul's time, that was a very small—indeed, minuscule—community. Paul was thus asking the pagans to drop out of a larger group for a much smaller, countercultural group. In this sense, there is indeed a counterpart in Paul to the duality of Israel and the nations in Judaism: it is the duality of the church and the world. But Paul sees nothing but perdition in the future of the pagans *unless* they become children of Abraham.

Again, this is generally in line with the eschatological expectations of the sectarian community whose scrolls were discovered at Qumran. The sectarians understood themselves as possessors of the true covenant, as sons of light or "sons of God's truth." In light of attempts to represent the early church as an inclusive community or Paul as an apostle of universal salvation, we must stress that the earliest followers of Jesus, including Paul, understood themselves in analogous terms—that is, in terms of salvation, as an *exclusive* community; they did not subscribe to anything remotely like modern religious pluralism. For the community reflected in the documents of Qumran, the enemies of God, the sons of darkness, would be destroyed. Paul uncannily echoes this language in his letter to the Philippians: "For many live as enemies of the cross of Christ." "Their end," Paul concludes remorselessly, "is destruction" (Phil 3:18–19). The unrighteous would not inherit the kingdom of God, he repeatedly warns his correspondents (1 Cor 6:9, 8:11, 10:6; see also Rom 2:12 and 2 Cor 2:15, 4:3).

Put another way, the understanding of salvation of both the Jewish community whose trove of scrolls was left at Qumran and the earliest church is sectarian. This means that the essential distinction is, in the words of E. P. Sanders, "between those outside the covenant . . . and those inside." For Paul, the promise of salvation is qualified by the demand for obedience, with the former depending on the performance or achievement of the latter for its fulfillment. Here, too, Paul's view on salvation is, as Sanders has observed, "typically Jewish." "Salvation by grace," Sanders explains, is for Paul "not incompatible with punishment and reward for deeds." "The gospel," Paul declares in Romans, "is the power of God for salvation to *everyone who has faith*" (Rom 1:16; emphasis added). Here, Paul links one's eternal destiny to one's willingness to believe in the Christian message. To the Corinthians, Paul observes that they will be saved by the gospel which they received "*if* [they] hold firmly to the message" (1 Cor 15:1–2; emphasis added). Only by obeying and believing, and persisting in obedience and faith, does one merit the reward of resurrection and eternal salvation. Paul promises the Romans that they will enjoy God's final kindness "*provided you continue in his kindness*" (emphasis added). The promise of salvation is thus provisional and dependent in part upon perseverance in the good. Should the Roman Christians fail to persevere, they will surely be "cut off" (Rom 11:22). Evildoers, he sternly warns, "will not inherit the kingdom of God" (Gal 5:21). Unpalatable though it may be to the modern sensibility, Paul clearly felt that those who failed to obey or believe in the Christian gospel, who refused to embrace the new covenant, would not have a place in the saved community. The pagans were doomed for perdition. As Sanders has summarized the matter, "What [Paul] actually thought is abundantly clear in passage after passage: apart from Christ, everyone will be destroyed; those who believe and participate in the body of Christ will be saved." Those fortunate few who belonged to Christ would be saved on the day of the Lord, and even nature and the cosmos itself would be transformed and liberated from bondage (Rom 8:21). Particularism—whether in nonsectarian Judaism, the Jewish group that authored the sectarian writings found at Qumran, or early Christianity—thus does not by any means imply permanent exclusivism, for the door to salvation within the saved community is always open.

Paul identified this saved community, the church, as "the body of Christ." Individually, each believer was a "member" of the body: "[12]For just as the body is one and has many members, and all the members of the body, though many, are one body, so it is with Christ. [13]For in the one Spirit we were all baptized into one body—Jews or Greeks, slaves or free" (1 Cor 12:12–13). There it is in a nub. The body has many, heterogeneous members, though it is one.

It followed, for Paul, that resurrection was a collective, or communal event. Put another way, the significance of Jesus' resurrection was hardly exhausted on Easter. It pointed forward to a *general* resurrection of the dead, of those who had embraced the true covenant by acknowledging Jesus as messiah and then participating in his death and resurrection. Just as Jesus rose on the third day, so would his body—the congregation of the faithful, the church—rise on the last day. Just as all died in Adam, all those who died in Christ would share in his resurrection: "for as all die in Adam, so all will be made alive in Christ" (1 Cor 15:22). The resurrection of the community, not the individual, is primary. Paul thinks of the body of Christ as eternal, in much the same way that the vision of the dry bones in Ezekiel 37 thinks of Israel as eternal (see Chapter 8, below).

Another idea is closely related to the mistaken notion that Paul believed everybody would be saved. This is the equally misguided idea that he believed that baptism abolished all religious, ethnic, economic, and sexual distinctions. Going even further, some scholars have argued that a condition of absolute social equality existed in the Pauline churches as a result of this baptismal theology. They rely principally on Gal 3:28: "There is no longer Jew or Greek, there is no longer slave or free, there is no longer male and female; for all of you are one in Jesus Christ." New Testament scholar Troy W. Martin has argued convincingly against this theory. He observes that it is only later interpreters—especially late twentieth-century ones—who see the Pauline communities as ideal, utopian communities that erased all distinctions of class, gender, and social station. Paul fully expected that ethnic, sexual, class, and slave/free distinctions would remain. What is at issue, Martin points out, is whether these distinctions have "any relevance for determining candidates for Christian baptism and entry into the Christian community." Martin concludes that, for Paul, they have no such relevance. Paul assumes that there will be a diversity of social roles and responsibilities in the body of Christ, and that this diversity will endure long after baptism (Rom 12:3–8; 1 Cor 7:1–16, 25–40; 11:2–16; 12:1–11, 28–31). "This verse," as Martin has summarized Gal 3:28 so nicely, "does not proclaim the absolute abolition of these distinctions but only their irrelevance for participation in Christian baptism." As Paul himself would put it: "For as in one body we have many members, and not all the members have the same function" (Rom 12:4).

Later interpreters of Gal 3:28 have argued that Paul meant to abolish all distinctions. But they do so by and large, not in order to explain what Paul meant, but to shore up current ideological and political agendas. Whatever one may think of such multicultural political agendas, they cannot fit into the world of the first century without falsifying Paul's meaning. Paul was a universalist neither in regard to salvation nor in regard to social organization.

PARTICIPATION IN CHRIST

If in Jesus' resurrection the end time had already begun, believers could in the interim begin to experience the shifting of the aeons and the new life it foreshadowed by "participating" in Jesus' death and resurrection. Both Albert Schweitzer and Sanders have recognized how important a category "participation" is in the thought of Paul. For Sanders, there is no doubt that the "heart of Paul's theology . . . the real bite of his theology lies in the participatory categories." Paul's concept of salvation, he goes on, "is basically cosmic and corporate or participatory." In light of the weight that "righteousness by faith" has been asked to bear since the Protestant Reformation in the sixteenth century, it is particularly important to underline Sanders' point. Since Luther, righteousness by faith has been seen as the center of Paul's theology. But most recent scholars have attempted to view Paul's writings through lenses appropriate to the first century rather than the sixteenth. So viewed, it becomes apparent that the goal of the Christian life is not first of all righteousness, which is theologically a corollary and, in the life of the believer, a side effect or secondary response to the primary end of religion. The aim of the believer's life is, rather, resurrection, and Christians share in Christ's resurrection by first participating in their Lord's suffering and death. As Paul puts it in Philippians 3,

> [10]I want to know Christ and the power of his resurrection and the sharing of his sufferings by *becoming like him* in his death, [11]if somehow I may attain the resurrection from the dead. (Phil 3:10–11; emphasis added)

Just as the Israelites had to suffer in Egypt and in the desert before arriving at Sinai, so must Paul and his listeners share in the afflictions their Lord bore before they partake of his glory. Here the aim is not righteousness per se but belonging to Christ, being "conformed" to him (Rom 8:29), being found "in" him, sharing in his sufferings and only then achieving the glory of the resurrection.

Paul will often declare that the sharing of Christ's crucifixion results in the dwelling of the Christian within Christ, or vice versa; it is this mutual indwelling that transforms the once dead sinner who is now raised to new life: "So if anyone is in Christ, there is a new creation: everything old has passed away; see, everything has become new!" (2 Cor 5:17). "I have been crucified with Christ," Paul tells the Galatians. "It is no longer I who live, but Christ who lives in me" (Gal 2:19–20). Schweitzer observed that the expression of being "in Christ" is almost formulaic in Paul. "It is no mere formula for Paul," he argues, however. "For him every manifestation of the life of the baptized man is conditioned by his being in Christ."

Schweitzer is certainly right about that, and he described this indwelling as a distinctively Pauline form of "mysticism." He might also have observed that this language deliberately harkens back to the thought-world of Second Temple Judaism, and even to early Israelite history. Paul surely meant this language to reverberate with allusion to God's palpable presence within the Temple and beforehand within the Tabernacle of Mosaic times. In his first letter to the Corinthians, he imagines each Christian as a minuscule Temple or a Tabernacle in which the Lord dwells: "Do you not know that you are God's temple and that God's Spirit dwells in you? If anyone destroys God's temple, God will destroy that person. For God's temple is holy, and you are that temple" (1 Cor 3:16–17).

In Paul's thinking, Christ's death atoned for sin, to be sure. But its main result was to have effected a change in lordships and sonships. Sanders summarizes the matter neatly: "Paul was thinking of the significance of Christ's death more in terms of a *change in lordship* which guarantees future salvation than in terms of the expiation of past transgression. . . . transgression does not constitute the problem. . . . [the] problem is not being under Christ's lordship." If they once lived under the lordship of sin and death, Christians now reside under the dominion of Christ, the sovereign Lord of life. Just so, Paul proclaims that faith and baptism have endowed the faithful, not with righteousness, but with sonship: "you are all children

of God through faith. . . . you belong to Christ" (Gal 3:26, 29). Believers
are linked to God, and can die to the power of sin, by dying with Christ. To
be raised one must, in the first place, be reckoned not as righteous, but as
"in Christ." To Paul's way of thinking, this is the essential and, in the end,
sufficient condition for salvation.

As already intimated, in Paul's theology the way in which Christians
come to die and thus to rise in Christ is through the ritual of baptism, as we
see in Romans 6:

> [3]Do you not know that all of us who have been baptized into Christ Jesus
> were baptized into his death? [4]Therefore we have been buried with him by
> baptism into death, so that, just as Christ was raised from the dead by the
> glory of the Father, so we too might walk in newness of life.
>   [5]For if we have been united with him in a death like his, we will certainly
> be united with him in a resurrection like his. [6]We know that our old self was
> crucified with him so that the body of sin might be destroyed, and we might
> no longer be enslaved to sin. [7]For whoever has died is freed from sin. [8]But if
> we have died with Christ, we believe that we will also live with him. (Rom
> 6:3–8)

What is central to this text and indeed to all of Paul's theology of salvation
is incorporation into the body of Christ, the communion of saints. Righteousness by faith, though not unimportant in Paul, is distinctly secondary;
in this text it is not mentioned at all. Rather, assimilation to or absorption
into the body of Christ is essential. This integration into the body of Christ
is undertaken expressly so that Christians can be buried with Christ in his
death and thus share in his victory over death and in the cosmic shift of
aeons.

For Paul, baptism is *the* ritual occasion for the believer to participate in
this cosmic transformation. It is there, on that occasion, that the person being baptized participates in Christ's death to the power and lordship of sin.
The ritual action establishes a link, a bond, between the savior and the
saved, which makes Christ lord and the baptized a son or daughter; it en-
dows the baptized with "member-ship" in the body of Christ, the mystical
body that will be raised on the last day: all are "baptized into one body" (1
Cor 12:13). "What takes place in Baptism," Schweitzer explains, "is the beginning of the being-in-Christ and the process of dying and rising again
which is associated therewith." Baptism is the ritual mode by which the

Christian participates in the epochal shift in aeons, from death to life. One plunges into the water under the dominion of wickedness and sin, naked to the assault of death; one rises in and under the authority of life, clothed in imperishability, having been rendered invulnerable to the sinister forces of the old aeon, awaiting final liberation. The newly baptized Christian dies and then comes again to life, mirroring the destiny of the Lord: "Therefore we have been buried with him by baptism into death, so that, just as Christ was raised from the dead by the glory of the Father, so we too might walk in newness of life" (Rom 6:4). It also mirrors the shift in aeons effected by Jesus' death and burial.

Baptism is thus the concrete way in which Christians are sealed and saved from death. Not "righteousness by faith" but being "in Christ," that is, a member of his mystical body, saves one from destruction and gives the baptized assurance of resurrection and salvation: "There is therefore now no condemnation for those *who are in Christ Jesus*" (Rom 8:1; emphasis added) — good news so liberating that Bach felt compelled to set the line to music in *Jesu, Meine Freude* (1723). Once denizens of the earthly kingdoms, slaves to the corruptible, they are now, already, citizens of heaven, and heirs of incorruptibility: "But our citizenship is in heaven, and it is from there that we are expecting a Savior, the Lord Jesus Christ" (Phil 3:20). Christians will be raised in the end because they are united with Christ in baptism. Having suffered with Christ, they will be glorified and raised with him on the last day.

WHAT KIND OF RESURRECTED BODY?

The text in which Paul responds to this question most directly is 1 Corinthians 15. When one reads that text, it appears very much as if those to whom Paul writes, or at least a segment of them, had denied the resurrection of the body: "Now if Christ is proclaimed as raised from the dead, how can some of you say there is no resurrection of the dead?" (1 Cor 15:12).

Who are making such denials? And on what basis? This chapter is a complicated treatise in itself, and many books have been written on it alone. One of the most successful of those recently published is Dale B. Martin's *The Corinthian Body*. Martin places 1 Corinthians 15 quite convincingly within the context of ancient Greek and Roman understandings of the composition of the body. On the basis of this literature, and his own close reading of the text, Martin concludes that one segment of the Corinthian community, an upper-class elite, fully looked forward to an afterlife. This part of the community also believed in the resurrection of Christ. About the general resurrection of the dead, however, they had some question. "What they question," Martin observes, "is the idea that human *bodies* can survive after death and be raised to immortality."

As we have already shown, Paul argues vehemently that *some* sort of bodily resurrection will occur and, indeed, that the truth of the gospel depends on this being so. The question is, as the doubters in Corinth asked, with what sort of body are they raised, and how is this possible? "But someone will ask, 'How are the dead raised? With what kind of body do they come?'" (1 Cor 15:35) — very possibly the verbatim question the Corinthian doubters asked. Martin reminds us here, crucially, that ancient thinkers did not think in terms of modern mind/body dualisms. Thus, though the body contains flesh and blood, it is also composed, for ancient thinkers, of heavenly substances, like "spirit" (*pneuma*). For Paul, or so Martin argues, the resurrected body will divest itself of the lower elements of its composition but retain the pneumatic elements, those it shares with the thinner, higher natures of the cosmos, like heavenly bodies. Earthly bodies, to use Paul's language, *do* contain elements of the heavenly, the glorious, the indestructible and immortal (1 Cor 15:40). As Martin puts it, "When Paul says that the resurrected body will be a pneumatic body rather than simply a psychic body or a flesh-and-blood body, he is saying that the immortal and incorruptible part of the human body will be resurrected — or . . . that the body will be raised, constituted (due to divine transformation) only by its immortal and incorruptible aspects, without its corruptible and corrupting aspects such as sarx [flesh]." This is what Paul means when he insists that "flesh and blood cannot inherit the kingdom of God, nor . . . the perishable inherit the imperishable" (1 Cor 15:50). The "perishable body puts on imperishability," and the mortal body "immortality" (1 Cor 15:54). "[42]So it is with the resurrection of the dead. What is sown is perishable, what is raised is imperishable. [43]It is sown in dishonor, it is raised in glory. It is sown in weakness, it is raised in power" (1 Cor 15:42–43).

Paul's opponents, then, did not depreciate the material or physical; they disparaged the body, or at least its "lower" elements, which it shared with the lower elements of the cosmos as a whole. What they doubted was that the lower elements would or could be raised.

In 1 Corinthians 15, Paul puts forward a defense of the resurrection of the body that derives first from Jewish apocalyptic literature. He so redefines the word "body," however, that the result represents something new. Nonetheless, it is important to stress that Paul clearly felt that the bodies sown and raised would be, somehow, the same. Indeed, the very use of the image of "seeding" suggests organic growth and development; the plant is different from the seed, yet the former grows out of the latter, owing to the surpassing power of their divine creator. The body that is sown is a physical body; "it is raised," to be sure, "a *spiritual* body" (1 Cor 15:44, emphasis added). Nonetheless it *is* a body. We are not dealing here with the immortality or transmigration of the soul or anything else of that sort.

The possibility of resurrection—the raising of the body by God—is thus once again rooted in the power of God at creation. If God could raise Adam out of dust, then he can surely raise a dead body at the general resurrection. The victory of God over death at the end again mirrors the primordial victory of the God of life at the beginning and reminds us that we owe our lives, before death and after, to the God who created all. We do not live, and will not live again, by nature alone.

For Paul, the resurrected body is a body very much like that of Jesus after his own resurrection: "Just as we have borne the image of the man of dust, we will also bear the image of the man of heaven" (1 Cor 15:49). As he puts it more clearly in another letter: our mortal body will be changed at the resurrection "that it may be conformed to the body of [Christ's] glory" (Phil 3:21). Here Paul traces the earthly paternity of Christians to Adam; their celestial lineage goes back to Christ, however, and it is with Jesus' resurrection, and their participation through baptism in that resurrection, that their own destinies have been sealed. For in Christ's death and resurrection victory, death has lost its power to harm. It has indeed been "swallowed up" (1 Cor 15:54) in God's triumph through Christ. Thus Christians can shout out, and even taunt death in joy and gratitude to the God who delivered them, again:

> Where, O death, is your victory?
> Where, O death, is your sting? (1 Cor 15:55)

A Journey to Sheol (and Back)

DID JESUS AND PAUL FIND
RESURRECTION IN THE BIBLE?

The belief that Jesus was resurrected and that his followers would be as well pervades the New Testament, as we have seen in detail in the previous two chapters. But we have also seen that something else pervades the New Testament: a heavy reliance on the Hebrew Bible, which it quotes or echoes incessantly and which is the only scriptures that Jesus, Paul, and all other early Christians knew (the term "New Testament" did not even exist until about a century and a half later). This, in turn, poses a conundrum. For in the Hebrew Bible — in the book, that is, that Christians would eventually come to call the "Old Testament" — we find almost nothing about an expectation that the dead would rise. Indeed, where it speaks of the future of the dead at all, the Hebrew Bible most often refers to their miserable abode, Sheol.

And yet, as we shall show, the source of the Christian belief in resurrection lay in nothing other than that very book. This is something most people do not know, but it is essential to anyone who wants to understand the Christian hope for eternal life and its connection to the Judaism out of which the messages of Jesus and Paul arose.

THE LAND OF NO RETURN

"Everyone who dies goes to Sheol," wrote Johannes Pedersen, a prominent scholar of the Hebrew Bible about eighty years ago, "just as he, if everything happens in the normal way, is put into the grave." To be sure, the same scholar's description of Sheol makes it clear that he does not believe that the dead cease to exist altogether, only that their existence is then altogether negative: "Firmness, joy, strength, blessing belong to the world of light; slackness, sorrow, exhaustion, curses belong to the realm of the dead." It would be hard to imagine anything further from an expectation of glorious resurrection than that! Over the intervening decades, many scholars have reiterated this grim view of the vision of existence after death in the Hebrew Bible. One of them employs as an example the dying King David's gruesome instruction to his heir designate, soon to be King Solomon, to do in David's old and once-trusted commander, Joab. Make sure, the old king warns Solomon, "that his white hair does not go down to Sheol in peace" (1 Kgs 2:6). Sheol, Pedersen explains, is "the shadowy, insubstantial underworld, the destination of all, good and bad without discrimination, where existence is wholly undesirable. The Hebrews in the classical period had no comfortable prospect of the hereafter." On this reading, the punishment does not lie in Joab's consignment to Sheol, for that is "the destination of all," but only in his being deprived of the chance to experience the full measure and contentment of old age. Solomon is to exact retribution upon Joab for the evil of "shedding blood of war in peacetime" (v 5), but the retribution itself consists simply of a descent sooner rather than later into the realm that consumes "good and bad without discrimination." For this is a worldview with "no comfortable prospect of the hereafter." It is, in sum, a worldview very different from that of the earliest Christians. Yet they, oddly enough, insisted that their own beliefs, including the belief in resurrection, had been foreshadowed in "the scriptures."

If this description of the Israelite Sheol sounds familiar, it is because it recalls numerous accounts of the netherworld from far-flung cultures, not least the related cultures of the ancient Near Eastern and Mediterranean worlds. One thinks, for example, of a fragmentary tablet in Akkadian (a language of Mesopotamia related to Hebrew) in which the hero Gilgamesh and his departed friend Enkidu are, however briefly, eerily reunited:

> "Tell me, my friend, tell me, my friend,
> Tell me the order of the nether world which thou hast seen."
> "I shall not tell thee, I shall not tell thee!

> (But) if I tell thee the order of the nether world
> which I have seen,
> Sit thou down and weep!"
> "[. . .] I will sit down and weep."
> "[*My body* . . .], which thou didst touch as thy heart rejoiced
> Vermin devour [as though] an old garment.
> [. . .] is filled with dust."
> He cried "[Woe]" and threw himself [in the dust],
> [Gilgamesh] cried, "[Woe!]" and threw himself in the dust.

Or consider this description of the "Land of No Return" from an Akkadian poem about the Mesopotamian goddess Ishtar's descent into the nether-world:

> To the house which none leave who have entered it,
> To the world from which there is no way back,
> To the house wherein the entrants are bereft of li[ght],
> Where dust is their fare and clay their food,
> (Where) they see no light, residing in darkness,
> (Where) they are clothed like birds, with wings for garments,
> (And where) over door and bolt is spread dust.

Texts like these profoundly reinforce the summary judgment of one scholar of ancient Mesopotamia that "the orthodox vision of the nether-world and existence there can be expressed in a simple word: gloom."

The same English term accurately renders the many classical Greek descriptions of the netherworld as well. And from this the inference may justly be drawn that in early Greek mythology, too, the dead still exist but they do not live. Their existence is one of unqualified and interminable unhappiness, unqualified and interminable hopelessness. The same aspect of hopelessness, nicely captured in the Akkadian term "Land of No Return," appears as well in biblical texts. Job's meditation on the frailty and impermanence of human life, for example, makes the same point:

> [7]Consider that my life is but wind;
> I shall never see happiness again.
> [8]The eye that gazes on me will not see me;
> Your eye will seek me, but I shall be gone.
> [9]As a cloud fades away,

So whoever goes down to Sheol does not come up;
[10]He returns no more to his home;
His place does not know him. (Job 7:7–10)

EXISTING WITHOUT LIVING

But just what and where is Sheol? This question has long occupied the minds and pens of scholars. The beginning of wisdom in answering the question is to avoid literalism, especially the variety that imagines that ele ments in the ancient Israelite worldview have close equivalents in ours. We are, in other words, confronting not just the formidable challenge of linguistic translation, but also—and more importantly—the even more difficult one of cultural translation. Complicating the task is the obvious fact that the range of conditions that the Hebrew Bible groups under the rubric of "death" includes many that we designate otherwise. As one scholar puts it, "those endangered feel that they are in Sheol already, they become rigid in the grip of the enemy." To understand the condition of those dispatched to Sheol (for we shall argue that not all the dead were), it will be useful to get a sense of the predominant metaphors by which the Hebrew Bible conveys the character of the grim abode of these dead.

Pedersen observes that "the ideas of the grave and of Sheol cannot be separated," since the dead are in both at the same time, "not in two different places." We shall soon have occasion to challenge this total identification of Sheol and grave, but in Pedersen's defense it can be said there is a common synonym for both the grave and Sheol: "Pit." Thus can the author of one of the most plangent of psalms describe himself as consigned not only to the grave, but to the realm of the dead in Sheol/the Pit, sated with God's fury and his fellows' contempt:

> [2]O Lord, God of my deliverance,
>> when I cry out in the night before You,
>> [3]let my prayer reach You;
>> incline Your ear to my cry.
> [4]For I am sated with misfortune;
>> I am at the brink of Sheol.
> [5]I am numbered with those who go down to the Pit;
>> I am a helpless man

> [6]abandoned among the dead,
>   like bodies lying in the grave
>   of whom You are mindful no more,
>   and who are cut off from Your care.
> [7]You have put me at the bottom of the Pit,
>   in the darkest places, in the depths.
> [8]Your fury lies heavy upon me;
>   You afflict me with all Your breakers. *Selah.*
> [9]You make my companions shun me;
>   You make me abhorrent to them;
>   I am shut in and do not go out.
> [10]My eyes pine away from affliction;
>   I call to You, O LORD, each day;
>   I stretch out my hands to You. (Ps 88:2–10)

Although the author of these verses is surely not yet dead in our sense, in his own view he already dwells—one hesitates to say "lives"—in the realm of the dead; he is in "the Pit." Here again, we run up against the problem of cultural translation. To us, people are either alive or dead. If they speak—reciting, for example, those plaintive lines from Psalm 88 quoted above—they are alive: end of story. They may be gravely ill, under lethal assault, or sentenced to capital punishment, but they are living nonetheless. The ancient Israelites thought in a markedly different way. They were quite capable of seeing just such an individual as dead. Or, to be more precise, they could do so in their poetic literature without implying that in a more prosaic genre (like historiography or religious law) they would make the same classification. In other words, for us, death is radically discontinuous with life, a quantum leap, as it were, lying between the two. For the poets who wrote the psalms, by contrast, the major discontinuity lay between a healthy and successful life, on the one hand, and one marked by adversity, in physical health or otherwise, on the other. The diagram below illustrates the difference:

a. Life → illness || death
b. Life || → illness → death

We are predisposed to think of death as involving two stages, one characterized by intense affliction but capable of reversal and a second one that is permanent and irreversible (see a). The psalmists, by contrast, saw illness as continuous with death and thought of the reversal of illness as so miraculous as to be in the nature of a return to life, an exodus from Sheol. The sick are closer to the dead than to the living (see b).

The imagery of grave and pit is only one component of the overlapping symbolic renderings of the netherworld in the Hebrew Bible. Some scholars, noticing that languages related to Hebrew lack the word "Sheol" but use the word for "land" or "earth" in the same way, draw attention to biblical texts in which the related Hebrew word (*'eretz*) seems to have a similar meaning. The book of Numbers, for example, speaks of the fate of a group of rebels against the authority of Moses and Aaron led by their own cousin, Korah:

> [32]The earth opened its mouth and swallowed them up. . . .[33]They went down alive into Sheol, with all that belonged to them; the earth closed over them and they vanished from the midst of the congregation. [34]All Israel around them fled at their shrieks, for they said, "The earth might swallow us!" (Num 16:32–34)

In the opinion of some scholars, the rich mythological resonance of this image of "the earth" opening its mouth to "swallow" the malefactors constitutes potent evidence that we are dealing with more than the ground as we might conceive it and must instead think of it in terms of Sheol. As they see it, an image so graphic and anthropomorphic as this, together with the threefold repetition of "earth," suggests that the term refers, if not to Sheol itself, then at least to its horrific and irresistible orifice in the terrestrial world, the route by which the doomed leave this world.

An earlier and highly memorable attestation of the earth's "swallowing" malefactors occurs in the Song at the Sea in Exodus 15, when such is the fate of Pharaoh's army:

> You put out Your right hand,
> The earth swallowed them. (Exod 15:12)

Here, another Hebrew word for "ground" (*'adamah*) is used, but it has the same meaning. In fact, it also appears in Moses' prediction of Korah's miraculous demise: "the ground opens its mouth and swallows them up" (Num 16:30). In this text, the earth or ground is entirely under God's control and serves as the agent of his righteous will. But there is still room to suspect that the language that describes the earth or ground as if it were a monster of some sort ("opens its mouth and swallows") may indicate that Sheol is animate, a malevolent, gruesome being, that is, rather than merely a place or a fate.

"WHEN MY LIFE WAS EBBING AWAY, I CALLED THE LORD TO MIND"

The lethal threat that monster represents is an important part of the story, but not the whole story. Herein, too, lies an irony. For all that scholarship may tell us that the dreary netherworld was a land of no return, much of our knowledge of it comes from people who claim to have returned from it or who pray that God will enable them to do so. Consider the spatial imagery of these lines:

> ²Hear my cry, O God,
>> heed my prayer.
> ³From the end of the earth I call to You;
>> when my heart is faint,
>> You lead me to a rock that is high above me.
> ⁴For You have been my refuge,
>> a tower of strength against the enemy.
> ⁵O that I might dwell in Your tent forever,
>> take refuge under Your protecting wings. (Ps 61:2–5)

Here, Nicholas Tromp detects "a clear antithesis between the unsteady mire of the netherworld and the safe rock." "The end of the earth," in other words, is not some distant terrestrial spot to which the psalmist has been driven; it is the deepest pocket of the netherworld, the outer reaches of Sheol. And to Tromp, the unnamed "enemy" from whom God has rescued the psalmist is none other than "the arch-enemy, Death, himself," a "rapacious monster," well-known from the mythology of Israel's neighbors. Whether the psalm really reflects so much living mythology is open to doubt, but Tromp's point about "the end of the earth" seems likely. The psalmist is calling upon God to bring him back from the underworld.

Along with the language of grave and of earth/ground, the terminology of water is also prominent in the description of the mortal threat that biblical psalmists hope to surmount (or claim to have already surmounted) by the grace of God. Here follows one poet's description of the challenges he faced:

> [5]For the breakers of Death encompassed me,
> The torrents of Belial terrified me;
> [6]The snares of Sheol encircled me,
> The coils of Death engulfed me. (2 Sam 22:5–6)

"Breakers" and "torrents" here serve as names for the chaotic and death-dealing rivers of the netherworld. A poem with a similar thrust has been put into the mouth of the fugitive prophet Jonah, adding a cosmic dimension to the latter's three-day plight in the belly of the fish by reference to these old mythic motifs:

> [3]He said:
> In my trouble I called to the LORD,
> And He answered me;
> From the belly of Sheol I cried out,
> And You heard my voice.
> [4]You cast me into the depths,
> Into the heart of the sea,
> The floods engulfed me;
> All Your breakers and billows
> Swept over me.
> [5]I thought I was driven away
> Out of Your sight:
> Would I ever gaze again
> Upon Your holy Temple?
> [6]The waters closed in over me,
> The deep engulfed me.
> Weeds twined around my head.
> [7]I sank to the base of the mountains;
> The bars of the earth closed upon me forever.
> Yet You brought my life up from the pit,
> O LORD my God!
> [8]When my life was ebbing away,
> I called the LORD to mind;
> And my prayer came before You,
> Into Your holy Temple. (Jon 2:3–8)

In keeping with the comic character of the book of Jonah, God commands
the enormous fish to vomit the swallowed prophet, thus rescuing him from
the lethal subterranean waters—and restoring him to divine service
whether he likes it or not (Jon 2:11).

In the case of the author of 2 Samuel 22, rescue from the overpowering
waters of Sheol comes in loftier imagery, the imagery of God as a fierce
warrior marching forth to combat his fearsome foe:

> [8]Then the earth rocked and quaked,
> The foundations of heaven shook—
> Rocked by His indignation.
> [9]Smoke went up from His nostrils,
> From His mouth came devouring fire;
> Live coals blazed forth from Him.
> [10]He bent the sky and came down,
> Thick cloud beneath His feet.
> [11]He mounted a cherub and flew;
> He flew on the wings of the wind.
> [12]He made pavilions of darkness about Him,
> Dripping clouds, huge thunderheads;
> [13]In the brilliance before Him
> Blazed fiery coals.
> [14]The LORD thundered forth from heaven,
> The Most High sent forth His voice;
> [15]He let loose bolts, and scattered them;
> Lightning, and put them to rout.
> [16]The bed of the sea was exposed,
> The foundations of the world were laid bare
> By the mighty roaring of the LORD,
> At the blast of the breath of His nostrils.
> [17]He reached down from on high, He took me,
> Drew me out of the mighty waters;
> [18]He rescued me from my enemy so strong,
> From foes too mighty for me.
> [19]They attacked me on my day of calamity,
> But the LORD was my stay. (2 Sam 22:8–19)

The LORD's laying bare of the seabed in verse 16 is especially illuminating.
It recalls the account in Genesis 1 of God's first creating the sky to divide

the waters and then draining the terrestrial waters into pools that he called "seas" so that the dry land could be seen (vv 6–7, 9–10). More directly, it recalls the great act of deliverance he performed for the Israelites escaping Egypt: "the LORD drove back the sea with a strong east wind all that night, and turned the sea into dry ground" until his chosen had crossed, only then ordaining that "the waters may come back upon the Egyptians and upon their chariots and upon their horsemen," drowning the murderous foe (Exod 14:21, 26). In the rather different account of these events in the poetic version (Exodus 15), it is again the blast of God's wind that does the arrogant enemy in. Here, however, as we have seen, an expression redolent of the netherworld characterizes their disappearing into the sea: "the sea covered them" and "the earth swallowed them" (Exod 15.10, 12). In 2 Samuel 22, this ancient creation imagery is applied to an individual's song of thanksgiving, and God's rescue of the miraculously delivered speaker from his formidable enemies is a rescue from Sheol seen as "the mighty waters" (vv 5–6, 17–18). The defeat of the terrifying foe is the defeat of an overreaching netherworld but also and equally the drying up of the chaotic waters that characterize it and threaten divine order and human life alike. Here again, salvation is both individual and cosmic. On the individual level, it involves the embattled psalmist's escape from the netherworld and restoration to life. On the cosmic level, it reflects the reestablishment of the divine authority that enables a life-enhancing world order to endure in the face of the ever-formidable forces associated with violent or unjust death. God's creation is itself an act of rescue from the overpowering forces of death.

We have now examined two very common but related images of Sheol, the subterranean world and the lethal waters. Other metaphors for the abode of the unfortunate dead can be treated more briefly. One of them, the expression "the gates of death," suggests a city in which Death — perhaps conceived as the Canaanite god of the same name (Mot) — reigns supreme, in all his grisly majesty. If so, the contrast underlying Ps 9:14–15 is especially suggestive:

> [14]Have mercy on me, O LORD;
> see my affliction at the hands of my foes,
> You who lift me from the gates of death,
> [15]so that in the gates of Fair Zion
> I might tell all Your praise,
> I might exult in Your deliverance.

The energizing contrast here lies between "the gates of death" and "the gates of Zion," between the lowest and highest points in the universe, as it were. In the former, the foe reigns supreme, afflicting the innocent speaker grievously and at will. In the latter, the LORD reigns, having "set up His throne for judgment" (v 8), and receives the grateful praise of the faithful he has delivered from death. "Gates of death" may refer not only to a subterranean city where evil works its will, but also and equally to Sheol as a prison.

In that light, consider the rich and reinforcing symbolism of these verses from another psalm:

> [10]Some lived in deepest darkness,
>> bound in cruel irons,
>>> [11]because they defied the word of God,
>>> spurned the counsel of the Most High.
> [12]He humbled their hearts through suffering;
>> they stumbled with no one to help.
> [13]In their adversity they cried to the LORD,
>> and He rescued them from their troubles.
> [14]He brought them out of deepest darkness,
>> broke their bonds asunder.
> [15]Let them praise the LORD for His steadfast love,
>> His wondrous deeds for mankind,
>>> [16]For He shattered gates of bronze,
>> He broke their iron bars.
> [17]There were fools who suffered for their sinful way,
>> and for their iniquities.
> [18]All food was loathsome to them;
>> they reached the gates of death.
> [19]In their adversity they cried to the LORD
>> and He saved them from their troubles.
> [20]He gave an order and healed them;
>> He delivered them from the pits.
> [21]Let them praise the LORD for His steadfast love,
>> His wondrous deeds for mankind.
> [22]Let them offer thanksgiving sacrifices,
>> and tell His deeds in joyful song. (Ps 107:10–22)

Much of the power of this stanza derives from its overlay of several dominant metaphors of Sheol, and we should be most unwise to attempt to unravel and separate them. The "pits" from which the LORD rescued the rebels humbled in suffering (v 20) recalls the language of the grave, as we saw above. The twice-mentioned "deepest darkness" (vv 10, 14) again suggests the grave, but also the primordial darkness and water that God triumphantly overcomes in the act of creation in Gen 1:2. The Hebrew word in question (*tzalmavet*), best known as the "shadow of death" in the King James Version of the twenty-third psalm (v 4), surely suggests death to the attentive hearer, even if that etymology is unscientific, as some scholars now believe. The "gates of death" suggests a city, as we have seen, specifically, the subterranean city that is the diametric opposite of the lofty city atop Mount Zion, in which the life-giving LORD reigns supreme and inviolable.

The references to "cruel irons," "gates of bronze," and "iron bars" depict something far more ghastly than a mere city, even one that is heavily fortified. They depict a prison, and so doing, they interpret the rescue/healing of the afflicted penitents as an act of liberation. The attentive reader of the Hebrew Bible may recall at this point a number of other texts, most memorably the story of Joseph, whom his brothers first resolved to murder and subsequently threw into a pit from which he was rescued, only to be enslaved and later imprisoned in Egypt—but then redeemed from these fates no less (Gen 37:18–28, 36; 39:20; 41:14). In this, of course, Joseph pre-enacts the experience of the whole people Israel a few generations later when they become the target first of Pharaoh's enslavement, then of his genocidal decree (Exod 1:8–22), only to survive both of these and to march proudly out of the house of bondage (Exod 13:17–14:31). Both of these cases—the one cast as biography, the other as national history—present in prose narrative the sort of liberation and deliverance celebrated in the poetic verses we have quoted from Psalm 107. That liberation or deliverance is a central theme of the entire Hebrew Bible, and it suffuses the traditional Jewish liturgy to this very day. It was also a major component of Judaism in the time of Jesus.

Our examination of various images of Sheol in the Jewish scriptures reinforces the point made earlier that literalistic efforts to locate the abode of the dead in space are misconceived. Grave, pit, underworld, utmost bounds of the earth, engulfing waters, subterranean city, prison—all these metaphors communicate a mode of existence, one that, in the literature we have been examining, characterizes people who have not "died" in our sense of the term at all. As Tromp aptly puts it, "those endangered feel that they are in Sheol already" because they live lives of weakness, defeat, depression, vulnerability, and the like. In passages that deal with the biblical netherworld, the difference between being dead and being almost dead—can *we* imagine a larger difference than that?—often evaporates before our very eyes. Thus can the despondent speaker in Psalm 88 say, "I am at the brink of Sheol" (literally, "my life has reached Sheol") and then three verses later tell the LORD, "You have put me at the bottom of the Pit, / in the darkest places, in the depths" (vv 4, 7). It is not the case that in the intervening two verses he has passed away or somehow changed his locale from the edge of Sheol to its deepest pit. Rather, his condition—agonizing misfortune infinitely compounded by God-forsakenness—is very much the condition of Sheol. Without God's intervention ("cut off from Your care," v 6), he is dead. And, remarkably, tragically, for the speaking voice of Psalm 88, unlike most of the comparable psalmists (especially the author of Psalm 107), God never intervenes. This poet remains "a helpless man, abandoned among the dead" (vv 5–6). All that differentiates him from them is his ability to call out to God to save him from Sheol. Unanswered (as he is), he is as good as dead.

COMMUNICATING WITH THE DEAD

The image of Sheol in the Hebrew Bible is of a place of intense loneliness, isolation, and abandonment. Psalm 88 once more puts it well, "You have put friend and neighbor far from me / and my companions out of my sight" (v 19). To judge by this literature, the land of the living and the abode of the dead are not in any communication whatsoever.

A number of biblical passages, however, augmented by archaeological studies, have emboldened some contemporary scholars to suggest an alternative view of the netherworld in Israelite thought. According to this view, the living were believed to be able to affect the dead (especially for the better), and the dead were deemed able, under certain ritual conditions and to some degree, to communicate with the living. These scholars, in other words, evoke a world in which the two realms are not nearly so separate as they appear in the psalms of lament or of thanksgiving, and death was not so final or so tragic as it appears in them. If they are right, such poems do not reflect the whole reality of the Israelite construction of death. They reflect instead certain segments of Israelite society at certain periods, but it would be a capital error to generalize from those segments and periods and to find the Israelite view of death in them alone. In particular, some scholars have conjectured that a cult of the dead had been long and widely practiced in ancient Israel, as in other ancient Near Eastern and Mediterranean societies, before various biblical sources acted to proscribe it relatively late in biblical history. Especially potent fuel for the conjecture comes from the confession that, according to Deuteronomy, an Israelite farmer is to make after depositing his tithe at the central sanctuary:

> [12]When you have set aside in full the tenth part of your yield—in the third year, the year of the tithe—and have given it to the Levite, the stranger, the fatherless, and the widow, that they may eat their fill in your settlements, [13]you shall declare before the LORD your God: "I have cleared out the consecrated portion from the house; and I have given it to the Levite, the stranger, the fatherless, and the widow, just as You commanded me; I have neither transgressed nor neglected any of Your commandments: [14]I have not eaten of it while in mourning, I have not cleared out any of it while I was unclean, and I have not deposited any of it with the dead. I have obeyed the LORD my God; I have done just as You commanded me." (Deut 26:12–14)

The traditional Jewish interpretation of the affirmation central to our concern (v 14) is that the farmer has not eaten of the tithed crop while in a state of mourning (those in the initial stage of mourning being thus forbidden to make the affirmation) nor used it to provide a casket or shroud for the deceased. Whatever other strengths it may have, the understanding this interpretation affords of the clause, "I have not deposited any of it with the dead," is forced, to say the least, and we should not be surprised that an alternative reading has been proposed. In light of the practice, known from many cultures, of feeding the dead to sustain them in the netherworld, the scholars in question have read verse 14 to forbid this *only* when the food is to be tithed: either it is tithed and thus set aside for the needy or it is offered to the dead, but not both. On this reading, under ordinary circumstances, circumstances that do not involve the tithe or kindred rituals, feeding the dead would have been altogether unobjectionable to the author of this text.

Other arguments for the same general point have come from archaeol-

ogy, for example the archaeology of the house in ancient Israel. Rachel S.
Hallote makes the point nicely:

> As families grew and shifted the space in the house was relocated. Occasion-
> ally additions were made, but in many cases floor plans remained identical
> for a century at a time. The older generations especially would move from
> room to room each time there was a new marriage or new birth. When a
> member of the oldest generation died, he would simply be given another
> space within the house—this time beneath its floors. His final resting-place
> kept him within the family unit in the most literal sense and allowed him to
> continue to participate in the life of the family and the household, even after
> death.

Given this incorporation and participation of the dead in the life of the
family, it stands to reason that Hallote sees in Deut 26:13–14 evidence that
"the Israelite desire to appease and please the dead by giving them the best
food available was irresistible."

Some scholars now go even further, arguing that the food offered to the
dead is sacrificial and the recipients of the sacrifice are thus the deceased.
In this reading, the departed are not so much dead (in our sense) as deified:
they become gods who command and receive the service of their descendants. However negatively the later biblical and post-biblical traditions
were to judge the phenomenon (and they judged it very negatively indeed), the cult of the dead would thus have been a major element of Israelite devotion in biblical times.

According to the dominant reconstruction of the cult of the dead, it involved communication in each direction. The living, especially the descendants of the deified departed, served the dead through sacrificial rituals, and the dead served the living by giving them information about the
future, and the like. Although necromancy, the verbal communication between the dead and the living, came to be strictly proscribed and attributed
to foreign influence (for example, Lev 19:31; 20:27; Deut 18:9–14), a number of texts have been interpreted in recent years to suggest that it was once
widely practiced and, according to some scholars, not viewed as an offense
to the God of Israel until relatively late. Thus, an oracle by the prophet Isaiah (eighth century B.C.E.) that predicts a terrifying siege of Jerusalem
arranged by God himself likens the victims to ghosts:

³And I will camp against you like David;
I will lay siege to you with a mound,
And I will set up siegeworks against you.
⁴And you shall speak from lower than the ground,
Your speech shall be humbler than the sod;
Your speech shall sound like a ghost's from the ground,
Your voice shall chirp from the sod.
⁵And like fine dust shall be
The multitude of your haughty people;
And like flying chaff,
The multitude of tyrants. (Isa 29:3–5)

The image of the dead evoked in verse 4 is hardly that of individuals who have passed into oblivion and are no more. Rather, the impression conveyed is that the dead have been humiliated, reduced not to silence but to a humble speech, barely detectable yet real. To be sure, the verse passes no judgment on those who might be tempted to consult these ghosts, except perhaps indirectly in the unflattering description of the latter: they are likened to those besieged.

The difference between this oracle, which speaks of ghosts as well-known beings, and the legal literature of the Hebrew Bible that strictly forbids Israelites to consult them, may be less extreme than first seems the case. For the legal materials do not deny the possibility that the dead may endure in some unspecified condition or even that they may have valid insights to communicate. Rather, where a rationale for the prohibition on necromancy appears at all (as in Deut 18:9–14), it is grounded in the assumption that the practice characterizes the wicked and idolatrous Canaanites and thus, if observed by Israel, compromises the chosen people's wholehearted trust in, and loyalty to, their covenanting God. When such consultation is *not* at issue (as it is not in the oracle at hand), the continued existence of the dead and their capacity to communicate a message to the living can be openly (if indirectly) acknowledged.

The best-known and most extensive account of necromancy in the Hebrew Bible is the story of Saul's desperate—yet successful—attempt to consult the departed Samuel on the eve of his own demise (1 Sam 28:3–25). Here we learn that Saul, Israel's first king, had altogether proscribed necromancy and yet sought in desperation the very sort of séance that he had forbidden. The tone is one of unrelieved tragedy.

> [4]The Philistines mustered and they marched to Shunem and encamped; and Saul gathered all Israel, and they encamped at Gilboa. [5]When Saul saw the Philistine force, his heart trembled with fear. [6]And Saul inquired of the LORD, but the LORD did not answer him, either by dreams or by Urim or by prophets. [7]Then Saul said to his courtiers, "Find me a woman who consults ghosts, so that I can go to her and inquire through her." And his courtiers told him that there was a woman in En-dor who consulted ghosts. (1 Sam 28:4–7)

In seeking out a necromancer, the king was violating his own decree, for "Saul had forbidden [*hesir*] [recourse to] ghosts and familiar spirits in the land" (v 3). The LORD's abandonment of his once chosen king is so thoroughgoing and irreversible that he even denies Saul the media that properly replace the forbidden practice—divinely inspired dreams, prophecy, and the paraphernalia of divination. Indeed, it is precisely the failure of the legitimate media that motivates Saul to seek a séance with the prophet of the LORD who had anointed him king in the first place but had also already deposed him:

> Samuel said to Saul, "Why have you disturbed me and brought me up?" And Saul answered, "I am in great trouble. The Philistines are attacking me and God has turned away [*sar*] from me; He no longer answers me, either by prophets or in dreams. So I have called you to tell me what I am to do." (1 Sam 28:15)

Consequently, it is a bit simplistic to say that Saul reverted to the necromancy that he had forbidden (*hesir*, v 3). Rather, in response to the LORD's turning away (*sar*, v 15) from him, he sought (and received) a séance with the prophet of the LORD who had been the agent of his being made king. And, from one point of view, the séance succeeds: the departed Samuel does indeed impart an oracle. Yet here, too, the note of tragedy is unbroken, for the oracle reiterates the desperate king's deposition from the throne and then adds the chilling message, "Tomorrow your sons and you will be with me," as a result of the impending and unstoppable Philistine victory (v 19). The evaluation of necromancy implied in this passage is too complex to be classified in a system that knows only the categories of fraudulent or legitimate. For here, consultation with the dead is both efficacious and forbidden. It yields a valid oracle, but the dead man who gives it is a prophet of the LORD who mostly just reiterates the prophetic pronouncement he rendered while alive. The procedure fails to reconnect the rejected supplicant with the God who has renounced him. It provides, in sum, no valuable new knowledge and no deliverance. The dead man cannot save.

The eerie meeting of Saul and Samuel—the rendezvous of the doomed and the deceased—contributes further evidence that in ancient Israel the dead were not always thought to have passed into oblivion. In 1 Samuel 28, the prophet and his message still exist, but only the message—the oracle of the LORD—survives in full force. The messenger himself is simply "an old man . . . wrapped in a robe," who is upset that he has been disturbed (vv 14–15) and whose only special claim is his status as a prophet of the LORD while he yet lived. Whatever the character of Samuel's subterranean abode (it is never actually called Sheol), the higher and more substantial reality lies not there, but above, in the realm of the living, where God's unfathomable will works itself out in history. That realm alone is the one to which the oracle is addressed. The wisdom of the dead prophet turns out to be essentially a reiteration of the final message he delivered to the king: the LORD has taken the kingship from Saul and given it to David (v 17). The only new information Samuel conveys is that the sinful and rejected king will die the next day (v 19). In 1 Samuel 28, the dead have no special wisdom, no mysteries to reveal, and no new prophecies to make. They do not in the least benefit the one who consults them.

1 Samuel 28 reminds us again that the patterns of religion generally regarded as normative in the Hebrew Bible reflect only a segment of the ancient Israelite population, many of whom doubtless once engaged without scruple in the very rites therein designated as deviant. Societies do not forbid practices that no one would think to perform. That being the case, the question before us is not whether some Israelites in some periods thought that there could be access to the dead. Our question, rather, involves the extent to which the biblical texts assume or approve of that belief and the corollary issue of the rough date at which the belief and its associated practices came to be seen as improper and disloyal to the God of Israel.

In support of their belief that the dead were thought to influence the lives of their descendants, some biblical scholars have turned to what may seem an unlikely source of evidence—biblical personal names. Here, they believe they have found convincing indications of a widespread belief in the survival and continuing power of deceased ancestors. On the basis of names like Abida (Gen 25:4), which can be parsed to mean "My Father Knows," Karel van der Toorn, for example, concludes that "deified ancestors . . . 'know' their descendants." Abiezer (Josh 17:2, "My Father Is Help") and Ahiezer (Num 1:12, "My Brother Is Help") show that the ancestors "are ready to 'help'" the descendants, just as names like Abishua (1 Chr 5:30, "My Father Is Deliverance") indicates that they "are ready . . . to 'come to their rescue.'" "Their help," argues van der Toorn, consists in "support," as demonstrated by the name Ahisamach (Exod 31:6, understood as "My Brother Offers Support") or in "kind judgement," as indicated by a name like Abidan (Num 2:22, meaning "My Father Gives Judgment"). He derives an important point from names like Abiasaph (Exod 6:24), which he understands to mean "The Father Has Added (a Child to the Family)" and Jokneam (Josh 12:22), which he translates as "May the Ancestor Create [Offspring]." All these he takes to "refer to the multiplication of descendants and the extension of the family by the deified ancestors."

On the basis of these names and others like them, van der Toorn draws a wide-ranging conclusion about the relationship of the dead to the living in ancient Israelite society: "dead kin were regarded as kind and benevolent. . . . The dead were believed to take care of their descendants from beyond the grave. Having reached a preternatural state, they used their powers for the good of their family. Not only did they symbolize the identity of that family; in the final analysis, they were also responsible for its continuing growth and welfare." This is a conclusion that depends rather heavily on van der Toorn's conviction that "the Israelites were usually aware of the religious significance of their personal names." There is room to wonder, however, how general this awareness was and how long it survived.

Some contemporary analogies may help to clarify the issue. How many speakers of English name their sons "Christopher" in the hope that the child will be one who "bears Christ," in conformity with the Greek and Latin etymologies of the name? And how many Jews who name their daughters "Esther" intend thereby to do honor to the goddess Ishtar, from which the name probably derives (as one Talmudic authority already recognized)?

One also has to reckon with the possibility that some of the names adduced in support of the deified ancestor hypothesis were already traditional before the emergence of Israel and do not necessarily reflect the dominant Israelite thinking in any period. Even if the knowing father or rescuing brother whom the name first honored really had been a deceased and deified ancestor, the name may well have been understood differently by the ancient Israelites who bore or recorded it. We also must consider the possibility that the names were either reinterpreted or perpetuated without concern for the meaning they would have if they were parsed as sentences. Indeed, van der Toorn's own reasoning would seem to require that precisely this second logical option did indeed take place. However early Israelites understood names like Ahiezer, Ahisamach, and Abidan, the relatively late biblical source in which they now occur surely did not believe that the names invoked a deceased but divine ancestor! And the same can be asserted with at least equal certainty about the author of Chronicles, the very late biblical author (late as authors of the Hebrew Bible go, that is) who dutifully records the name Abishua, for example. Indeed, Abidan appears as the name of a figure in rabbinic Judaism in the early third century C.E. Are we to imagine that his name was still understood to refer to a deified ancestor who gave judgment for his descendants? Everything we know about rabbinic Judaism forces us to answer firmly in the negative.

The issue is thus not whether the names lost their connections with deities (assuming they ever had them) but when. The mere existence of names that can be construed to refer to divinized ancestors does not demonstrate that Israelites throughout the First Temple period (roughly 1000–586 B.C.E.) generally and without condemnation worshiped dead ancestors.

Another piece of evidence in support of the theory of the deified dead in ancient Israel needs to be considered. That is of the use of the term 'elohim to describe the being(s) that the necromancer sees "coming up from the earth" in 1 Sam 28:13. Usually translated in other contexts as "God" or "gods," the term might, maximally, indeed be taken as evidence for the deification of the dead. A more minimal interpretation, however, accords much better with Israelite religion as far as the latter can be reconstructed. On this reading, 'elohim functions like the English word "spirit," which can denote anything from God to an angel, a demon, a ghost, the tone of an organization, or an alcoholic beverage. The word, in short, can mean many things, and the connotations of one of its usages cannot be legitimately extended to the others. That the dead were *'elohim* in some biblical texts does not in the least imply that they were divine in the same way the God of Israel (Yʜwʜ, conventionally rendered "the Lᴏʀᴅ," as is our practice in this discussion) was, or even his local rivals (Baal, for example) were thought to be, nor that they were the recipients of sacrifice, the addressees of prayers, benefactors of their worshipers, or anything of the kind. They may well have been thought to be as debilitated and inert as the book of Psalms (and other biblical literature) describes them.

THE PASSAGES THAT AREN'T THERE
(AND WHAT THEY TELL US)

Let us imagine what the narratives and laws of the Hebrew Bible would look like if they reflected a segment of ancient Israelite culture in which phenomena such as ancestor worship and necromancy actually had long been deemed acceptable and practiced widely, as many scholars now claim it was. Consider as our first illustration Isaac, when he has confronted the death of his father Abraham and his own appointment to continue the family line (Gen 26:1–5). Here, if anywhere, "the Israelite desire to appease and please the dead" through food offerings and other sacrifices would surely be "irresistible." So would the son and heir's desire to receive his father's counsel as he attempted to step into the latter's shoes and faced challenges strikingly similar to his, like the threat of a potentially lecherous king eager to absorb his wife into the harem (Gen 12:10–20; 20; 26:6–11). In this case, no less than in that of Saul on the eve of the battle that would end his life, Isaac would surely have felt an irresistible urge to make use of a necromancer to raise the shade of the departed and thus to secure the intervention of the knowing, helping, rescuing, and judging god that his father had become upon death. Indeed, given the exquisite narrative artistry of the storytellers of Genesis, one can imagine without much difficulty a heartbreaking rendezvous between Isaac and Abraham, like that of Odysseus with his mother, asking for information about his long-missed father. Or—a better analogy still—one can picture an Israelite equivalent of the scene in Vergil's *Aeneid* in which the proto-Roman hero Aeneas, under the guidance of the Cumaean Sybil, at long last meets with his beloved father Anchises in the netherworld. The Israelite authors did not write Homeric or Vergilian epic, of course, but if consultation with the dead were a widespread and acceptable part of their religious heritage, would they not have devised a roughly equivalent rendezvous of Abraham and Isaac, or at least something that anticipates it, however dimly? And if calling on the dead ancestor were a longstanding, widespread, acceptable Israelite practice, should we not expect it to appear here if anywhere?

The same can be asked of the next generation in the family line of Israel, of Jacob, when his father Isaac dies (Gen 35:28–29). Had all outstanding issues in the immensely complicated relationship between the two been resolved while the father yet lived? Would Jacob not have still wished more than most sons to "appease and please" the father he had once deceived grievously, plunging him into uncontrollable trembling (Gen 27:1–45)? Would he not have set forth rich fare at the latter's grave—if not out of guilt, then certainly out of a desire to treat his father's ghost as any good Canaanite/Israelite son would be expected to? And would Jacob not have wanted to secure Isaac's blessing one more time, this time when it would perhaps be all the stronger, coming from the realm of the divinized dead? If so, then surely he, too, would have sought out the appropriate practitioner to raise his father's shade and perform the requisite and, at that period, thoroughly unobjectionable rites.

Since the initial infertility of the matriarch is an important issue in each of the three Patriarchal generations in Genesis (for example, 15:1–6; 25:20–21; 29:31; 30:1–2), as well as in the stories of Samson (Judg 13:2), Hannah (1 Sam 1:4–11), and Naomi (Ruth 1:11–13), one would expect to find many remnants of the appeal to the divine ancestor who is responsible for "the multiplication of descendants and the extension of the family by the deified ancestors." Here, too, should we not expect to read that the proper sacrifices and libations were offered, the divine ghost of the ancestor served with food, the appropriate necromancer enlisted, and the hoped-for blessing of fertility thus extended?

The same questions could be asked about Joshua, the successor of Moses, whose charisma he has assumed (Num 27:20), or about Rehoboam, the son of King Solomon, whose harshness and intransigence lost him the major part of his father's realm (1 Kgs 12:1–24)—indeed, about dozens of biblical characters, too many to list here, in need of appeasing, pleasing, consulting, and benefiting from their ancestors.

Yet the actual literary evidence is stunning. For not a single such narrative exists, and our thought experiment remains purely theoretical. To be sure, the Hebrew Bible records a variety of burial practices, from the humble Moses' interment in an unknown grave (Deut 34:5–6) to the proud Absalom's erection of a monument to keep his memory alive in the absence of a son (2 Sam 18:18). Biblical authors were also willing to record practices very much at odds with the continuing Israelite tradition, such as the forty days of embalming for Jacob in Egypt and the subsequent seventy days in which the Egyptians mourned the patriarch from whom Israel took its name (Gen 50:2–3). More importantly, the narratives speak unabashedly of esteemed ancestors' engaging in practices that were later fiercely opposed, even anathematized. Consider Abraham's willingness to perform a child sacrifice (Gen 22:1–19; compare Lev 20:2–5; Deut 12:29–31) or Jacob's marriage to two sisters (Gen 29:21–30; compare Lev 18:18). Or, again, consider the lack of embarrassment or apologetic about the patriarchs' consecrating sanctuaries outside the one central sanctuary that came to be seen as exclusively legitimate (for example, Gen 12:7–8; 21:33; 28:18–19; compare Deut 12:1–27). Yet nowhere do we find a narrative describing the allegedly "irresistible" and altogether legitimate feeding of the dead or sacrificing to the supposedly deified ancestors. Similarly, other than Saul's tragically unproductive consultation with Samuel at En-dor, we find no explicit narrative about a consultation with the departed—many places where the theory says they ought to be but none where they are.

Biblical law offers no more support than narrative for this hypothesis. To be sure, as we have seen, Deut 26:14 can be plausibly construed to imply that food deposited with the dead is a problem only if it is then offered for the tithe. This is at most a plausible implication; the text may simply mean that the foods offered are clear of any association with wrongdoing, such as offerings for the dead. But if this text does imply that feeding the dead was acceptable, why, again, is there no attestation of the practice in biblical narrative, and why no other law similarly restricting but not prohibiting this putatively irresistible practice? We can imagine, for instance, that the firstborn of flock and herd to which the LORD lays claim, according to more than one Pentateuchal source (for example, Exod 13:11–13; 22:28–29; 34:19–20), would, for the same reason, be ineligible to feed to the dead, and the farmer would be sternly cautioned against thinking otherwise. Similarly, laws that regulate freewill offerings (for example, Lev 7:16–18) might warn against the designation for this purpose of meat left for the dead, or, in forbidding such sacrifices to be eaten after the morrow, might include offering them to the deceased in the same prohibition. But, once more, this is not the case, and the evidence in the legal corpora for this supposedly widespread and long legitimate practice remains limited to exactly one clause in Deuteronomy.

Necromancy, on the other hand, is indeed prohibited, though explicitly only in law codes that historians tend to date to a relatively late period (Lev 19:31; 20:27; Deut 18:9–14). An argument from silence could thus suggest that necromancy had been thought quite legitimate early on and was prohibited only in the wake of the reforms of Kings Hezekiah and Josiah (late eighth to late seventh centuries B.C.E.) and the centralizing, royalist party they championed. This requires us, of course, to discount the report that "Saul had forbidden [recourse to] ghosts and familiar spirits in the land" (1 Sam 28:3). If this report is without a basis in historical fact, it is difficult to see why the narrator would want to portray Saul this way at all. For Israel's first king is (to understate drastically) not generally depicted as foreshadowing those two admired reforming monarchs, who are, in fact, descended from the very man in favor of whom he was deposed, King David. That Saul is depicted as engaging in necromancy is indeed an important piece of evidence for the reconstruction of this aspect of the religion of Israel, but so is the fact that he is reported to have proscribed necromancy three centuries before the reforms of Hezekiah and four before the kindred reforms of Josiah. It may well be that on this point Hezekiah and Josiah were actually traditionalists, harking back to older patterns of Israelite religion that had become obscured—much as the biblical narratives about them insist (2 Kgs 18:1–8; 22:1–2; 23:19–25).

The conclusion to which the data impel us is that for those ancient Israelites who produced the Hebrew Bible, Sheol seems generally to have remained as lifeless, as remote, and as inaccessible as the psalms of thanksgiving and of lament portray it. Those who entered it were thought to be cut off from the land of the living, from the intimacy of kith and kin, and from the life-giving participation in the worship of the LORD, whom (as many a psalm tells us) the dead do not praise. The groups whose views are reflected in the Hebrew Bible did not think that the dead played a continuing, active role in the household, and they did not regard them as divine or powerful. The archaeological evidence indicates that the dead were on occasion offered food, though it is unclear for how long and how often this was done or whether the practice reflects the strength or the weakness of the departed. The literary evidence in the form of the Hebrew Bible, by contrast, gives scant indication that the practice existed at all and expresses no explicit approval of it in any period. That there were sectors of Israelite society that thought otherwise, or periods in which the alternative evaluation of feeding the dead prevailed, need hardly be denied. But neither should it be denied that these were not the sectors or the periods whose views are commonly reflected in the Hebrew Bible, in any of the periods of its composition.

RETURNING FROM THE LAND OF NO RETURN

There are two striking ironies about Sheol. One is the disparity between how little we actually know of it and how much attention it commands in the scholarly literature. As we shall see in the next chapter, references to Sheol are far less numerous than one might think, and they are clustered only in specific genres. One reason that so many scholars have felt constrained to turn to Canaanite and other non-Israelite sources to fill in the picture of the abode of the dead, in fact, is precisely the uninterest of the Hebrew Bible in such matters. In our judgment, however, it is eminently misguided to seek to overcome that uninterest, importing this or that Canaanite or Mesopotamian item into Israel and even into the Hebrew Bible on the slenderest of textual or archaeological evidence. Instead, we should *respect* the uninterest, viewing it as characteristic of the nature of Israelite religion as it is reflected in the Hebrew Bible and doubtless to some degree outside it as well. For, whatever the social reality (which is always more complex than any literary treatment, including those in the Hebrew Bible, indicates), the focus of that *book* is not on the world of the dead, but on that of the living, specifically, on the people Israel and their complicated relationship with their God in history. This historical focus perforce leads to a continual glance backward toward ancient and long dead figures like Abraham, Isaac, Jacob, Moses, and King David, but not because the deceased ancestors have become gods or are possessed of wisdom to offer to those who consult them, or because they offer deliverance to the descendants who pray and sacrifice to them, or because they might disrupt those who fail to feed or otherwise honor them. Rather, in the Hebrew Bible the ancestors matter because it was to them that God's promise was believed to have been first given, to them that the norms of the God-pleasing life were revealed (whether they succeeded in living up to them or not), and because in dealing with them God made known his ways. These ancient figures are not gods who, from some other world to which they went at death, now rescue, bless, and instruct. They are altogether mortal and altogether fallible human beings whom God rescued, blessed, and instructed in their lifetimes, in this world. If a focus of attention in the history of Israelite religion ever lay on the dead and the esoteric power or wisdom that some believed they possessed, it is all the more significant that in the Hebrew Bible itself, the focus lies principally in two very different places. It lies on this life and the ever-present possibility of obedience to God's known will established in public revelation. And it lies on the indefeasible promises that God made to such people as the national and dynastic founders, the patriarchs of Genesis, and to King David. If those individuals had ever been conceived as deified ancestors who are sources of rescue, blessing, or instruction, in the Hebrew Bible they have become recipients of promises from the true God, promises that even death ultimately could not defeat.

We have already seen the second striking irony about Sheol. For all that modern scholars and some biblical authors describe it as the land of no return, it is often mentioned in the context of praising God precisely for bringing people back from there or asking that he do so. Consider the Song of Hannah (1 Sam 2:1–10), a poem ascribed to Samuel's mother when God has at long last enabled her to overcome her infertility. Our concern lies with a verse in the middle of the poem:

> The LORD deals death and gives life,
> Casts down into Sheol and raises up. (1 Sam 2:6)

The most natural reading of the claim that the LORD "raises up" from Sheol is that he reverses death, resurrecting the denizens of the netherworld just as he reverses other cruel fates mentioned in Hannah's hymn, such as hunger and barrenness. The injustice that resulted in the dispatch of some innocent individuals to Sheol will be reversed when the LORD establishes the reign of justice that the hymn celebrates throughout. Such a reversal is not yet the same as the expectation that Jesus and the early Christians had that God would soon raise the dead and deliver a last judgment. The Song of Hannah and similar texts in the Hebrew Bible do not envision a general resurrection at all, or a last judgment, or even a gift of eternal life to those raised from the dead. But they begin to point toward the set of convictions underlying the understanding of death and life in the Jewish circles out of which Jesus and Christianity emerged.

4

WHO GOES TO SHEOL—
AND WHO DOES NOT

WHEN AND WHY SHEOL IS MENTIONED

In our last chapter, we cited the scholarly view that "everyone who dies goes to Sheol" so that the netherworld is "the destination of all, good and bad without discrimination, where existence is wholly undesirable." If this is so, then Qohelet (also known as Ecclesiastes) was surely correct when he wrote that "the same fate is in store for all" (Qoh 9:2), namely, death and the "wholly undesirable" existence that goes with it.

For Qohelet, this is a sad thought, one that seems to offend his sense of justice. And well it should. For if the conventional view (widely held by scholars of the Hebrew Bible today) is correct, and Sheol was thought to be the abode of the wicked and righteous alike, then any belief in the ultimate justice of God in the Hebrew Bible is thrown into severe doubt. Sheol in that case would house not only Hitlerian tyrants like the Babylonian king whose delicious arrival there the book of Isaiah mockingly envisions (14:3–21) or the pharaoh whose descent thereto Ezekiel similarly but more graphically foretells (Ezek 32:17–32). Rather, it would necessarily also house the revered patriarch Abraham, though he died "old and contented" (Gen 25:8); the great liberator and law-giver Moses, whose "eyes were undimmed and his vigor unabated" even at death (Deut 34:7); and even Job, the man who survived unspeakable suffering to find his life restored, dying like Abraham "old and contented" (Job 42:17). If Sheol is the destiny of all, these three must (in the minds of those who wrote and heard about them) even now be enduring a "wholly undesirable" existence, no less than the self-deifying but doomed Babylonian and Egyptian oppressors of Israel whom the prophets taunted.

In a theological universe in which everyone eventually goes to Sheol, then, God may demand justice from people all he wants, but he does not practice it himself. In the last analysis, he decrees the same fate for saint and for sinner. If that was a thought that troubled Qohelet, it outraged Abraham. When, for example, God announced his plan to destroy Sodom, Abraham protested. "Far be it from You to do such a thing, to bring death upon the innocent as well as the guilty," he said to the LORD, "so that innocent and guilty fare alike. Far be it from You! Shall not the Judge of all the earth deal justly?" (Gen 18:25). When death is punishment, it is a gross injustice that the innocent should die.

There is, however, ample room to wonder whether in Israelite thought as reflected in the Hebrew Bible, Sheol really was assumed to be the universal destination. Were that the case, one might reasonably expect the term to occur very often in the Hebrew Bible, indeed to be mentioned nearly as often as death itself, since all who die go to Sheol. In fact, however, it occurs fewer than seventy times (as opposed to one thousand times for the root *mwt*, "die/death"), and, as Philip Johnston points out, its distribution is illuminating:

> The term occurs mostly in psalmodic, reflective and prophetic literature, where authors are personally involved in their work. By contrast, it appears only rarely in descriptive narrative, and then almost entirely in direct speech. In particular, "Sheol" never occurs in the many narrative accounts of death, whether of patriarchs, kings, prophets, priests or ordinary people, whether of Israelite or foreigner, of righteous or wicked. Also, "Sheol" is entirely absent from legal material, including the many laws which prescribe capital punishment or proscribe necromancy. This means that "Sheol" is very clearly a term of personal engagement.

The "personal engagement" that Sheol reflects is the struggle against the powerful and malignant forces that negate life and deprive it of meaning. Is death itself inevitably one of these forces? It would be unwise to classify death (in the modern, biologistic sense of a cessation of animation) so. For in the Hebrew Bible, death is malign only to the extent that it expresses punishment or otherwise communicates a negative estimation on the life that is ending. As Ruth Rosenberg puts it, "There was no turning back from natural death, and the grave, as a human destination, is conspicuously devoid of negative connotations in the [Hebrew] Bible, and often contemplated with composure." Thus, however much Sheol may be conceived in the imagery of the grave, "in the Bible the concept of the grave and Sheol or its semantic equivalents were consistently kept apart." When the psalmist says to the LORD, "You will not abandon me to Sheol, /or let Your faithful one see the Pit" (Ps 16:10), he is therefore not asserting the absurd notion that God will forever spare him from death. Rather, Rosenberg argues, he is expressing his faith that, "You [God] will not let your faithful servant die an untimely, evil death."

Rosenberg casts this critical but usually overlooked distribution in terms of the dichotomy of natural and unnatural. "Whenever death is due to unnatural causes, Sheol is mentioned," she writes; "whenever death occurs in the course of nature, Sheol does not appear." The distinction is not, however, native to the Israelite worldview but can easily be replaced by one that is—namely, the ubiquitous distinction between God's anger and his favor. If the circumstances of death do not suggest divine anger, then death (whether we judge it to be natural or unnatural) need not be feared, and "personal engagement" to avert it is utterly unnecessary. Sheol, in sum, very often has to do with punishment, and those who die in God's good graces, their lives fulfilled through his blessings, therefore have no reason to think that they will be dispatched to that "wholly undesirable" existence in the dark, dank netherworld. Poets who believe that their existential adversity has brought them into the shadow of death have good reason to plead that God spare them Sheol and to thank him for doing so when the lethal adversity subsides. But the texts about the deaths of Abraham, Moses, and Job, whose last days are undeniably blessed by God's providential intervention, give no hint that at that moment they fear Sheol, for their impending deaths do not negate God's evident and abundant favor. They die with lives fulfilled and seem to face no future terrors or miseries whatsoever.

A major focus of that favor—especially important, as we are about to see, in the case of Abraham and Job—is family, particularly the continuation of one's lineage through having descendants (preferably many of them) alive at one's death. Many expressions, some of them idiomatic, communicate this essential mode of divine favor. The idiom "He was gathered to his kin" or "to his fathers" seems originally to have derived from burial practices.

But in the Hebrew Bible it need not literally refer to interment in the family grave or to secondary burial any longer, since it is used of Abraham (Gen 25:8), for example, whose deceased blood relatives all lay in Mesopotamia. It is revealing, but not surprising, that the expression never occurs together with a mention of a descent to Sheol. The reason is evident: Sheol is anything but a locus of familial reunion. Those who go down to it are said to feel isolated and abandoned, and the absence of kin in the descriptions of the group imprisoned there is striking. Ezekiel's elaborate depiction (Ezek 32:17–32), for example, portrays once mighty warriors, some still in "their battle gear" (v 27), now reduced to powerlessness in the face of the great leveler. Like soldiers in wartime, they are far from parents, wives, and children. If being "gathered to one's kin/fathers" refers to the afterlife, it is not an afterlife in the misery of Sheol.

Similar points can be made about a similar idiom for dying in the Hebrew Bible, "he slept/he lay with his fathers." If the Hebrew verb in question is translated as "slept," it fits with the identification of death with sleep that we meet elsewhere in the Hebrew Bible. Note, for example, that the prophet Elisha revives the Shunammite lady's son, "laid out dead on his couch," after his aide Gehazi's failed attempt to bring him back and his report that, "the boy has not awakened" (2 Kgs 4:31–32; discussed in more detail in Chapter 7). Much later, in the Judaism of the rabbis of Talmudic times (about 50–500 C.E.), sleep will be conceived as a kind of miniature or temporary death. As one saying in the Talmud puts it, "sleep is one-sixtieth of death."

Translated as "he lay [with his fathers]," the Hebrew expression in question again recalls the burial practices in which the deceased remains with his or her kin, whether in the house or in hewn niches. Though that is probably the origin of the expression, this idiom, too, does not now refer exclusively to family burial, since it is used (to give but one example) of Moses, whose ancestors presumably lay in Egypt when he was placed to rest in a grave that "no one knows . . . to this day" (Deut 31:16; 34:6). With very few exceptions, the expression is used for those who died peacefully, whereas the expression "he died," for example, is most characteristically used of kings (whether judged good or wicked) who perished violently. On either translation, the expression itself gives no grounds whatsoever for assuming that one who "slept/lay with his fathers" did so in Sheol, which is, as we have seen, almost always the destination of those who die violently, unjustly, in punishment, prematurely, or with a broken heart.

We say "almost always" because, despite the arguments we have just developed, a handful of passages affirm that Sheol is the end point for everyone. Especially unambiguous is Ps 89:49:

> What man can live and not see death,
>> can save himself from the clutches of Sheol?

Note the equivalence here of death and Sheol, with the clear implication that individuals, no matter how they have died, cannot escape the dreary netherworld. In cases like this, the course of wisdom is openly to confront the contradiction between those passages that assert that Sheol is indeed the destination of all human beings and those more numerous passages that affirm the possibility of a fortunate end to life. It is remarkable that the former passages are so few and that the differentiation of terminology is so consistent. This suggests that the inconsistency is best seen as a tension between two competing theologies. The one that sees Sheol as the universal destination comports well with ancient Mesopotamian and Canaanite notions of ultimate human destiny as one of pure gloom. This conception survives in a few places in the Hebrew Bible, but it is very much at odds with most of the relevant texts there, which instead assume a distinction between those who go to Sheol and those who die blessed, like Abraham, Moses, and Job. Another way to state this is to say that the Hebrew Bible displays a tension between an older notion of Sheol as the ultimate destination of all humankind, on the one hand, and a bold and younger affirmation of the LORD as savior, on the other. This second assertion eventually culminated in a proclamation of the God of Israel as the one who is powerful even over the dismal netherworld and the forces that impel people toward it. But the development toward that point was neither inevitable nor linear, and remnants of the older view remained even in relatively late texts, like the passage in Qohelet that we have mentioned.

What exactly was the fate of those fortunate enough to avoid the netherworld? Where, if not Sheol, did the ancient Israelites who wrote of their lives and heard their tales believe *them* to have gone? On this, the Hebrew Bible is strikingly silent and forces us into conjecture. As for actual practice (as opposed to the biblical ideals), it is not hard to imagine that the deposits of food for the dead that we discussed in the previous chapter were intended to nourish the deceased in another place, where (with the proper assistance of the living) their experience would be very different from the torments of Sheol that psalmists pray God to spare them or thank him for so doing. Perhaps the food and similar gestures of attention of the living were thought to mitigate the misery of Sheol. Whatever the case, it is highly instructive that the Hebrew Bible is so severely reticent about describing the existence of the dead, and there is, as we have seen, ample room for disagreement with the claim that the dead were generally thought to be in communication with the living in ancient Israelite religion.

In the case of those in the Hebrew Bible who die blessed, there is nonetheless survival of a certain, but very important, sort. If we examine the deaths of such people, we see that their survival actually lies not in their transport to a different world like the Christian Heaven but in their lineage (including, in some cases, the larger lineage that is the whole people of Israel). Thus Abraham dies after arranging the marriage of his favored son Isaac and begetting, in addition to the firstborn Ishmael, six other sons, some of them (like Isaac and Ishmael) destined to beget great nations in fulfillment of God's explicit promise to the founding patriarch (Gen 25:1–18; 12:2; 17:20; 21:18; 28:3–4). And so, too, Job lives "to see four generations of sons and grandsons" (Job 42:16). This, in turn, is strikingly reminiscent of the dying Jacob, who tells his son Joseph, "I never expected to see you again, and here God has let me see your children as well," or of Joseph himself, who "lived to see children of the third generation of [his son] Ephraim" (Gen 48:11; 50:23). These instances of the viewing of the future lineage are hardly coincidental or irrelevant to our topic. For, in all these cases, the individual dies fulfilled, the divine promises richly (and unexpectedly) realized at the end of a stormy life, long marked by infertility or other intergenerational problems. The viewing of the distant descendants so prominent in the cases of Job, Jacob, and Joseph establishes the happiness of the individual's destiny at the time of his death. Dying within the blessing of God, the patriarch faces his final destiny with composure, altogether unlike those who, dying outside the blessing of God, face the misery of Sheol, with justified trepidation and despondency. The fulfillment of the blessed individual's life survives him and continues to testify to his final felicity—and to his God's steadfast faithfulness to his pledged word.

In the case of Moses, the matter is only somewhat different. His death notice (Deuteronomy 34), to be sure, mentions nothing of his descendants, of whom little is known in any case. But the promises made to and through Moses never centered on his own personal lineage anyway. Indeed, in the episode of the golden calf, Moses declines the LORD's offer to make an Abrahamic "great nation" of him in replacement of the sinning Israelites:

> [9]The LORD further said to Moses, "I see that this is a stiffnecked people. [10]Now, let Me be, that My anger may blaze forth against them and that I may destroy them, and make of you a great nation." [11]But Moses implored the LORD his God, saying, "Let not Your anger, O LORD, blaze forth against Your people, whom You delivered from the land of Egypt with great power and with a mighty hand. [12]Let not the Egyptians say, 'It was with evil intent that He delivered them, only to kill them off in the mountains and annihilate them from the face of the earth.' Turn from Your blazing anger, and renounce the plan to punish Your people. [13]Remember Your servants, Abraham, Isaac, and Israel, how You swore to them by Your Self and said to them: I will make your offspring as numerous as the stars of heaven, and I will give to your offspring this whole land of which I spoke, to possess forever." [14]And the LORD renounced the punishment He had planned to bring upon His people. (Exod 32:9–14)

It is clear that the Mosaic promises center on the lineage of Abraham, Isaac, and Jacob, that is, the whole Israelite nation, and not on Moses' own progeny. Thus, when "the LORD showed him the whole land" (Deut 34:1) just before Moses died and the Israelites began to take possession of it, the scene is remarkably reminiscent of Jacob's, Joseph's, and Job's viewing several generations of descendants just before their own deaths. In the Deuteronomic theology, the fulfillment of Moses' life continues and remains real, visible, and powerful after his death. It takes the form of Israel's dwelling in the promised land and living in deliberate obedience to the Torah book he bequeathed them, for all their generations (for example, Deut 31:9–13; Josh 1:6–8). In Deuteronomy, all Israel has become, in a sense, the progeny of Moses.

SHEOL IS NOT HELL

Nothing distorts the proper understanding of Sheol in the Hebrew Bible more than the traditional Jewish and Christian understanding of the afterlife as a locus for reward or punishment. If one examines the circumstances that result in one's assignment to biblical Sheol in the Hebrew Bible, it soon becomes evident that they far exceed punishment for moral infractions. Sheol, though an unhappy place, is no hell. (The terminology is confusing here, because in rabbinic Judaism, the word "Sheol" becomes a synonym of *Gehinnom*, the Jewish counterpart to the Christian "Hell"). Rather, it is best conceived as a kind of continuation of the end of the deceased's life. If the deceased has died prematurely, violently, bereft of children, rejected by God, or broken-hearted, he or she faces Sheol (which, as we noted in Chapter 3, an individual can begin to experience even on this side of the grave). Thus, the national ancestor Jacob, having (as far as he knows) lost to the jaws of a wild beast his beloved Joseph, the son of his old age, "refused to be comforted, saying, 'No, I will go down mourning to my son in Sheol'" (Gen 37:35). It would be a capital error to interpret either Joseph's or Jacob's anticipated presence in Sheol as punitive, as if God (whom he does not mention here) were punishing them for this or that sin. Joseph's is owing to his ostensibly having died a violent and premature death, one that is not followed by a proper burial or mitigated by the continuation that comes from having children. Each of these conditions alone could bring him to Sheol. Cumulatively, they make his presence there close to certain. As for Jacob's own anticipation of joining him in the miserable netherworld, here the operative factor is a broken heart, the unending ache caused by the loss of his favorite child. In each case, that of the (putatively) mauled son and that of the inconsolable father, Sheol is not a punishment from God or any other agent. It does not come in response to sin; it is the continuation of the depressing circumstances that existed at the time of the individual's death.

Were Sheol the universal destination, we should expect to find in the Hebrew Bible many statements similar to Jacob's in the mouths of others whose deaths, or anticipated deaths, are mentioned. This is rarely the case, however; one cannot equate dying with going to Sheol. In those accustomed to the familiar Jewish and Christian duality of Garden of Eden/ Gehinnom, Heaven/Hell, this instinctively raises the question of where those go who die a fortunate death—a peaceful death, that is, one that takes place at a ripe old age, the decedent having lived to see a multitude of thriving descendants and possessing the assurance of a decent burial. Deriving from the question of where we go after we die, the question is, in fact, misconceived when posed to the Hebrew Bible. For the Hebrew Bible displays very little interest in this question. It is much more likely to focus on the question of whether God's blessing (especially the blessing of children) was or was not realized in the decedent's life. If it was, then death can be, in Rosenberg's words, "contemplated with composure." The decedent's life has come to fulfillment; there are no lasting deficits, no unresolved issues to impede its fortunate completion. If it was not, however, then the decedent is in the domain of Sheol. The binary opposite of Sheol in the Hebrew Bible is thus not some Israelite version of the Garden of Eden or Heaven; it is, rather, a life that is enveloped in the blessing of God and gives persuasive testimony to that blessing.

In other words, Sheol can be thought of as the prolongation of the unfulfilled life. There is no equivalent prolongation of the fulfilled life precisely because it is fulfilled. The prolongation of those who die fulfilled comes, rather, not in the form of residence in a particular place, a joyful antipode to the miserable Sheol, but in the form of descendants, such as those three or four generations that Jacob, Joseph, and Job are privileged to behold just before they die. It also comes in the form of the survival of the decedent's "name" (*shem*), which is itself closely associated with his lineage. As James L. Kugel observes, the name can express the immortal dimension of the self: "Quite unlike the body, a person's 'name' in this sense is altogether immune to the inroads of time. A name, in this abstract sense of the sum total of all a person's deeds, is immutable, so that eventually that name is all that remains of our earthly existence; years, centuries after our death, the name—in this abstract sense—is what we are, what our life amounted to." To this, we should add that the name sometimes seems to affect things even after death:

> The memory of the righteous is a source of blessing,
> But the name of the wicked rots away. (Prov 10:7)

The name or the memory, in short, survives the person or, to put it more precisely, the person survives in the name as in the descendants. There is no good reason to think that the righteous whose memory is a source of blessing were generally thought to endure the miseries of Sheol nonetheless.

If the Jewish and Christian theologies of postmortem reward and punishment cause us to misunderstand Sheol in one way, a hasty harmonization to the patterns inferred (not without uncertainty) from Mesopotamian and Canaanite texts induces a misunderstanding in the other direction. For this can mislead us into thinking that without exception all who die — which is to say, all who live — end up in that gloomy place. On this reading, the texts in the Hebrew Bible that speak of the life fulfilled by the promise of God cannot be taken seriously, or must at least be relegated to the penultimate stage, for the dreary, Godless existence in the netherworld is the end that awaits everyone. If this is the case, then, one must understand the book of Job, for example, not to end, as it actually does:

> [11]All his brothers and sisters and all his former friends came to him and had a meal with him in his house. They consoled and comforted him for all the misfortune that the LORD had brought upon him. Each gave him one *kesitah* and each one gold ring. [12]Thus the LORD blessed the latter years of Job's life more than the former. He had fourteen thousand sheep, six thousand camels, one thousand yoke of oxen, and one thousand she-asses. [13]He also had seven sons and three daughters. [14]The first he named Jemimah, the second Keziah, and the third Keren-happuch. [15]Nowhere in the land were women as beautiful as Job's daughters to be found. Their father gave them estates together with their brothers. [16]Afterward, Job lived one hundred and forty years to see four generations of sons and grandsons. [17]So Job died old and contented. (Job 42:11–17)

Rather, we should be obliged to presume that Job's restoration from affliction was temporary, so that the fuller and more accurate account of his end would have a final verse after verse 17 above that might read: "Then he went down to Sheol, to the land of slackness, sorrow, exhaustion, and curse, where there is no joy, strength, or blessing, to the dark pit in which the abandoned lie and in which no one praises the Lord and all are forever cut off from His care and from which no one returns." It is patently evident that this hypothetical verse radically changes the entire meaning not only of the passage to which it has been appended but of the book as a whole. It transforms a happy ending into a sad one (the same could be said about the ends of the stories of Abraham, Jacob, Joseph, Moses, and many others as well). Fortunately, this verse does not exist, and to concoct such a spurious closing is to miss one of the most salient features of the ancient Israelite understanding of death and life. The conclusion to the book of Job and kindred happy endings entail a very different understanding of death from the one in which the gloomy underworld is the universal destination. They advance, rather, a bold theology, a theology that robs death of any necessary connection with the dreariness of the netherworld and offers instead the possibility of a happy ending to individual existence. To imagine that the Hebrew Bible consistently maintains that *all* human beings go eventually to Sheol, never to be redeemed therefrom, is thus to fail to reckon with the redemptive dynamics of many narratives found in that book, as if the authors of those conclusions wrote with their fingers crossed behind their backs, composing happy endings but actually thinking that the happiness was short-lived and the end was everlasting misery. Unfortunately, this is a widespread failure among scholars of the Hebrew Bible, secular and religious alike. Happy endings are sometimes the hardest to accept.

As we have seen, however, some vestiges of the older view, the view that all who die end up in Sheol, linger. Qohelet (to cite an extreme example) appeals to the universality of the unfortunate death and thus the unfulfilled life to bolster his overall skepticism about the redeeming God (Qoh 9:2). But, on balance, the Hebrew Bible is remarkably consistent in speaking of the opposite, the possibility of a meaningful life ending in a fortunate death, and of redemption after unspeakable tragedy.

What has happened with the biblical Sheol, it seems to us, is that the affirmation of faith in the omnipotent and rescuing God of Israel, against whom not even the most formidable of enemies can ultimately stand, has collided with the brute fact of death, with all the negative denotations that death generally had in Mesopotamia and Canaan. Something had to give. What gave was not the faith in the limitless power of the Rock of Israel and their redeemer. What gave was death. The result, however, was neither that death disappeared, as if humans were rendered immortal, nor (at this point) that the dead rose in judgment, with the worthy among them then awarded eternal life. Rather, to adapt the prophet Hosea, death gave up its plagues, and Sheol, its pestilence. Death would remain universal, but not everyone who died would experience it as a plague. Sheol would remain pestilential, but not everyone who died would go there. There is thus a duality to the general view of death in the Hebrew Bible that is different from the duality of those resurrected to "eternal life" and those resurrected to "everlasting abhorrence" known from later Jewish tradition (Dan 12:2) and from Christianity, to be sure, but that also anticipates the later patterns in an important way. The pattern predominant in the Hebrew Bible is the duality of the death that closes a fortunate life, conceived theologically as one blessed by God, and the death that prolongs an unfortunate life, one lived, for whatever reason, outside the blessing of God.

DEATH DEFANGED

We have argued that in the Hebrew Bible there is no antipode to Sheol in the sense of a heavenly locale to which the blessed go after death—no postmortem Heaven or Garden of Eden to which those loyal to God can look forward. This should not, however, be taken to mean that there is no spatial antipode to Sheol available in this life. As we have seen and shall see again in detail in the next chapter, the Temple in Jerusalem was conceived as just such a paradise-like place where God, for all his purity and holiness, is nonetheless available on earth and his blessing is abundant. Now we can add that there is also another antipode to Sheol, another heavenly state available in this world, though one that, like descendants or the name/memory, cannot be located in space so readily. It lies in the story of Israel's relationship with God, the history of redemption, which centers on the establishment or restoration of familial and national continuity through the efficacious word of the LORD. At the individual level, redemption through the acquisition of descendants (or a good name) is available to all, from the humble but God-fearing midwives for whom God "established households" (Exod 1:21) to the great non-Israelite patriarch Job, whom God enabled to reestablish his household after unparalleled tragedy. At the communal level, however, the redemption is manifested in the history of redemption that came to constitute the prime self-identification of the people Israel, the people whose liturgical life continually proclaimed that God, who was their rock and their redeemer, could in the end overcome even the horrors and terrors of death.

5

HEAVEN ON EARTH

THE TEMPLE AS THE GARDEN OF EDEN

In the previous chapter, we were at pains to argue that there is no positive antipode to Sheol in the sense of a place, like the Jewish Garden of
Eden or the Christian Heaven, to which the fortunate dead arrived to experience everlasting happiness. Instead, we advanced the claim that the
happiness of such figures after death had a great deal to do with the fact
that their deepest identities were inextricably embedded in the continuation of their families. The death of an individual has a different meaning in
a culture that instinctively understands the self in familial and thus transgenerational terms more than we in the modern West do. It is thus no coincidence that the report of Abraham's death, for example, is sandwiched
between two sets of genealogies of his descendants and that the account of
Job's follows the report that he "lived . . . to see four generations of sons and
grandsons" (Job 42:16). For the most part, the postmortem fulfillment of
those who die in a state of blessing is realized in the form of the happy continuation of the family of which they were, and forever remain, a generational link.

This leaves us, then, with an asymmetrical structure that the analogies
with Heaven and Hell, or with the Garden of Eden and Gehinnom, can
only obscure. The casual reader of the Hebrew Bible in a Christian or post-
Christian culture can perhaps be excused for thinking that in the worldview of that book, the Garden of Eden has, in fact, disappeared, only to be
restored in the fullness of time, when resurrection reverses the death sen-

tence on Adam (Gen 3:22–24). This is, after all, the foundation of a central Christological claim from the time of the apostle Paul on (for example, Rom 5:12–21). Within the context of the Hebrew Bible, however—and all the more so in rabbinic Judaism—this view is highly misleading; it has done great damage to the efforts of scholars and laypeople alike to understand the issues. One exception to this interpretation, the Wisdom tradition known from books like Proverbs, could, in fact, identify its goal, the life of Wisdom, with the Tree of Life and thus see the Tree of Life as still eminently accessible:

> She [i.e., Wisdom] is a tree of life to those who grasp her,
> And whoever holds on to her is happy. (Prov 3:18)

In the rabbinic tradition, Wisdom having long beforehand been equated with Torah, the Torah in turn came to be identified with the Tree of Life through which God, in the words of the familiar blessing of the Jewish prayer book, "planted eternal life within us." This is not to say that either Jewish Wisdom literature or the rabbinic tradition held that those who practice and study Wisdom or Torah never die—a palpable absurdity. It does suggest, rather, that Wisdom and Torah were thought to retard or mitigate death in some important sense. The point is that in the framework of Wisdom/Torah, the Edenic condition is not so lost at present as the familiar Christian reading claims. Something of the happiness that Jews and Christians would later associate with heaven could still be experienced, but on this side of death.

Another, more widely attested and symbolically resonant concept of Eden appears in passages like the following from Ezekiel:

[11]The word of the LORD came to me: [12]O mortal, intone a dirge over the king of Tyre and say to him: Thus said the Lord GOD:

> You were the seal of perfection,
> Full of wisdom and flawless in beauty.
> [13]You were in Eden, the garden of God;
> Every precious stone was your adornment:
> Carnelian, chrysolite, and amethyst;
> Beryl, lapis lazuli, and jasper;
> Sapphire, turquoise, and emerald;
> And gold beautifully wrought for you,

Mined for you, prepared the day you were created.
¹⁴I created you as a cherub
With outstretched shielding wings;
And you resided on God's holy mountain;
You walked among stones of fire.
¹⁵You were blameless in your ways,
From the day you were created
Until wrongdoing was found in you.
¹⁶By your far-flung commerce
You were filled with lawlessness
And you sinned.
So I have struck you down
From the mountain of God,
And I have destroyed you, O shielding cherub,
From among the stones of fire.
¹⁷You grew haughty because of your beauty,
You debased your wisdom for the sake of your splendor;
I have cast you to the ground,
I have made you an object for kings to stare at.
¹⁸By the greatness of your guilt,
Through the dishonesty of your trading,
You desecrated your sanctuaries.
So I made a fire issue from you,
And it has devoured you;
I have reduced you to ashes on the ground,
In the sight of all who behold you.
¹⁹All who knew you among the peoples
Are appalled at your doom.
You have become a horror
And have ceased to be forever. (Ezek 28:11–19)

Here, the prophet Ezekiel (early sixth century B.C.E.) predicts and justifies
the downfall of the Phoenician city-state Tyre, as the mighty forces of the
neo-Babylonian Empire sweep to the west and south. As is often the case in
the ancient Near East, the kingdom is identified with its ruler, but it is the
further identification of the king of Tyre that attracts our attention. For underlying Ezekiel's oracle is a variant of the story of Eden so much better

known from the version that appears in Genesis 3. A blameless creature inhabiting "Eden, the garden of God" grows arrogant, attracts God's wrath, and, cast to the ground, has "ceased to be, forever." The differences, however, are illuminating and warn against the facile assumption that Ezekiel knows of the version in Genesis. For one, whereas Adam is childlike, lacking the knowledge of good and evil, the mythic figure with whom the king of Tyre is identified, is "full of wisdom"(v 12). A second difference is that Adam is very much a human being, formed "from the dust of the earth" (Gen 2:7), whereas Ezekiel's primal man is a cherub, a Godlike being who dwells not on the earth that Adam is bidden to till and to tend as a garden (Gen 2:15) but "on God's holy mountain," that is to say, the cosmic capital from which the deity exercises sovereignty over his universal domain. It is this last point that may account for the high degree of overlap between the precious stones found in Eden in Ezek 28:13 with those on the breastplate of the Israelite high priest in Exod 28:17–20. The primal man in Ezekiel is the special attendant of God, dwelling in the latter's Temple, the palace of the ruler of the world, in intimate association with him.

The most revealing aspect of Ezekiel's oracle for our purposes is its identification of the Temple on "God's holy mountain" with "Eden, the garden of God" (vv 13–14). This builds, in turn, upon the conception of the Temple as paradise—the world in its ideal state, the world as its creator hoped it would be—which has deep and wide resonance not only in Israel, but throughout the ancient Near East as well.

The biblical archaeologist Lawrence E. Stager notes, for example, an Assyrian text that speaks of the performance of the sacred ritual of the *akitu*, or New Year's festival, in a "Garden of Plenty," which seems to be a counterpart of the Israelite Garden of Eden. In Babylonia and Egypt as well, monarchs went to great lengths to procure exotic botanical specimens for their capital gardens with the goal to "signif[y] the ecumenic sovereignty of the ruler." It is in this tradition that Stager places the report that Solomon, king of Judah and Israel and builder of the great Temple of Jerusalem, "discoursed about trees, from the cedar in Lebanon to the hyssop that grows out of the wall" (1 Kgs 5:13). "Since cedars do not grow beyond the Lebanon and the Amanus [that is, far to the north of Jerusalem], they could have been transplanted and cultivated in Jerusalem only under the most propitious conditions, such as irrigated gardens secluded behind stone or brick walls might provide." The psalms offer evidence that the

Temple was the focus of at least some of Solomon's horticultural initiatives:

> [13]The righteous bloom like a date-palm;
>> they thrive like a cedar in Lebanon;
>> [14]planted in the house of the LORD,
>> they flourish in the courts of our God.
> [15]In old age they still produce fruit;
>> they are full of sap and freshness,
>> [16]attesting that the LORD is upright,
>> my rock, in whom there is no wrong. (Ps 92:13–16)

In Stager's understanding, given the geographical limits in which wild cedars are found, the first verb in verse 14 must be translated not as "planted," but as "transplanted." Solomon, or some comparable royal patron, has brought fruitful date palms and exotic, majestic cedars into the Temple, reinforcing both its divine owner's "ecumenic sovereignty" and the paradisiacal character of his palace.

The key point is that in the ancient Near East, gardens, especially royal gardens, were not simply decorative. They were symbolic, and their symbolic message was very much involved with that of the Temple in or near which they were not infrequently found. Gardens present and preserve natural things in a form that is so unnatural that it is free from chaos, decay, and death. Like temples, they are walled off from quotidian reality, with all its instability and irregularity and the threats these pose, and thus they readily convey, in William Wordsworth's memorable phrase, an intimation of immortality.

In the case of the great temple city of Jerusalem, there is a connection with the Garden of Eden that is more specific—and highly revealing. Genesis 2 speaks of four streams that branch off from the river that "issues from Eden to water the garden" (vv 10–14), of which two are readily identified as the major rivers of Mesopotamia, the Tigris and the Euphrates. Another, the Pishon, is unknown. But the remaining stream, the Gihon (whose name seems to mean "Gusher") bears the name of the spring below the City of David whose waters flow eastward to the Kidron Valley, where, as Stager points out, they "irrigated the gardens and parks planted . . . by kings of the Davidic dynasty." It is, in fact, to this very spring that David orders his son and designated successor Solomon transported on the royal mule to be anointed king (1 Kgs 1:32–40). The Gihon is also the source of the "gently flowing waters of Siloam" that possessed such significance for Isaiah, the great prophet of Judah in the eighth century B.C.E. For Isaiah, these waters symbolized the quiet trust characteristic of authentic faith in the God of Israel, in contrast to the "mighty, massive waters of the Euphrates" that symbolized the king of Assyria and his military forces (Isa 8:5–8). As Stager puts it, "these quiet, cosmic waters emanating from the primordial deep signified the orderliness and tranquility of God's creation on which humans should rely."

The paradisiacal character of the Gihon thus draws upon a rich store of mythic materials deeply connected to the ancient Near Eastern theology of temples. Especially in the Zion theology of Judah, the Temple is not only the capital building of the universe but the place where God's protective care is manifest, tangible, and inviolable:

> ⁶O LORD, Your faithfulness reaches to heaven;
>> Your steadfastness to the sky;
>> ⁷Your beneficence is like the mountains of El;
>> Your justice like the great deep;
>> man and beast You deliver, O LORD.
> ⁸How precious is Your faithful care, O God!
> Mankind shelters in the shadow of Your wings.
> ⁹They feast on the rich fare of Your house;
>> You let them drink at Your refreshing stream.
> ¹⁰With You is the fountain of life;
>> by Your light do we see light.
> ¹¹Bestow Your faithful care on those devoted to You,
>> and Your beneficence on upright men. (Ps 36:6–11)

In this extraordinarily artful psalm about God's succor and protection of the faithful and just, the mythic connections are patent. "Mountains of El" in verse 7 alludes to the abode of the Canaanite creator god with whom the Israelite deity was not infrequently identified to one degree or another. The reference to "Your house" (v 9) establishes that the locus of the LORD's succor and protection is indeed the Temple, and the "refreshing stream" from which he gives his faithful to drink, and even more, the "fountain of life" (v 10) evoke again the mythos of the waters of Jerusalem that we have been discussing. In this connection, we must not overlook the fact that the phrase rendered "refreshing stream" (*nachal 'adaneykha*) includes the plural of "Eden" and might be translated more accurately (if less poetically) "Your stream of delights" or "the stream of Your delights." Presumably, the source of this Edenic stream lies in the "fountain of life" whose terrestrial manifestation is the Gihon spring from which the royal and temple city drew its drink.

This, in turn, raises the question of how the "fountain" is related to "life." Unfortunately, Psalm 36 never tells us directly. A practical answer does come to mind, however. That humankind "feast on the rich fare" in the Temple (v 9) may be taken for a poetic reference to their consuming the sacrificial offerings. The drink mentioned in the same verse would then refer simply to the accompanying beverage, and the "fountain of life" would designate the source of this liquid sustenance, and no more. The practical answer, though probably accurate on one level, is excessively prosaic for so poetic and intense a meditation on the part of our psalmist and fails to reckon with the density of mythological allusion that we see in his poem. A better, or at least fuller, explanation of the fountain of life appears in the vision of the future Temple in Ezekiel:

[1]He led me back to the entrance of the Temple, and I found that water was issuing from below the platform of the Temple—eastward, since the Temple faced east—but the water was running out at the south of the altar, under the south wall of the Temple. [2]Then he led me out by way of the northern gate and led me around to the outside of the outer gate that faces in the direction of the east; and I found that water was gushing from [under] the south wall. [3]As the man went on eastward with a measuring line in his hand, he measured off a thousand cubits and led me across the water; the water was ankle deep. [4]Then he measured off another thousand and led me across the water; the water was knee deep. He measured off a further thousand and led me across the water; the water was up to the waist. [5]When he measured yet another thousand, it was a stream I could not cross; for the water had swollen into a stream that could not be crossed except by swimming. [6]"Do you see, O mortal?" he said to me; and he led me back to the bank of the stream.

[7]As I came back, I saw trees in great profusion on both banks of the stream. [8]"This water," he told me, "runs out to the eastern region, and flows into the Arabah; and when it comes into the sea, into the sea of foul waters, the water will become wholesome. [9]Every living creature that swarms will be able to

live wherever this stream goes; the fish will be very abundant once these waters have reached there. It will be wholesome, and everything will live wherever this stream goes. [10]Fishermen shall stand beside it all the way from Engedi to En-eglaim; it shall be a place for drying nets; and the fish will be of various kinds [and] most plentiful, like the fish of the Great Sea. [11]But its swamps and marshes shall not become wholesome; they will serve to [supply] salt. [12]All kinds of trees for food will grow up on both banks of the stream. Their leaves will not wither nor their fruit fail; they will yield new fruit every month, because the water for them flows from the Temple. Their fruit will serve for food and their leaves for healing." (Ezek 47:1–12)

In this strange, and strangely detailed, vision, waters arise from under the Jerusalem Temple itself and, like those of the Gihon, flow down to the east. In this case, however, they flow not merely to the nearby Kidron Valley, but much farther, ever deepening as they go, until they reach the Dead Sea. That body of water derives its English name from the fact that it is so saline that fish and plants cannot survive in it; in Hebrew, it is the "Salt Sea." In this vision, its lethal, saline character, however, is miraculously undone, and "the water will become wholesome," or, more literally, "will be healed" (v 8). The result is that the once dead sea will swarm with living things, fish will become as abundant as they are in the Mediterranean (the "Great Sea" of verse 10), and fruit trees will grow on its once arid and forbidding banks. These will not be ordinary trees, to be sure. For their leaves will not wither, nor their fruit give out; rather, they shall be renewed every month—all "because the water for them flows from the Temple." Indeed, just as these supernatural trees will result from the healing effects of the Temple waters, so will their leaves, in turn, serve as medicine to cure the ailing (v 12). The trees will serve as agents of the healing and revivification that originates in the Temple of Jerusalem. They will be an antidote to the poison of disease and death.

The Temple vision in Ezekiel 40–48 results, then, in more than simply a reconstructed Temple and a reconstituted Israelite polity centered upon it. It results as well in a vision of the redeemed life that has striking points in common with notions of paradise that appear in the story of the Garden of Eden in Genesis 2–3. The trees whose leaves never wither and whose fruit never fails present us with the tantalizing temptation to draw a connection to the Tree of Life, which, had Adam been permitted to taste it, would have rendered him immune to death (Gen 3:22–24). Perhaps the Tree of Life was analogous to a fountain of youth, protecting not only against death but also against the age-related withering and failing that usually precede it. In light of the source of those trees in the Temple, one is at least equally inclined to connect them with the description of the righteous transplanted into the House of the LORD at the end of Psalm 92. In the psalm, as we saw, the righteous or the trees to which they are likened do reach "old age," but even so they "still produce fruit" and even retain the physical appearance of youth.

The implication of the imagery of healing waters and ever-fruitful trees is clear. The Temple serves, among many other things, as a survival of the primal paradise lost to the profane world, the world outside the sanctuary ("profane" is from the Latin, *pro* + *fanum*, "sanctuary"), and as a prototype of the redeemed world envisioned by some to lie ahead. It connects the protological and the eschatological, the primal and the final, preserving Eden and providing a taste of the life of intimacy with God that the Talmudic rabbis would come to call the World-to-Come.

IMMORTALITY IN THE HOUSE OF THE LORD

We have now sketched out a chain of associations consisting of the miraculous spring in the Temple, the healing and rejuvenating waters it puts forth, the supernatural trees and other new life that it miraculously and unexpectedly produces, and of course, the mode of being of the righteous and faithful in the Temple at which the chain begins. It is this last link that, in turn, brings us back to the question of the "fountain of life" in Ps 36:10. The evidence suggests that the Temple, too—properly approached and respected—was thought to be an antidote to death, bestowing a kind of immortality on those who dwell there in innocence, purity, and trust.

This notion of the Temple as the locus or source of immortality may, in fact, be the point of the conclusion to the enigmatic little poem that is Psalm 133:

> A song of ascents. Of David.

> [1]How good and how pleasant it is
> that brothers dwell together.

> ²It is like fine oil on the head
> running down onto the beard,
> the beard of Aaron,
>   that comes down over the collar of his robe;
> ³like the dew of Hermon
> that falls upon the mountains of Zion.
> There the LORD ordained blessing,
> everlasting life.

Here, fraternal unity (or perhaps reunion after estrangement) is likened to the oil that anoints the high priest. This, in turn, evokes a further simile, to the dew that falls on Hermon, a mountain in ancient Israel's far north that, reaching an altitude of more than ninety-two hundred feet, readily collects the precipitation that is all too rare throughout most of that arid land. In the psalm, the point is not that the precipitation descends on Hermon, but rather it (or Hermon-like dew in general) then falls upon the parched lands around Jerusalem. "Mountains of Zion" appears nowhere else in the plural in the Hebrew Bible, but "Mount Zion" is, of course, well-known as the name of the Temple Mount. In the Judahite temple theology, Zion possesses a mystique that one would never suspect from its mere physical reality. Therefore, we must not waste time trying to figure out how the dew of Hermon can descend upon the mountains of Zion 120 miles to the south. The geography maps out spiritual, not terrestrial, realities.

The dew that is the specific manifestation of divine bounty is a good analogy to the healing waters that issue from the Temple on Zion in Ezekiel 47. In Psalm 133, too, Zion is the place from which "the LORD ordained blessing, / everlasting life" (v 3). What precisely this last phrase means is, of course, a huge question. Most likely, it denotes the goodness of life in fraternal concord that the psalm begins by extolling. If so, the point is that this blessing rests upon a divine promise akin to or associated with the promises centering on the priestly service in the Temple and on God's promise of protection for his holy mountain, Zion, the spiritual center of the Israelite-Judahite brotherhood. The term "everlasting life" connotes neither individual immortality nor the result of a collective resurrection, but it still adds an important note. *Individual Israelites* die, and do not rise from the grave, but the collective promise of life to the *people Israel* that emanates from Zion shall endure forever. Here, as often, Zion serves as a spatial image of the liberation from the ravages of time and decay that characterize ordinary human life.

If we formulate the matter in this way, Psalm 133 seems to support the common view that the Hebrew Bible knows nothing of immortality as we understand it today, except as something placed out of our reach by man's first disobedience in the Garden of Eden. We want to argue, however, that this formulation, while not altogether erroneous, is incomplete in significant ways and thus misleading. For it fails to reckon with the Edenic character of the Temple itself, in particular, with the fact that death is as alien to the Temple, indeed as repugnant to the Temple, as it is to Eden. No one in the Hebrew Bible longs to die in the Temple or to be buried there, and for good reason: a dead body is a prime source of ritual contamination (Lev 21:1–4; Numbers 19). This is why Jewish law to this day forbids *kohanim* (men of priestly descent from the line of Aaron) to approach a dead body except to attend to the nearest of kin. Holiness and death are at odds; there is something like a magnetic repulsion between them. In Psalm 133, the Temple Mount is the place at which God ordained the blessing of eternal life; no thought is given to the reality—so evident to us—that those who visit there will ultimately die, the promise of eternal life notwithstanding. That consideration is as alien to the psalm as a corpse is to the Temple, or disobedience is to the Garden of Eden.

The implication of the paradisiacal character of the Temple that we have been developing is that the paradigm of Genesis 3 must not be overgeneralized, as it usually has been because of the role that chapter plays in the Christian drama of salvation. The familiar Christian use of Genesis 3 is temporal: the opportunity for immortality lay in the past and is unavailable now. Psalm 133 and its kindred literature offer a paradigm that is spatial: death is the norm outside Zion and cannot be reversed, but within the temple city, death is unknown, for there God has ordained the blessing of eternal life. To journey to the Temple is to move toward redemption. It is to leave the parched land of wasting and death for the fountain of life and the revival and rejuvenation it dispenses.

This conception of the Temple as paradise, the place rendered inviolable by the pervasive presence of God, explains one of the more striking features of Temple-oriented devotion in the Hebrew Bible. We are referring to the longing to remain in the Temple so often expressed by psalmists, their desire to spend their lives there, the reluctance to leave for the more familiar world marked by the murderous designs of the enemy and kindred menaces. Some of this can probably be explained by the status of sanctuaries in Israelite law, where they served as places of asylum for those unjustly accused and fearful of retaliation. Sanctuaries or altars served a legal function similar to that of the "cities of refuge" to which someone who has committed homicide without malice aforethought could escape the vengeance of the victim's blood-avenger (Num 35:9–34; Deut 19:1–13). Within the sanctuary lies life; outside it lurks death.

Within the Temple also lies innocence. Although worshipers experience therein the rich bounty of a gracious God, they do not enter by grace alone. Their lives must qualify them for admittance and residence, as demonstrated by compositions like Psalm 15:

> A psalm of David.
>
> [1]LORD, who may sojourn in Your tent,
>   who may dwell on Your holy mountain?
> [2]He who lives without blame,
>   who does what is right,
>   and in his heart acknowledges the truth;
>   [3]whose tongue is not given to evil;
>   who has never done harm to his fellow,
>   or borne reproach for [his acts toward] his neighbor;
>   [4]for whom a contemptible man is abhorrent,
>   but who honors those who fear the LORD;
>   who stands by his oath even to his hurt;
>   [5]who has never lent money at interest,
>   or accepted a bribe against the innocent.
> The man who acts thus shall never be shaken.

Many scholars classify poems like this one as "entrance liturgies," on the assumption that their origins lay in ceremonies in which priests guarding the entrance to the Temple precincts set forth the moral prerequisites for admission. The didactic affirmation with which Psalm 15 closes goes even further. It ascribes the very inviolability of the Temple Mount to the exemplary person who is ethically qualified to dwell there. Those whom the "entrance liturgy" qualifies for admittance become like the eternal and impregnable sanctuary into which they then come. They "shall never be shaken" (*lo'-yimmot*, v 5). Psalm 125 extends the same assurance to those who trust in the LORD, whatever their location:

> ¹Those who trust in the LORD
>> are like Mount Zion
>> that cannot be moved [*lo'-yimmot*],
>> enduring forever.
> ²Jerusalem, hills enfold it,
>> and the LORD enfolds His people
>> now and forever. (Ps 125:1–2)

The Temple in Jerusalem is the symbolic representation of the secure and protected life of those who trust in God and strive to live the morally up-right life he demands.

The converse of the Edenic life within the Temple precincts is the dan-ger that awaits without. The author of the celebrated Twenty-Third Psalm tells us that God "spread[s] a table for me in full view of my enemies." No wonder the thought appeals to him that he will "dwell in the house of the LORD / for many long years" (vv 5–6). And no wonder the author of Psalm 84 proclaims:

> Happy are those who dwell in Your house;
>> they forever praise You. (Ps 84:5)

At the conclusion of the same poem, the author draws together a number of themes that we have been developing—God's grace and bounty, the moral innocence of those who trust in him, and his reliable protection of them—in a similar paean to life in the holy shrine:

> ¹¹Better one day in Your courts than a thousand [anywhere else];
>> I would rather stand at the threshold of God's house
>> than dwell in the tents of the wicked.
> ¹²For the LORD God is sun and shield;
>> the LORD bestows grace and glory;
>> He does not withhold His bounty from those who live without blame.
> ¹³O LORD of hosts,
>> happy is the man who trusts in You. (Ps 84:11–13)

Poems such as these we have been examining attest to the sense of tran-scendence that the worshipers in the Temple experienced. There they rejoiced to find a world that is a sign of contradiction to the nastier and more familiar world of everyday life. Or, to be more precise, they rejoiced over the Temple reality with a keen awareness of the mundane reality from which they had been rescued. In the Temple, instead of want, they found surfeit; instead of abandonment, care; instead of pollution, purity; instead of victimization, justice; instead of threat, security; instead of vulnerability, inviolability; instead of change, fixity; and instead of temporality, eternity. If this sounds like the Garden of Eden or the World-to-Come of rabbinic tradition, or the Heaven of Christianity, that is surely no coincidence, for the Temple is the source of much of the imagery out of which these ideas grew. The outstanding difference, of course, is that the experience of the worshipers in the Temple lies on *this* side of death. To the extent that it anticipates the World-to-Come or Heaven, it is exactly that—an anticipation, a pre-enactment, a preview of what Judaism and Christianity (but not the Hebrew Bible, until quite late in its history) promise lies on the far side of death for those privileged to have it. To say that these spiritual experiences are, in the last analysis, this-worldly and thus irrelevant to our topic is shortsighted. They are very much experiences of another world, fleetingly available to those granted the ecstasy of worship in the House of the LORD. That is a world in which the worshipers are praising God forever (Ps 84:5), in marked contrast to "the dead [who] cannot praise the LORD" (Ps 115:17). The Temple is the antipode of Sheol, as life is the opposite of death, and the praise of God is the opposite of personal oblivion.

When we characterize this experience of the Temple in Jerusalem as an intimation of immortality, we must be careful to note that we are not dealing here with some ancient Israelite analogy to the immortality of the soul as that idea is expressed in Greek philosophical sources (later, of course, to find a home as well in Jewish, Christian, and Muslim theology). Those who shelter in the House of the LORD do not survive death as indestructible disembodied spirits, their bodies alone having passed away. Rather, they survive the very real threat of death—the utter demise of the *entire* person—because of the special intervention of God, and they survive in bodily form. Were it not for God's just and gracious rescue, they would have been destroyed. Those delivered from death to live in the Temple thus affirm that they depend on their relationship with their God for their very lives; they cannot rely on any inherently immortal dimension of the self to withstand the fate he has generously spared them. In this, as we shall see, the escape from death that they claim to have experienced exhibits striking affinities with resurrection as it emerges in Judaism and passes into Christianity as well.

Since the Temple serves as the antipode to Sheol, the locus of life against the Godforsaken realm of the dead, it stands to reason that longing for the Temple can also represent a longing for immortality. The parade example of this is a text we discussed briefly in Chapter 3, the Psalm of Jonah:

> ³He said:
> In my trouble I called to the LORD,
> And He answered me;
> From the belly of Sheol I cried out,
> And You heard my voice.
> ⁴You cast me into the depths,
> Into the heart of the sea,
> The floods engulfed me;
> All Your breakers and billows
> Swept over me.
> ⁵I thought I was driven away
> Out of Your sight:
> Would I ever gaze again
> Upon Your holy Temple?
> ⁶The waters closed in over me,
> The deep engulfed me.
> Weeds twined around my head.
> ⁷I sank to the base of the mountains;
> The bars of the earth closed upon me forever.
> Yet You brought my life up from the pit,
> O LORD my God!
> ⁸When my life was ebbing away,
> I called the LORD to mind;
> And my prayer came before You,
> Into Your holy Temple.
> ⁹They who cling to empty folly
> Forsake their own welfare,
> ¹⁰But I, with loud thanksgiving,

> Will sacrifice to You;
> What I have vowed I will perform.
> Deliverance is the LORD's! (Jon 2:3–10)

The placement of this song of thanksgiving in the mouth of Jonah is somewhat discordant because the fugitive prophet recites it from the belly of the fish but praises the LORD for having already rescued him from the netherworld. Presumably, within the context of the whole book of Jonah within its present shape, we are to think of the LORD's provision of "a huge fish to swallow Jonah" (Jon 2:1) as the act that rescued the drowning prophet from death, lifting him out of Sheol.

For our purposes, the most interesting feature of the Psalm of Jonah is its geography. Sheol (or "the pit") is the farthest point down. It lies at "the base of the mountains" (v 7). At the other extreme—presumably up high, though the text never specifies its direction—stands the "holy Temple," and it is there to which the dying prophet's prayer arrives, to precipitate this miraculous deliverance (compare Ps 18:5–7). It is instructive that the most painful thought Jonah has as he descends into Sheol is that he will never again gaze upon the Temple (v 5). More than anything else, this is the feature that represents the utter reality, the utter finality, of his death. Fortunately, things never reach that point. Although "there is no praise of You among the dead; / in Sheol, who can acclaim You?" (as Ps 6:6 puts it), Jonah can at least *remember* the LORD in Sheol and call upon him to rescue him from there. The rescue comes to its fulfillment in the place that the prophet thought he would never glimpse again and to which his prayer from the netherworld arrived—the Temple, and it is there that he praises his deliverer, offering thanksgiving sacrifices (vv 8–10). To move from Sheol to the Temple is to move from death to life. To long to gaze upon the Temple is to long for life itself.

ADAM FORESEES THE DESTRUCTION OF THE TEMPLE

The connection of the Temple with the Garden of Eden that we have been examining survived the Roman destruction of the Temple in 70 C.E. and can still be detected in subsequent rabbinic literature. It underlies, for example, a striking rabbinic observation about the expulsion of Adam, which happened, it will be recalled, because of the LORD's anxiety that humanity might become immortal:

> 22And the LORD God said, "Now that the man has become like one of us, knowing good and bad, what if he should stretch out his hand and take also from the tree of life and eat, and live forever!" 23So the LORD God banished him from the garden of Eden, to till the soil from which he was taken. 24He drove the man out [*waygaresh*], and stationed east of the garden of Eden the cherubim and the fiery ever-turning sword, to guard the way to the tree of life. (Gen 3:22–24)

This particular instance of rabbinic interpretation of the Hebrew Bible (the phenomenon is known as "midrash" and will occupy us again, especially in Chapter 13) interprets "drove out" (*waygaresh*) as "broke" or "crushed" (*wayyagres*), thus connecting the expulsion from Eden to a verse from Lamentations:

> He has broken [*wayyagres*] my teeth on gravel,
> Has ground me into the dust. (Lam 3:16)

Lamentations, it will be recalled, is a book about the agony of Fair Zion. It commemorates the destruction of Jerusalem and its Temple and for that reason is chanted in synagogues to this day on the evening of Tish'ah Be'Av, the fast day that tradition associates with the destruction and that is thus the saddest day of the Jewish year. On the basis of this wordplay, then, a midrash deduces that when God "drove the man out" of the Garden of Eden, "he showed him the destruction of the Temple." It is not simply that the two catastrophes (each involving an expulsion into exile) are similar. Nor is it simply the case that the primal, universal catastrophe anticipates (and is perhaps even repeated in) the historical, national catastrophe generations later. Rather, the two events—the loss of the potential for immortality and the destruction of the Edenic refuge from death—are deeply interconnected and draw upon the same elements in the symbolic universe of ancient Israel. The Temple concretizes and re-presents Eden, with its potential for immortality, and the loss of the Temple is the loss not only of tangible, material intimacy with God but also of the life that is inextricably associated with such a spiritual relationship. The destruction of the Temple recapitulates the expulsion from Eden.

Conversely, the image of redemption from exile and rehabilitation of the promised land can draw upon the imagery of Eden restored (e.g., Ezek 36:33–36; Isa 51:3). The destruction of the Temple that the midrash imagines Adam to have foreseen as he was being driven out of Eden is not the last word, either for the prophets or for the rabbis. In each case, an astonishing restoration reverses the tragedy, real and wrenching though the latter is. The loss of Eden, like the loss of the Land of Israel, proves to be temporary when God finally acts to close the tragic parenthesis in history. The return to the miraculously restored Zion is a return to the world as God created it to be.

"YOU WILL RECEIVE ME WITH GLORY"

We have seen that the intimations of immortality in the Temple are only that—intimations and not the confident expectation that the experience of protection afforded in it will forever be the empirical reality. To be sure, the literature of Temple devotion that we have been examining knows nothing of a departure from the inviolable precincts into the world of the raging enemy—except, of course, in the form of prayers that the protection continue and such a departure never occur. In this sense, and this sense alone, we can say that the worshipers dwell in a world without death. But we know, and they occasionally feel, that the sanctuary they have been granted will come to an end, that they will eventually be turned out of their Edenic asylum and, separated from the source of life, will surely die. Although the rhetoric of Temple devotion is indeed one of life and not death, of eternity and not temporality, we are entitled nonetheless to point out that death comes even to those who find refuge in the Temple.

In the Hebrew Bible and perhaps outside it as well, however, there are hints of another ancient Israelite perspective, one that seems to look forward to a continuation of divine protection even after death. To be more specific, these are passages that seem to speak of individuals whose earthly lives end without death. The best known describes the departure of the prophet Elijah after the commissioning of his successor, Elisha:

> [1]When the LORD was about to take Elijah up to heaven in a whirlwind, Elijah and Elisha had set out from Gilgal. [2]Elijah said to Elisha, "Stay here, for the LORD has sent me on to Bethel." "As the LORD lives and as you live," said

Elisha, "I will not leave you." So they went down to Bethel. ³Disciples of the prophets at Bethel came out to Elisha and said to him, "Do you know that the LORD will take [*loqeach*] your master away from you today?" He replied, "I know it, too; be silent."

⁴Then Elijah said to him, "Elisha, stay here, for the LORD has sent me on to Jericho." "As the LORD lives and as you live," said Elisha, "I will not leave you." So they went on to Jericho. ⁵The disciples of the prophets who were at Jericho came over to Elisha and said to him, "Do you know that the LORD will take [*loqeach*] your master away from you today?" He replied, "I know it, too; be silent."

⁶Elijah said to him, "Stay here, for the LORD has sent me on to the Jordan." "As the LORD lives and as you live, I will not leave you," he said, and the two of them went on. ⁷Fifty men of the disciples of the prophets followed and stood by at a distance from them as the two of them stopped at the Jordan. ⁸Thereupon Elijah took his mantle and, rolling it up, he struck the water; it divided to the right and left, so that the two of them crossed over on dry land. ⁹As they were crossing, Elijah said to Elisha, "Tell me, what can I do for you before I am taken [*'ellaqach*] from you?" Elisha answered, "Let a double portion of your spirit pass on to me." ¹⁰"You have asked a difficult thing," he said. "If you see me as I am being taken [*luqqach*] from you, this will be granted to you; if not, it will not." ¹¹As they kept on walking and talking, a fiery chariot with fiery horses suddenly appeared and separated one from the other; and Elijah went up to heaven in a whirlwind. ¹²Elisha saw it, and he cried out, "Oh, father, father! Israel's chariots and horsemen!" When he could no longer see him, he grasped his garments and rent them in two. (2 Kgs 2:1–12)

As is generally the case in the stories of Elijah and Elisha, the major emphasis lies on the defiance of nature characteristic of these wonder-working itinerant prophets. Elijah's parting of the Jordan, reenacting both Moses' splitting of the Sea of Reeds and the latter's successor Joshua's stopping the waters of the Jordan (Exod 14:21–31; Josh 3:9–4:24), confirms anew his supernatural authority and, more importantly, the limitless power of the God who grants it. Here, the question of authority is especially pertinent, because Elijah is about to commission a successor. The miracle of Elijah's ascent to the sky in a whirlwind validates the "difficult thing" that Elisha has requested, a "double portion" of the prophet's spirit. The language recalls the law that specifies the "double portion" as the firstborn son's inheritance (Deut 21:17) and thus underscores Elisha's status as the sole successor to the man he calls "father" (2 Kgs 2:12). From now on, it will be Elisha who serves as the head of the "disciples of the prophets."

Where was Elijah after he "went up to heaven in a whirlwind" (v 11)? The Hebrew word *shamayim* is better rendered "sky" than "heaven," because the latter term suggests a paradisiacal abode unknown in the Hebrew Bible. There is, in fact, no reason to think that Elijah is here assumed into heavenly glory, rewarded for his service, or brought into the company of other righteous servants of God. Rather, the God of Israel, whose throne several texts locate in the sky, whisks his servant Elijah away from the earth and toward his own mysterious and unapproachable abode.

That Elijah should leave the earth in this eerie fashion is altogether congruent with the presentation of him elsewhere in Kings. Unlike most prophets, for example, we know nothing of his paternity; no father's name is given. His introduction into the narrative also sounds the notes of numinous power and abrupt appearance that resound throughout the narrative, until his abrupt disappearance after parting the Jordan that we have just seen:

> Elijah the Tishbite, an inhabitant of Gilead, said to Ahab, "As the LORD lives, the God of Israel whom I serve, there will be no dew or rain except at my bidding." (1 Kgs 17:1)

The mysterious closeness to God, manifest in the awesome display of divine power at the end of Elijah's earthly life, accounts for his eerie transport into the sky. To speculate about his destination is as fruitless as speculating about his origin or the way in which he acquired those miraculous powers. Indeed, so little is known about his destination that we cannot safely say even that he never died. Perhaps 2 Kings wants us to think that death followed his miraculous disappearance.

Jewish tradition, beginning perhaps as early as the late prophet Malachi (Mal 3:23–24), sees the matter differently. It conceives Elijah as a prophet who never died and thus continually stands ready to serve as the messenger or human agent of heavenly reconciliation. To this day, the Jewish liturgy voices the petition that God send Elijah to announce the good news of comfort and deliverance. But where the Tishbite resides in the interim (if, that is, he did not die) is something the biblical sources never address. The story of Elijah's translation into the sky testifies to the power of God over death, but it says nothing about the nature of immortality.

The other passage about an earthly life that seemingly ends without death is equally mystifying but even more cryptic:

> [21]When Enoch had lived 65 years, he begot Methuselah. [22]After the birth of Methuselah, Enoch walked with God 300 years; and he begot sons and daughters. [23]All the days of Enoch came to 365 years. [24]Enoch walked with God; then he was no more, for God took [*laqach*] him. (Gen 5:21–24)

The seventh figure in the Priestly (P) antediluvian genealogy, Enoch has the shortest longevity—only 365 years. The number recalls the solar year and has suggested a connection to "the Mesopotamian Enmeduranna, who is the seventh king before the Flood" and whose "capital city was the ancient center of the sun god." One has the sense that there was once a much larger and richer account of Enoch's premature disappearance, heavily mythological in character, which has been lost. Perhaps something of that material lies behind the massive amount of Enoch literature that Jews authored between (roughly) the third century B.C.E. and the sixth century C.E. What is beyond dispute, however, is that our text has suppressed whatever myth had circulated, leaving commentators guessing ever since about the cause of Enoch's early disappearance. The great biblical and Talmudic commentator, Rashi (eleventh century), for example, thought that "God took him" prematurely in order to prevent him from sinning, presumably in the pandemic corruption that resulted in the great flood.

It is less clear whether the "taking" in question signified something other than death. As another commentator, Abraham ibn Ezra (twelfth century) and others point out, the same verb (*laqach*) appears in Jonah's death wish (Jon 4:3) and in the LORD's announcement of Ezekiel's wife's impending death. The latter passage is especially germane because God is the subject of the verb (Ezek 24:16). The assumption, by no means secure, that God's taking Enoch was of the same order as his taking Ezekiel's wife would compel us to interpret the former's earthly end simply as death. In that case, the absence of the verb "to die" in Gen 5:24 (in contrast to Jon 4:3 and Ezek 24:18) in favor of the softer and more ambiguous term "was no more" (*'eynennu*) may suggest a tenderer attitude on God's part, as befits the innocent man whose end the verse reports—but nothing more. Consider the telling contrast the Targum Onkelos (an ancient Aramaic translation of the Torah) makes merely with the addition of these few words: "for the LORD had caused him to die."

This rabbinic insistence that Enoch's body indeed died (whatever God did with his soul) may well originate in reaction to the Jewish Enoch literature already mentioned. The book of Jubilees (second century B.C.E.) gives this account:

> [22]... And Enoch bore witness against all of them. [23]And he was taken from among the children of men, and we led him to the garden of Eden for greatness and honor. And behold, he is there writing condemnation and judgment of the world, and all of the evils of the children of men. [24]And because of him none of the water of the Flood came upon the whole land of Eden, for he was put there for a sign and so that he might bear witness against all of the children of men so that he might relate all of the deeds of the generations until the day of judgment. [25]And he offered the incense which is acceptable before the LORD in the evening (at) the holy place on Mount Qater. (Jub 4:22–25)

Here we see a striking foreshadowing of the rabbinic notion that the destiny of the righteous lies in the Garden of Eden. But we also hear an echo of the more ancient identification of that magic place with the Temple. Enoch is not simply rewarded by being whisked off to paradise. Offering sacrificial incense, he also serves there as a priest. Most likely, the sweet savor of the incense corresponds to the rectitude of his own earthly life, which must have brought a kindred pleasure to God. The life he has after "he was taken from among the children of men" not only rewards, but also continues and even enhances the direction of his life beforehand. He enacts symbolically in ritual the ethical character of his godly conduct.

Finally, we must consider passages from two psalms that seem also to speak of a future life for the upright after they have died. The first appears in Psalm 49:

> [15]Sheeplike they head for Sheol,
>   with Death as their shepherd.
> The upright shall rule over them at daybreak,
>   and their form shall waste away in Sheol
>   till its nobility be gone.

¹⁶But God will redeem my life from the clutches of Sheol,
    for He will take me [*yiqqacheni*]. (Ps 49:15–16)

The translation of the notoriously difficult verse 15 comports well with the overall theme of the poem: the futility of wealth and social status in the face of inevitable death. If "Death" (v 15) refers to the Canaanite god of that name (Mot), then we are to see a contrast between those whom Death leads to Sheol and the psalmist himself, whom God redeems and "takes." If so, Death/Mot has now been assigned a *moral* function in God's world: it/he leads those who are arrogant, self-satisfied, and materialistic to the miserable netherworld to which they have condemned themselves, but he has no authority over those who humbly trust in God. Verse 16, as clear textually as its predecessor is opaque, nonetheless admits of some semantic ambiguity. Does it affirm that God will not allow the psalmist to remain in Sheol when he has died or that he will prevent him from descending thereto in the first place? Either way, the same ambiguity as to the destination that we saw in connection with Elijah and Enoch remains, signaled by the presence of the same verb, "to take." Where does God "take" the faithful servant who relies on him, rather than on wealth and status, for his ultimate felicity? We again find no answer.

The other passage in Psalms is also ambiguous:

²³Yet I was always with You,
    You held my right hand;
    ²⁴You guided me by Your counsel
    and will receive me [*tiqqacheni*] with ['*achar*] glory.
²⁵Whom else have I in heaven?
And having You, I want no one on earth.
²⁶My body and mind fail;
    but God is the stay of my mind, my portion forever.
²⁷Those who keep far from You perish;
    You annihilate all who are untrue to You.
²⁸As for me, nearness to God is good;
    I have made the Lord GOD my refuge,
    that I may recount all Your works. (Ps 73:23–28)

The main uncertainty lies with the second line of verse 24. The rendering above understands '*achar* to be a preposition meaning "with," a rare usage, to be sure, but one for which there is persuasive evidence. The future tense ("will receive") seems called for, since the psalmist is speaking of the decline of his own "body and mind," which, in striking contrast to the demise of those far from God, does not sever his relationship with God. If it was generally thought that "they who descend into the Pit / [do not] Hope for Your grace" (Isa 38:18), it is all the more striking that this psalmist continues emphatically to regard God as his rock and his refuge even in the face of death.

To be sure, it is possible to read the psalmist's words as expressing confidence in God only despite death and not after it. But to do so is to vitiate the force of the contrast between those distant from God and untrue to him, whom God "annihilates" so that they "perish," on the one hand, and the speaker himself ("As for me . . ."), on the other (vv 27–28). The psalm resolves the problem of the wicked who prosper and the innocent who suffer the way the Hebrew Bible usually resolves it—not with an intellectual insight, but with confidence that God will dramatically turn the tables, righting the wrong that has caused the psalmist such grief. In Psalm 73, the turning of the tables involves the annihilation of the unfaithful, whereas the psalmist has God as his "portion forever." The prosperity of the wicked is transient; the felicity of the faithful, eternal.

As in the cases of Enoch, Elijah, and Psalm 49, we cannot say where it is that God will receive/take the speaker of Psalm 73 with glory. Since the emphasis lies on God as refuge rather than the destination of the dying, we surely distort the message of the psalm if we focus on the "place" in which its author enjoys his unending closeness to God. Rather, it would seem that all of these texts that speak of the enigmatic "taking" are expressing a belief that whether spatial or not, it is in God's power to provide an antipode to the misery of Sheol. Although some—perhaps most—are "sent down" to Sheol (e.g., 1 Kgs 2:9), others God "takes" himself, continuing his reliable protection of those who find refuge in him at or even beyond the point of death.

CONFIDENCE IN THE FACE OF DEATH

The conclusion we drew about the intimations of immortality in the House of the LORD applies no less to the texts about Elijah, Enoch, and the psalmists that we have just examined. Here, too, if God's "taking" involves survival after death or disappearance, the analogy with resurrection is stronger than that with immortality of the soul as the term has usually been understood. For these four texts do not speak of any indestructible core of the self that endures in a disembodied state even after the flesh and bones have rotted away. Rather, they speak of an active intervention of God, snatching up to the sky the person found worthy (Elijah), taking him before his time and still in his innocence (Enoch), redeeming him from the power of Sheol (Psalm 49), or receiving him with glory, in contrast to the wicked whom God annihilates (Psalm 73).

In all these cases, one must not miss the powerful theme of special grace. In each instance, the person might have died as others do, with as much or as little hope for the future as they have. In the cases of Enoch and especially the two psalmists, there is also an important note of judgment. Presumably, it is because "Enoch walked with God" that "God took him" (Gen 5:24). One psalmist's confidence that "He will take me" (Ps 49:16) stands in pointed contrast with the dreary fate of those who foolishly trust in their wealth. The other psalmist's expectation that God will receive him "with glory" (Ps 73:24) is the correlative of his confidence that the wicked, though at present thriving, shall nonetheless be overthrown (e.g., "How suddenly are they ruined," v 19). In these two psalms, it is not too much to speak of an eschatological dimension, as long as we bear in mind that the final judgment comes not at the end of history, but at the end of the psalmist's own experience, that is, at the end of his life. His death is his personal eschatological moment. It attests to the long-delayed justice of God. As we shall see, the same must be said for the biblical expectation of a resurrection of the dead, when it at last appears unambiguously around the second century B.C.E.

It would be simplistic, then, to polarize immortality and resurrection. For one thing, doing so obscures the critical point that there is a version of immortality that is quite close to resurrection. To be sure, this is not the version on which philosophers from Plato to Maimonides to Kant (and beyond) have focused—the version that posits an immaterial and imperishable soul. Rather the version of immortality of which the literature in the Hebrew Bible speaks concentrates on almost the diametric opposite, a painfully vulnerable "life" (*nepesh*) that God will take or redeem—or so its possessor hopes—whereas others less worthy will descend into Sheol without hope. Secondly, even when a full-blown expectation of resurrection develops, one should not assume that those who hold it think that people simply do not exist between death and resurrection. "Many of those that sleep in the dust of the earth will awake," one reads in Dan 12:2, in language that suggests inactivity ("that sleep") rather than nonexistence or the miserable fate of those dispatched to Sheol. Later, the survival of the deceased even before their resurrection becomes a staple of rabbinic thought. In one particularly touching account, God is said to devote a quarter of each day to teaching Torah to little children who have died.

Finally, the aspiration to immortality that we have been exploring exhibits another connection to resurrection, and this lies in the fact that when the expectation of resurrection arises in Judaism (and then in Christianity), resurrection is still only the prelude to something greater and more permanent. This is "eternal life," as the book of Daniel puts it (12:2), or, to use the familiar rabbinic expression, life in the World-to-Come. Since this new life is thought to follow upon resurrection, it must entail embodiedness: people come back in the flesh. But the flesh in which they come back is necessarily different from the kind they knew in their mortal life, for now they have become immune to death and the bodily infirmities associated with it. There is no second death for those awarded eternal life. Once raised from the dead, they are granted immortality, and the flesh in which they are raised can only be analogous, and not identical, to the sort of flesh that characterized them beforehand. Their new life is thus not a mere continuation of the old but rather a radical transformation of it, a perfecting of the self in a world distinguished from this one by its perfection.

Although the longing for immortality that we have been exploring in this chapter does not envision resurrection, neither does it envision life in a disembodied state. Rather it tends to imagine embodied persons immune to the ravages of disease, death, scarcity, injustice, and enmity, living forever in a perfected world, the world symbolized, most commonly, by the Temple. That post-biblical Jews, believing in resurrection, and Christians as well continued to cherish the old literature that so vividly expressed this longing for immortality is thus hardly surprising.

6

HOW BIRTH REVERSES DEATH

INDIVIDUAL AND FAMILY IN BIBLICAL ISRAEL

In our previous chapter, we noted in passing that the death of an individual has a different meaning in a culture that understands the self in familial, transgenerational terms. In such cultures, we must recognize the difficulty of separating individuals from their families (including, ultimately, the extended family that is the nation). If, in fact, individuals are fundamentally and inextricably embedded within their families, then their own deaths, however terrifying in prospect, may not be thought to have the finality that death carries in a culture with a more individualistic, atomistic understanding of the self, like the culture of the modern West. What we are asserting here is something more radical than the truism that in the Hebrew Bible, parents draw consolation from the thought that their descendants will survive them, just as, conversely, parents are plunged into a paralyzing grief at the thought that their progeny have perished (for example, Gen 37:33–35; Jer 31:15). This is, of course, the case, and probably more so in the ancient world, where children were the support of one's old age, than in modern societies, where the state and the pension fund fill many roles previously concentrated in the family. Our point, rather, is that the self of an individual in ancient Israel was entwined with the self of his or her family in ways that are foreign to the modern West, and became foreign to a substantial degree already long ago.

Let us take as an example the passage in which Jacob is granted "the blessing of Abraham," his grandfather, according to the prayer of Isaac, his father, to "possess the land where you are sojourning, which God assigned to Abraham" (Gen 28:1–4). The blessing on Abraham can obviously be altogether and satisfactorily fulfilled in the latter's descendants. Thus, too, can Ezekiel envision the appointment of "a single shepherd over [Israel] to tend them — My servant David," who had passed away many generations before (Ezek 34:23). Can we see in this a plain-sense prediction that David, king of Judah and Israel, will be raised from the dead? To do so is to move outside the language of the text and the culture of Israel at the time of Ezekiel, which does not speak of the resurrections of individuals at all. But to say that Ezekiel means only one who is "like David" — a humble shepherd boy who comes to triumph in battle and rises to royal estate, vindicating his nation and making it secure and just — is not quite the whole truth, either. For biblical Hebrew is quite capable of saying that one person is "like" another or descends from another without implying identity of some sort. The more likely interpretation, rather, is that Ezekiel here predicts the miraculous appearance of a royal figure who is not only *like* David but also *of* David, a person of Davidic lineage, that is, who functions as a revived David. This is not the resurrection of a dead man, to be sure, but neither is it the appearance of some unrelated person who only acts like David, or of a descendant who is "a chip off the old block." David is, in one obvious sense, dead and buried, and his death is final and irreversible. In another sense, harder for us to grasp, however, his identity survives him and can be manifested again in a descendant who acts as he did (or, to be more precise, as Ezekiel thought he acted) and in whom the promise to David is at long last fulfilled. For David's identity was not restricted to the one man of that name, but can reappear to a large measure in others who share it, especially if they share his flesh and blood.

This is obviously not reincarnation. For that term implies that the ancient Israelites believed in something like the later Jewish and Christian "soul" or like the notion (such as one finds in some religions) of a disembodied consciousness that can reappear in another person after its last incarnation has died. In the Hebrew Bible, however, there is nothing of the kind. The best approximation is the *nephesh*, the part of the person that manifests his or her life force or vitality most directly. The term has traditionally (and very misleadingly) been translated into English as "soul," but it must not be overlooked that unlike the "soul" in most Western philosophy, the biblical *nephesh* can die. When the non-Israelite prophet Balaam expresses his wish to "die the death of the upright," it is his *nephesh* that he hopes will share their fate (Num 23:10), and the same applies to Samson when he voices his desire to die with the Philistines whose temple he then topples upon all (Judg 16:30). Indeed, "to kill the *nephesh*" functions as a term for homicide in biblical Hebrew, in which context, as elsewhere, it indeed has a meaning like that of the English "person." As Hans Walter Wolff puts it, *nephesh* "is never given the meaning of an indestructible core of being, in contradistinction to the physical life   capable of living when cut off from that life."

And there is a very good reason for that. As Aubrey Johnson observes, "The Israelite conception of man [is] as a psycho-physical organism." It would seem to follow that if a person were ever to return "as a psycho-physical organism," it would have to be not through reincarnation of the soul in some new body, but through the resurrection of the body, with all its parts reassembled and revitalized. For in the understanding of the Hebrew Bible, a human being is not a spirit, soul, or consciousness that happens to inhabit this body or that—or none at all. Rather the unity of body and soul (to phrase the point in the unhappy vocabulary that still presupposes the problematic dichotomy) is basic to the person. It thus follows that however distant the resurrection of the dead may be from the understanding of death and life in ancient Israel, the concept of immortality in the sense of a soul that survives death is even more distant. And, from the standpoint of the Hebrew Bible, whatever the problems with the doctrine of resurrection—and they are formidable—the problems with disembodied immortality are even greater.

The self in ancient Israel is not only embodied. It is also embedded within the family in ways that are as profound as they are alien to most modern readers, even deeply religious readers. Robert Di Vito points out that "salient features of modern identity, such as its pronounced individualism, are grounded in modernity's location of the self in the 'inner depths' of one's interiority rather than in one's social role or public relations." Cautioning against the naïve assumption that ancient Israel adhered to the same conception of the self, Di Vito develops four points of contrast between modern Western and ancient Israelite thinking on this point. In the Hebrew Bible, "the subject (1) is deeply embedded, or engaged, in its social identity, (2) is comparatively decentered and undefined with respect to personal boundaries, (3) is relatively transparent, socialized, and embodied (in other words, is altogether lacking in a sense of 'inner depths'), and (4) is 'authentic' precisely in its heteronomy, in its obedience to another and dependence upon another."

Although Di Vito's formulation is overstated and too simple—is every figure in the Hebrew Bible, even David, presented as "altogether lacking in a sense of 'inner depths'"?—his first and last points are highly instructive and suggest that the familial and social understanding of "life" in the Hebrew Bible is congruent with larger issues in ancient Israelite culture. "Life" and "death" mean different things in a culture like ours in which the subject is not so "deeply embedded . . . in its social identity" and in which authenticity tends to be associated with cultivation of individual traits at the expense of conformity, and with the attainment of independence and self-determination.

The contrast between the ancient Israelite and the modern Western constructions of personal identity is glaring when one considers the structure of what Di Vito calls "the patriarchal family." This "system," he tells us, "with strict subordination of individual goals to those of the extended lineal group, is designed to ensure the continuity and survival of the family." In a society like ancient Israel, in which "the subject . . . is deeply embedded, or engaged, in its social identity," "with strict subordination of individual goals to those of the extended lineal group," the loss of the subject's own life and the survival of the familial group cannot but have a very different resonance from the one most familiar to us. For even though the subject's death is irreversible—his or her *nephesh* having died just like the rest of the body/soul—his or her fulfillment may yet occur, for identity survives death. God can keep his promise *to* Abraham or his promise to Israel associated with the gift *of* David even after Abraham or David as an individual subject has died. Indeed, in light of Di Vito's point that "the subject . . . is comparatively decentered and undefined with respect to personal boundaries," the very distinction between Abraham and the nation whose covenant came through him (Genesis 15; 17), or between David and the Judahite dynasty whom the LORD has pledged never to abandon (2 Sam 7:8–16; Ps 89:20–38), is too facile.

THE FUNCTIONAL EQUIVALENT OF RESURRECTION

Our examination of personal identity in the earlier literature of the Hebrew Bible thus suggests that the conventional view is too simple: death was not final and irreversible after all, at least not in the way in which *we* are inclined to think of this matter. This is not, however, because individuals were believed to possess an indestructible essence that survived their bodies. Rather, it is because the boundary between individual subjects and the familial/ethnic/national group in which they dwelt, to which they were subordinate, and on which they depended was so fluid as to rob death of *some* of the horror it has in more individualistic cultures, influenced by some version of social atomism. In more theological texts, one sees this in the notion that subjects can die a good death, "old and contented . . . and gathered to [their] kin," like Abraham, who lived to see a partial—though only a partial—fulfillment of God's promise of land, progeny, and blessing upon him, or like Job, also "old and contented" after his adversity came to an end and his fortunes—including progeny—were restored (Gen 25:8; Job 42:17). If either of these patriarchal figures still felt terror in the face of his death, even after his afflictions had been reversed, the Hebrew Bible gives us no hint of it. As we saw in Chapter 4, death in situations like these is not a punishment, a cause for complaint against God, or the provocation of an existential crisis. But neither is it death as later cultures, including our own, conceive it.

Given this embeddedness in family, there is in Israelite culture, however, a threat that is the functional equivalent to death as we think of it. This is the absence or loss of descendants. It is in this light that we should understand the association the book of Proverbs makes between Sheol and infertility:

> ¹⁵The leech has two daughters, "Give!" and "Give!"
> Three things are insatiable;
> Four never say, "Enough!":
> ¹⁶Sheol, a barren womb,
> Earth that cannot get enough water,
> And fire which never says, "Enough!" (Prov 30:15–16)

The three items analogized here to "a barren womb" are all redolent of death—Sheol (the dark, miserable netherworld), parched earth that cannot sustain life, and a raging fire that consumes everything and everybody in its way. Given such associations, we can better understand why the future patriarch Abraham's childlessness evokes such anxiety:

[1]Some time later, the word of the LORD came to Abram in a vision. He said,

> "Fear not, Abram,
> I am a shield to you;
> Your reward shall be very great."

[2]But Abram said, "O Lord GOD, what can You give me, seeing that I shall die childless!" (Gen 15:1–2)

All the reward in the world—wealth, longevity, even having God as one's personal protector—cannot compensate for childlessness. In this light, we can understand better the full weight of the gruesome test to which Abraham is put when at last his childlessness has been reversed and he has the promised son. The proof that Abraham truly "fears God," that he places obedience to the divine command above his personal welfare, is that he is willing to sacrifice even that promised son (Gen 22:11–12). As Rabbi David Kimchi, a thirteenth-century commentator, puts it, Abraham loved Isaac even more than he loved himself "and yet all this love and affection were as nothing in his eyes" when God ordered him to offer up his beloved son.

Given the central role of children in the identity of parents in ancient Israelite culture, we have a credible clue as to the meaning of the common punishment formula, "that person shall be cut off [*venikhretah*] from his kin" (for example, Gen 17:14). The rabbinic opinion that this punishment (which the rabbis call *karet*) involved both a premature death and childlessness may well be close to the mark in the Hebrew Bible as well. As Donald J. Wold notes, the penalty constitutes "a divine curse of extinction" that entails the death of children and not simply the absence of them. It is akin to the death of one's self; indeed, in the context of the Hebrew Bible, it is a form of the death of one's self.

The book of Job is an instructive case in point. Job's miseries begin not with lack of children, like Abraham's great test, but with the loss of his children, which provokes suicidal thoughts and an existential and theological crisis that has continued to reverberate through the millennia (Job 1:13–19; Job 3). Here, bereavement of progeny is the functional equivalent of death, and here, too, the patriarch's restoration inevitably entails his recovery of his seven sons and three daughters (Job 42:13; compare 1:2). To us, of course, the loss has not been made good, because these are not the same children who died at the onset of the tale. But this objection only demonstrates the distance between our individualistic and nonfamilial construction of personal identity and the highly collective and familial concept that underlies these ancient Israelite narratives. For the epilogue, which speaks of Job's restoration, gives no indication whatsoever that grief about his deceased first set of children impaired his contentment at the time of his own death. The tragedy of the mortality of individuals cannot but attract the attention of the modern reader. The interest of the ancient narrator lies, however, in the restoration of Job through the return of his family.

If childlessness is the equivalent of death, what is the equivalent of resurrection? The stories about Abraham and Job, and of many other figures, male and female, throughout the Hebrew Bible, provide the answer: *birth* is the reversal of death and thus to a large degree the functional equivalent of resurrection (or of afterlife in general) in later cultures, including our own. The births of Abraham's first heir, Ishmael, and then of the promised son, Isaac, render God's promise of a reward to Abraham credible, just as the birth of Job's new brood in the epilogue is the comic counterpoint to the tragic death of his first set of children in the prologue. In these stories, it is not death but birth that is God's last word, and the continuance of the family enables the patriarch to die fulfilled.

Similarly, in the book of Ruth, one of the great masterpieces of biblical narrative artistry, a tale that begins with famine, expatriation, and death is transformed into one of abundance, return home, integration of the alien, and, most of all, birth. Naomi, bereft of husband and sons alike, acquires a surrogate daughter in the Moabitess Ruth, who in faithfulness to her Israelite mother-in-law "left [her] father and mother and the land of [her] birth," as Ruth's husband-to-be, Boaz, puts it, "and came to a people [she] had not known before" (2:11). Through Ruth—now married to Boaz and on her way to becoming a matriarch of the House of Judah and even of its royal line—Naomi, herself apparently past her childbearing years, becomes the equivalent of a mother (4:11–12; 1:12–13; 4:16–17). The deaths of her husband and sons, which occasioned her calling herself Mara ("bitter") in place of Naomi (derived from a word for "pleasantness," "sweetness"), have now been reversed, and she is once again "Naomi" (1:19b–21; 4:17). "Shaddai has made my lot very bitter," she had once told the women of Bethlehem, using a rare name of God. "I went away full, and the LORD has brought me back empty" (1:20–21). But by the end of story, when Ruth has given birth, Naomi, too, has been brought back full. As in Job, so here the tragedies of the first chapter are reversed, and more, in the last. God's last word is life, not death.

The tales of Abraham, Job, and Ruth and Naomi, though much more developed in narrative artistry than most, are hardly unique within the Hebrew Bible. In more rudimentary form (though perhaps epitomizing longer oral formulations), the pattern in which birth reverses death can be found in many other stories. Its earliest attestation (in terms of literary order, whatever the chronology of composition) lies in the folk etymology of Adam and Eve's third son, whom the latter named "Seth [*shet*], meaning, 'God has provided [*shat*] me with another offspring in place of Abel,'" whom Cain had killed (Gen 4:25). Twenty-three generations later, Judah, ancestor of Boaz and thus of the royal line from which David would hail, loses two sons, the second because of a refusal to fulfill the requirement of the surviving brother, "to provide offspring for his brother" (Gen 38:9; see Deut 25:5–10). Having refused to release his third son for fear the same fate would befall him, too, and mistaking his widowed daughter-in-law for a prostitute, Judah inadvertently fulfills the requirement himself. In the end of this strange and disquieting tale, full of odd twists and unexpected reversals, the man who lost two sons gains twins, as the widow whose in-laws neglected her gives birth to the boys who will carry on her father-in-law's tribe and her late husband's name. And this, let it not be forgotten, is the tribe from which King David's dynasty would someday spring.

A few chapters later, Jacob loses (as far as he knows) his beloved son Joseph; the sight of the latter's bloody tunic plunges him into mourning and depression (Gen 37:31–35). As in the story of Naomi and Ruth, so here death is conjoined with famine and expatriation, as the surviving sons of Jacob (minus his other beloved son, Benjamin, Joseph's only full brother) leave the promised land and descend into Egypt in search of grain. When they return without Simeon, who Joseph has demanded be kept as a hostage in lieu of Benjamin, Jacob understandably sees himself bereft of *two* sons, and, to add insult to injury, he now faces the demand to release a third as well. Yet it is precisely the release of the third son that eventually restores the other two, saves the family from famine, and reunites it after a long estrangement. The pattern of death and revival that underlies the

Joseph story is nicely highlighted by Jacob's response to his sons' report that "Joseph is still alive; yes, he is ruler over the whole land of Egypt." "His heart went numb, for he did not believe them," the narrator relates. "But when they recounted all that Joseph had said to them, and when he saw the wagons that Joseph had sent to transport him, the spirit of their father Jacob revived" (Gen 45:26–27). As in the case of Abraham and Isaac, so here the life of the father is entwined in that of the son.

Jacob's own apparent death and revival here encapsulates the underlying movement of the entire tale, a tale of the apparent death of children reversed through the providential restoration of them to their grieving father. Since the comic resolution focuses on the same children lost in the tragic opening, the pattern is more reminiscent of the binding of Isaac (Gen 22:1–19) than of the books of Ruth and Job. For those books close with the birth of *new* children rather than the restoration of those lost in the first chapter of each book. Too much, however, should not be made of the difference. For in each case, a death—apparent, real, or threatened—is reversed, and a parent gains or retains progeny after death has made its terrifying presence known. In fact, in the case at hand, Jacob, who thought he had lost two sons, acquires two *new* sons, when on his deathbed, he adopts Joseph's children as his own (Gen 48:5–7). Birth again qualifies and diminishes the finality of death.

These examples show that the construction of personal identity in biblical Israel renders problematic the conventional claim that the Pentateuch in particular, and the Hebrew Bible in general (with the exception of a few late passages), offers no expectation of survival after death. A more accurate generalization is that the hope for survival centers on the family, including (eventually) the extended family that is the nation, the whole House of Israel. If this seems to offer twenty-first-century people scant consolation in the face of their own inevitable death, as it indeed does, this is primarily because modern constructions of personal identity perceive higher and more rigid boundaries between the subject and the social group, especially the involuntary grouping that is the family. When the emphasis lies on the individual and his or her power of self-determination, as it generally does in modern Western thought, then the loss of the individual to death will inevitably seem catastrophic and irreversible (unless, of course, it can be reversed through resurrection), and the survival of the family through new births offers nothing more than purely psychological consolation, of whatever worth. To the modern Western mind of the sort we are describing, it seems right to say that in the last chapters of the respective books, Naomi, Ruth, and Job recover psychologically from the deaths reported in the first chapters. They carry on and rebuild. But to imply, as those biblical tales do, that the births of Ruth's son Obed and Job's seven new sons and three new daughters *overcome* the deaths of Elimelech, Mahlon, Chilion, and Job's first set of seven sons and three daughters seems to be missing the point badly. To us, the shadow of death always overcasts the happiness that the books of Ruth and Job predicate of Naomi and Job at the end of their travail. We look in vain for some acknowledgement that the newfound or recovered felicity is not absolute, since death is. The authors of these books thought otherwise.

The notion that the continuation of the family constitutes the expectation of survival in the Hebrew Bible—birth thus serving as the reversal of death—can lead to a misunderstanding that needs to be confronted immediately. Since the family carries on after the death of one of its members, it might be thought that the form of survival to which this pattern best corresponds is immortality: the core of the indestructible self is simply embedded in a larger unit and thus survives with that unit, even after the individual subject has irreversibly perished. If that is the case, then death becomes inconsequential, and the subject can face it with equanimity and tranquility, certain of the survival that his or her continuing family guarantees.

The stories that we have examined suggest, however, a different and far more pessimistic vision and, with it, a stormier and less complacent mode of spirituality. For in the stories of Abraham, Jacob, Judah, Ruth, and Job, death indeed threatens. It threatens not only individual subjects but also the family itself. In other words, given the construction of personal identity in the Hebrew Bible, infertility and the loss of children serve as the functional equivalent of death. Striking at each generation of the patriarchs of Genesis, and then at Judah in the next, childlessness in one or both of these modes threatens to terminate the family, thus evoking the terror that later generations (including our own) feel in the face of their personal deaths. That individuals in ancient Israel felt that same terror cannot be gainsaid; such terror is in plentiful evidence in the Psalms. Nonetheless, and despite a long tradition of viewing the sin of Adam and Eve (and the mortality thought to go with it) as the most memorable event in Genesis, the great enemy in that book is not death as we think of it at all (still less is it sin), but death in the twin forms of barrenness and the loss of children.

THE NAME SURVIVES DEATH

A key idiom for this larger, more encompassing understanding of death involves the notion of the loss of one's "name" (*shem*). Here we must revert to the book of Proverbs:

> The memory [*zekher*] of the righteous is a source of blessing,
> But the name of the wicked rots away. (Prov 10:7)

As William McKane puts it: "The *zekher* or *shem* is in effect an indirect prolongation of a man's influence and authority beyond death . . . The contrast is between the beneficent persistence of the righteous man's vitality expressed in his enduring influence on the life of his community, and the process of decay which induces the memory of the wicked to rot away to nothingness." We would add, however, that the community in which the effect of that "beneficent persistence" is felt is very often the family that hails from the deceased. The name is closely associated with the patrimonial land of the person's family. We find a fine example of this in the plea of the five daughters of Zelophehad to Moses:

> [3] Our father died in the wilderness. He was not one of the faction, Korah's faction, which banded together against the LORD, but died for his own sin; and he has left no sons. [4] Let not our father's name [*shem*] be lost to his clan just because he had no son! Give us a holding among our father's kinsmen! (Num 27:3–4)

Without a son, Zelophehad's name and the real estate with which it was associated are endangered. Fortunately for him and for his daughters, the LORD instructs Moses to allow the hereditary land of a man who dies without sons to pass to his daughters (Num 27:5–8; but see the qualification in 36:1–12). As long as the dead man's descendants survive on his hereditary holding, his name survives. If he lacks descendants or the land is alienated from his lineage, his name perishes.

The same logic underlies the institution of levirate marriage, which requires the brother of the deceased to marry his widow (Deut 25:5–10). "The first son that she bears shall be accounted to the dead brother, that his name [*shem*] may not be blotted out in Israel," Deuteronomy tells us (25:6). In this way, the late brother can beget a child even after his death, and one of the most dreaded aspects of his own demise, the extinction of his name through the lack of a son, can be reversed. By a kind of legal fiction, his family brings something of their dead kinsman back to life. Birth again reverses death. Levirate marriage is a mode of redemption of the dead.

These considerations illuminate the curious story of the provision of David's son Absalom for his own continuance after death:

> Now Absalom, in his lifetime, had taken the pillar which is in the Valley of the King and set it up for himself; for he said, "I have no son to keep my name [*shem*] alive." He had named [*shem*] the pillar after himself, and it has been called Absalom's Monument [*yad*] to this day. (2 Sam 18:18).

An interesting Canaanite parallel has led some to suggest that the expression translated above as "keep my name alive" actually refers to cultic invocation of a deified ancestor even in this text. The analogies with Zelophehad's daughters and with levirate marriage, however, argue that the issue is instead one of memorialization and the perpetuation of the name. Absalom takes preemptive action against the threat of extinction that death and childlessness jointly pose. Indeed, the closest parallel to this verse actually lies in the LORD's promise to eunuchs who observe the Sabbath:

> I will give them, in My House
> And within My walls,
> A monument [*yad*] and a name [*shem*]
> Better than sons or daughters.
> I will give them an everlasting name [*shem*]
> Which shall not perish. (Isa 56:5)

In this instance, God's promise to the Sabbath-observant eunuchs functions as the equivalent of levirate marriage for those biologically precluded from having children. The name, God assures the eunuchs, is the equivalent of the descendants they cannot engender; it thus guarantees that they shall not lack an "everlasting" continuance. God once again arranges things so that death is not final in all its aspects, and something of the deceased survives his physical demise.

In this chapter and the two that preceded it, we have seen a number of different ideas of the defeat of death. In Chapter 4, we argued that a significant body of texts in the Hebrew Bible suggests that not everyone was thought to go to Sheol, the miserable netherworld. Rather, it was possible for an individual to experience a fortunate death at the end of a fulfilled life, whose very fulfillment meant that no future misery lay in store. In Chapter 5, we explored texts that speak of the Temple as a place of everlasting life and others that speak of God's "taking" a person at or before death, though no destination is specified and we cautioned against the assumption that something like the Christian "Heaven" is what these authors had in mind. Lastly, in this chapter we have seen how the survival of descendants or of the name of the deceased was thought to counteract death. It is not wise to imagine how all these variant ideas and images fit together: they may not. The Hebrew Bible is a collection of diverse writings from different periods and different sectors of society, and we shall quickly lose our appreciation of its parts if we try to resolve all the contradictions and flatten the texts into one univocal system. What we can say with considerable certainty, however, is that death was not always thought to be God's last word.

A FORETASTE OF RESURRECTION

The mode of spirituality that befits the worldview of the texts that we have been discussing in this chapter is light-years away from untroubled confidence in the survival of an indestructible core, whether of the individual self (the "soul") or of the larger kin group. Rather, it is one that fervently hopes against hope for continuation after death and the fertility, safety, and memorialization that make it possible. It also seeks divine protection against the death-dealing forces that threaten the family by closing wombs, destroying male fertility, and taking children away. Just as creation in the vision of the Hebrew Bible is not a steady state of serenity but rather a precarious order maintained or renewed in the face of potent and malevolent chaos; and just as righteousness is often, perhaps usually, seen as vindication against powerful and successful evildoers and their false accusations; so is the continued life of the family a *triumph* over the forces of death, a *vindication* against evil, and therefore a consequence of *struggle*. It is a turning back of the very real and deadly forces of adversity, the forces

that rob one of progeny and name. In these aspects of triumph and reversal, the phenomena in the Hebrew Bible that we have been describing
foreshadow the resurrection of the dead much more than they do the immortality of the soul.

In the previous chapter and this one, we have examined two antipodes
to Sheol, the first focused on worship in the LORD's Temple, and the second on lineage and the miraculous origin and survival of the larger lineage
that is the people Israel. Our argument has been that these serve as symbols
of continuation and thus call into question the heavy-handed claim that
the Hebrew Bible always regards death as inevitable and in accordance
with the divine will. These two antipodes are not only symbols, however;
they are also the means by which certain types of continuation despite
death can be acquired. The two come together strikingly in a psalm that
memorably expresses the view of felicity in the Hebrew Bible:

> A song of ascents.
>
> [1]Happy are all who fear the LORD,
> > who follow His ways.
> [2]You shall enjoy the fruit of your labors;
> > you shall be happy and you shall prosper.
> [3]Your wife shall be like a fruitful vine within your house;
> > your sons, like olive saplings around your table.
> [4]So shall the man who fears the LORD be blessed.
>
> [5]May the LORD bless you from Zion;
> > may you share the prosperity of Jerusalem
> > all the days of your life,
> > > [6]and live to see your children's children.
> May all be well with Israel! (Psalm 128)

Although the psalmist does not affirm or even mention immortality or resurrection, it is very much to be doubted that he thought the felicity of
which he sang ended at the grave.

THE DEATH AND RESURRECTION
OF THE PROMISED SON

"PICK UP YOUR SON"

The intimate connection of infertility with death, and of childbirth and familial survival with resurrection, that we developed in our previous chapter appears nowhere in the Hebrew Bible with greater clarity than in 2 Kgs 4:8–37, the story of the great lady of Shunem and the wonder-working prophet Elisha ben Shaphat. The tale is deceptively simple. The wealthy woman, we are told, urges the prophet to stop at her house for a meal, and soon the practice becomes regular whenever the prophet is in town (vv 8–9). After a while, at her suggestion, she and her husband provide him with a furnished apartment in their house as well. In gratitude for her patronage, Elisha has his servant Gehazi summon the woman so that he may ask how he might reciprocate, offering to speak to the commander of the army on her behalf. Her reply stresses her satisfaction with her life as it is and her disinclination to seek special favors: "I live among my own people." "The fact is," Gehazi then observes, ominously, "she has no son, and her husband is old." This prompts the prophet to summon her again and to predict that "next year, you will be embracing a son"—a most unlikely prospect, to be sure, as her incredulous response brings out: "Please, my lord, man of God, do not delude your maidservant." Yet Elisha's prediction comes true, and soon we hear of the little boy in the fields with his father and the reapers (vv 13–18).

The happy ending proves no ending at all, for death reverses the miraculous fertility of the devout but childless woman and her elderly husband.

"Oh, my head, my head!" the stricken boy cries to his father, who instructs a servant to carry the child to his mother. But it is too late: "And the child sat on her lap until noon; and he died" (vv 19–20). Joy has tarried for a few years, but now the wealthy couple is plunged back into the darkness of childlessness from which the miracle-working "man of God" had all too briefly delivered them.

The great lady of Shunem does not, however, give up. Concealing her mission from her husband, she finds Elisha and accosts him, "in bitter distress." "Did I ask my lord for a son?" she challenges the prophet. "Didn't I say: 'Don't mislead me'?" Perhaps underestimating the gravity of the situation or overestimating his own powers, Elisha dispatches Gehazi with instructions to touch the boy's face with the prophet's staff. But the woman will not accept an underling, and she and the prophet return to her home together (vv 22–30).

Meanwhile, Gehazi, following Elisha's instructions, fails in his assignment: "there was no sound or response." The prophet's staff is no substitute for his person, and his assistant lacks the master's charismatic gift. "The boy has not awakened," Gehazi reports to Elisha when the latter has arrived (v 31). Then the prophet, alone with the dead boy in the room that symbolizes the couple's devotion to God (v 21), first prays to the LORD, and then through the miraculous power of his own body, resuscitates the child. Having instructed Gehazi to summon the woman again, he tells her, "Pick up your son." She prostrates herself at his feet, picks up the resurrected boy, and leaves (vv 32–37).

The reader dependent on a summary like this one just provided is, alas, likely to miss the rich intertextual resonance of the story. The most striking connection is to the stories of the birth and near-sacrifice of Isaac (Gen 18:1–15; 22:1–19), where specific points of diction suggest that we may be dealing not merely with a similar theme, deeply rooted in Israelite culture, but with actual literary dependence as well. Both stories begin with the note of extraordinary hospitality, Abraham's to his three angelic (or divine) visitors, and the great lady's to the itinerant prophet (Gen 18:1–8; 2 Kgs 4:8–11). Gehazi's first remark—"she has no son, and her husband is old [*ve'ishah zaqen*]"—recalls Sarah's response to the annunciation of Isaac's conception. "And Sarah laughed to herself, saying, 'Now that I am withered, am I to have fertility—with my husband so old [*va'doni zaqen*]?'" (2

Kgs 4:14; Gen 18:12). It is unclear whether Sarah's laugh is born of joy or of disbelief, but in the narrative of Genesis 18, the LORD takes it as the latter:

> [13]Then the LORD said to Abraham, "Why did Sarah laugh, saying, 'Shall I in truth bear a child, old as I am?' [14]Is anything too wondrous for the LORD? I will return to you next year [*ka'et chayyah*], and Sarah shall have a son." (Gen 18:13–14)

And, if the connection to Genesis 18 is no coincidence, the author of 2 Kings 4 takes the annunciation of Isaac's conception the same way, as indicated by the Shunammite's response to the news of her own impending pregnancy: "She replied, 'Please my lord, man of God, do not delude your maidservant'" (v 16; compare v 28). In each case, the mother's incredulity communicates the unnaturalness of the conception that is about to take place. In the case of the Shunammite mother, something even more unnatural will take place—the resurrection of her son from the dead.

Living, as we do, in an age that has seen great advancements in the treatment of infertility, we are, of course, inclined to place these events in completely different categories from those of the ancients. The birth of a first child to a childless couple (one or both of whom is old or has always been infertile, to boot) is surely a cause for joy and wonder, we are likely to say, but not an impossibility like the resurrection of a dead person. But the placement of the Shunammite woman's objections suggests that at least to the author of 2 Kings 4, the two unlikely events were much closer in kind than they appear to us, perhaps even identical. Both the birth of a child to an infertile couple and the resurrection of a dead person testify to the triumph of the wonder-working God (and the validity of his wonder-working prophet, the "man of God") over the cruel course of nature. Each is a humanly inexplicable reversal of the seemingly inevitable sequence of events whose last word is death. Each represents a victory of life over death.

The possibility that Genesis 18 and 2 Kings 4 stand in a genetic relationship is enhanced by the use of the rare and enigmatic construction *ka'et chayyah* ("next year") in the two stories. In fact, the term occurs in these texts *alone*, twice in each chapter (Gen 18:10, 14; 2 Kgs 4:16, 17). Robert L. Cohn astutely points out an additional connection in the arrangement of the physical space in which the two annunciation scenes take place. Both Sarah and the Shunammite are standing at the "entrance" or "doorway" (*petach*) when the unbelievable good news comes (Gen 18:10; 2 Kgs 4:15). The unnamed son of the Shunammite woman and her aged husband thus becomes a kind of Isaac, the promised heir of an otherwise amazingly fortunate couple whom infertility has tragically deprived of the future that extends beyond their individual lives. If so, then the death and resurrection of the unnamed son corresponds markedly to the near-sacrifice of Isaac (the event known in Jewish tradition as the *aqedah*, or "binding"). Isaac's death is not reversed by a miracle-working prophet, to be sure, but it is miraculously averted by a heavenly being's dramatic intervention. As the messenger of the glad tidings, the "angel of the LORD" (Gen 22:11, 15) is the equivalent of the "man of God" (2 Kgs 4:9, et al.). The former averts a death, the latter reverses a death, but each acts to guarantee that the couple's line survives and that they have descendants, which is to say, continuation after their individual deaths.

In the rabbinic lectionary as it has come down in the Ashkenazic tradition (the tradition of Jews from northern and eastern Europe), 2 Kgs 4:1–37 is the prophetic complement (*haftarah*) to the weekly Torah portion that extends from Genesis 18 through 22 (*parashat vayyera'*). It thus corresponds to the section of the Pentateuch that recounts the events with which we have been comparing it, from the annunciation of Isaac's miraculous conception to his equally miraculous rescue from death at the hands of his ever-obedient father. In both the Torah portion and its accompanying *haftarah*, a family confronts two threats to its continuation—sterility and death—and in each case God reverses the ostensibly hopeless situation, defeating the forces of annihilation and granting a future to a lineage that had seemed doomed. The two threats appear very different to us, to be sure, for the Shunammite boy's resurrection seems more miraculous than the sparing of Isaac. Perhaps it seemed so to the ancient audience as well, but it is doubtful that the author of 2 Kgs 4:8–37, if he indeed knew of Genesis 18 and 22, sought to heighten its effect by adding resurrection to birth on the register of miracles. More likely, he wrote his story with that of Isaac in mind, only in the framework of a new institution characteristic of his own time and place, the miracle-working prophet, or "man of God." The latter, and not God directly or an angel, is the instrument by which God's unlikely promise of life comes about—whether in the face of death or after death. The point is not resurrection per se; it is the mastery of God and his prophet over the death-dealing power of nature.

There is, however, another, more noteworthy difference between Genesis 22 and 2 Kgs 4:8–37. Whereas the binding of Isaac ends with Abraham's return to Beersheba (Gen 22:19), the story of the Shunammite woman ends when, Elisha having worked his resurrection, "She came and fell at his feet and bowed low to the ground; then she picked up her son and left" (2 Kgs 4:37). The *aqedah*, in other words, terminates with the return of Abraham from his last trial; no mention is made of the boy's mother, and, indeed, the original promise of offspring to Abram, which Genesis 22 unmistakably reflects, had never designated any given woman as the matriarch of the "great nation" to stem from him (Gen 12:2–3; compare 13:14–17; 15:1–6). Sarai's offer of her bondwoman Hagar as a surrogate mother, occasioned by her own sterility (16:1–2), thus violated no aspect of the Abrahamic promise. And God's subsequent annunciation of Isaac's birth by Sarah (to which Sarai's name had been changed) is, as we have remarked, an extraordinary intervention. As such, it elicits laughter from each of the aged parents-to-be (17:17; 18:12).

There is an interesting pattern in the doubled rescue of Abraham and Sarah from the oblivion with which, first, their childlessness and, second, their new loss of Isaac threatens them. Preceding both the annunciation of the promised son's conception in Genesis 17–18 and his rescue from death in chapter 22 are stories of Hagar's near loss of her own son—the *aqedah* of Ishmael, so to speak. In Genesis 16, the slave woman, pregnant with Abraham's first son, flees into the wilderness in hopes of escaping her resentful mistress Sarai's oppression. The hopes, alas, fail, and an angel sends Hagar back to further mistreatment—only with the crucial qualification that she, too, will fall heir to the Abrahamic promise of innumerable progeny and shall bear a powerful son whose very name (meaning "God heeded") testifies to her rescue (vv 9–11). In the variant of the same story that appears in Genesis 21, a much more developed and powerfully narrated version, Ishmael undergoes his own *aqedah* in a more intense way, driven into the wilderness by Sarah's jealousy and God's instruction to Abraham to obey his wife. The rub is that the patriarch has, oddly, ill-equipped his secondary wife and infant son (as he is characterized in this text), giving them only "some bread and a skin of water" to sustain them in the desert until they reach their unspecified destination (vv 9–14).

Predictably, the water runs out, and the mother, putting her baby under a bush, "sat down at a distance, a bowshot away; for she thought, 'Let me

not look on as the child dies'" and then "burst into tears." Unpredictably—
unless, of course, one remembers that Israel's God is no less renowned for
rescuing from death than from childlessness—an angel intervenes, announces that "God has heeded the cry of the boy where he is" (vv 16–17),
and re-presents the promised son, now delivered from death, to his mother:

> [18]"Come, lift up the boy and hold him by the hand, for I will make a great
> nation of him." [19]Then God opened her eyes and she saw a well of water.
> She went and filled the skin with water, and let the boy drink. (Gen 21:18–19)

"Come, lift up the boy" is highly reminiscent of Elisha's parting charge to
the Shunammite woman, "Pick up your son" (2 Kgs 4:36), which in turn
reflects her husband's order to the servant when the boy was first stricken,
"Carry him to his mother" (v 19). The presentation of the revived child to
his grieving mother—whether recovered from lethal dehydration like Ishmael or literally resurrected from the dead like the unnamed Shunammite
boy—underscores the intimate connection between birth and revival. Or,
to state the converse, it draws our attention again both to the connection
between the infertility that, in different ways, accounts for each son's birth,
and to the death that threatens to rob each mother of her promised child,
proving God's word and his reputation for deliverance unreliable and
dashing her hopes for continuation beyond her own time.

FOUR LITTLE STORIES WITH ONE BIG MESSAGE

The placement of the story of Elisha in Shunem in its current literary location sheds further light on the deeper dynamics of life and death that the
story unfolds. The tale abuts two stories of miraculous feedings. In the first
(2 Kgs 4:1–7), a widow of "one of the disciples of the prophets" has become
impoverished, and a creditor is about to seize her two sons as debt slaves. In
response, Elisha miraculously manages to fill every vessel in sight with oil,
and when the oil has stopped, he instructs her, "Go sell the oil and pay your
debt, and you and your children can live on the rest."

The parallels of this brief miracle story with the ensuing story of the
childless couple are patent, though at times the relationship is inverted.
Whereas Elisha in the first little tale produces food for an impoverished
woman, at the beginning of the longer story that follows, a wealthy woman
produces food for the prophet (2 Kgs 4:8). Whereas in the first narrative,
the woman has children but no husband or food, in the second she has

husband and food, but no children, and this, too, calls for a remedy. In the opening tale, the widow is about to lose her two sons, but Elisha averts this and proclaims that she and they now have the means to "live." In the sequel, Elisha gives the wealthy lady of Shunem one son twice, first by curing her infertility and then by resurrecting the child she has borne and lost. In each case, the survival of the family is threatened, in the first by poverty and enslavement, in the second by sterility and death. And in each case the prophet steps into the breach to ensure that mother and children stay together, that the integrity and continuity of the family is preserved.

By prefacing the story of the childless couple of Shunem with the tale of the destitute widow, the author or redactor of 2 Kings 4 has done more than simply to enhance our appreciation of the dynamics of the latter story. He has also connected the tale with more distant texts (whether intentionally or not) in ways that further illuminate the underlying concepts of life and death. For to the astute reader of the Hebrew Bible, the widow's fear that she will lose her two sons cannot but recall other mothers who faced similar threats—Eve, for example, who loses Abel to murder and Cain to exile, or Rebecca, who tells Jacob to flee from Esau's murderous revenge: "Let me not lose you both in one day" (Gen 4:1–16; 27:45).

But the particular conditions that motivate the action, poverty (which in that cultural context means lack of food) and enslavement, suggest that the closest analogy actually lies with events later in Jacob's life, specifically with the famine that takes his sons to Egypt. When Joseph demands that Simeon be held as a hostage until Jacob releases his beloved son Joseph's only full brother, Benjamin, the thematic commonalities become even more striking:

> [36] Their father Jacob said to them, "It is always me that you bereave: Joseph is no more and Simeon is no more, and now you would take away Benjamin. These things always happen to me!" [37] Then Reuben said to his father, "You may kill my two sons if I do not bring him back to you. Put him in my care, and I will return him to you." [38] But he said, "My son must not go down with you, for his brother is dead and he alone is left. If he meets with disaster on the journey you are taking, you will send my white head down to Sheol in grief." (Gen 42:36–38)

It is finally Judah—having already lost two sons of his own, making his daughter-in-law a double widow (Gen 38:6–11)—who, as the famine worsens, secures Benjamin's release from his doting father's grasp (Gen 43:1–14).

In sum, the little seven-verse narrative of Elisha and the impoverished widow in 2 Kgs 4:1–7 encapsulates in the context of one small family the dynamics of life and death that engulf the entire nation—itself represented as a man and his twelve sons—in Genesis. Seen in this light, the movement in 2 Kings 4 from the widow's tale to the events in Shunem takes on added resonance. For with it, the threat to familial survival moves from enslavement to infertility to death, and this is also the movement that underlies Pharaoh's assaults upon Israel in Exodus 1 as well. First, the tyrant reduces the special nation to slavery, setting taskmasters over them and putting them to work on the royal store cities. When that fails, he instructs the midwives to destroy all male babies—a decree that, given the patrilineal assumptions of the time, ensures that in another generation no Israelite children will be born and the troublesome nation will become extinct. Finally, the midwives having defied the king's command, Pharaoh orders the boys thrown into the Nile, so that only the girls shall live (vv 8–22). As in 2 Kings 4, so in Exodus 1, enslavement has escalated into death. And in Exodus, as in Kings, though the suffering is real and no justification for it is offered, God yet triumphs over it. Neither slavery nor death has the last word.

Now let us turn our attention to the little story that follows the tale of Elisha's resurrection (2 Kgs 4:38–41). Like the more developed tale that precedes it, this one, too, deals with a famine and the prophet's miraculous remedy for it. In this case, the prophet instructs his servant to make a stew, which, given the slim pickings, happens to include as a prime ingredient the gourds of a wild vine. The effect is literally deadly:

> [40]While they were still eating of the stew, they began to cry out: "O man of God, there is death in the pot!" And they could not eat it. [41]"Fetch some flour," [Elisha] said. He threw it into the pot and said, "Serve it to the people and let them eat." And there was no longer anything harmful in the pot. (2 Kgs 4:40–41)

The odd locution "there is death [*mavet*] in the pot!" connects this mininarrative of a mere four verses to the longer story of resurrection that it follows. Just as Elisha reversed the death of the Shunammite's son, so does he instantaneously provide an antidote for the poisonous gourds. How, precisely, flour was able to counteract the toxin is unknown; this, too, is probably intended to be viewed as a miracle. Indeed, the very fact that there was flour to be had at all in a time of famine, when the disciples of the prophets were reduced to foraging for foodstuffs, is most likely intended as another example of the prophet's supernatural gifts. The display of those gifts is, in fact, the unifying theme of the entire chapter. Seen in this light, the tale of the resurrection of the Shunammite boy is not only the longest story in the chapter; it also constitutes a refocusing of the theme of the prophet's powers more specifically on the power to reverse death.

Finally, we must deal with the fourth little tale in 2 Kings 4, which brings to a close the chapter that focused on the story of the resurrection of the Shunammite couple's promised son. Here Elisha proves able to feed a hundred people with but twenty loaves of bread (2 Kgs 4:42–44). Like Sarah and the Shunammite lady, his attendant is skeptical: "How can I set this before a hundred men?" But the prophet, who sees the situation from the divine and not the natural perspective, is adamant: "Give it to the people and let them eat. For thus said the LORD: They shall eat and have some left over." And "as the LORD had said," so it was. The impossible reversal happened.

Here in this shortest narrative of 2 Kings 4, we see the familiar theme that has dominated the previous tales of the chapter: menacing shortage followed by miraculous provision. The development over the course of the chapter is revealing and suggests connections to the story of the people Israel that dominates the Hebrew Bible. The first tale, of the widow in debt, takes place in the context of a nuclear family: a woman without a husband is about to lose her two sons. The second tale, the long narrative about Elisha in Shunem, also takes place in the context of family: a woman and her husband without a son lose and then recover the boy with whom God wondrously graces them. The third story, about the lethal stew, takes place in a larger grouping, the prophet and his disciples. This group serves as the prophet's family: Elisha, like his predecessor Elijah and unlike other prophets, seems to have neither wife nor children. Note that his "disciples" are literally "sons of the prophets" (2 Kgs 4:38). If so, of course, it is not a natural family, but, as it were, a supernatural one, a family founded on the charisma of the master and his ability to provide for his disciples. Finally, in this last tale, the miraculous feeding of the "people" (2 Kgs 4:42–44), we sense the rescue of a larger group, neither a nuclear family nor (probably) a prophetic brotherhood but some other "people," whose life depends on the prophet's divine powers to overcome shortage and deliver them from impending starvation. In this, the incident reminds us of the reason given in Deuteronomy for another miraculous provision of food, the manna, supplied "in order to teach you that man does not live on bread alone, but that man may live on anything that the LORD decrees" (Deut 8:3). That 2 Kgs 4:42–44, considered as a self-contained narrative, anticipates this more national understanding of the miraculous deliverance from starvation is properly open to doubt. The idea makes eminent sense, however, when the narrative is placed in the larger canon of the Hebrew Bible.

The major threats to well-being in all these tales in 2 Kings 4—enslavement, infertility, death, and starvation—are, as we have seen, deeply interconnected in the narratives of the Hebrew Bible that have a national focus as well. It is especially instructive that these include the narratives of the birth of the *'am*, the people par excellence, Israel, in Genesis. In each of these four narratives, the theological point is the same: God's power to reverse life-threatening adversity is uncanny and absolute, and some of it has been committed into the keeping of a wonder-working prophet. To us today, who have seen enslavement, famine, and infertility overcome but no one resurrected, the story of the restoration of the dead boy seems to fall into a different category from the other miracles in 2 Kings 4. But there is no reason to think that the original audience or readership thought it did, and much reason to believe that they saw all these threats to well-being as capable of reversal at the hands of a "man of God." Resurrection in 2 Kings 4 is indeed a miracle, but it is precisely the capacity to perform miracles that defines the "man of God," and it is by the miracles of God that the ever-dying, ever-reviving people of Israel lives.

A LOOK AHEAD

Having looked backwards at the rich connections of the story of the resurrection in Shunem with those of Israel's own origins, we must now shift directions briefly and ask in which sense the story anticipates the Jewish and Christian teachings about the resurrection of the dead as these will develop a few centuries later. The similarities with the story of Jesus as it appears in some of the gospels are evident: a mother hears an amazing prophetic prediction of the birth of a son, who is indeed born just as predicted but then tragically dies and is miraculously resurrected. One cannot discount the possibility that the story in 2 Kings 4 helped to shape the way the authors of these gospels told the story of Jesus. After all, 2 Kings 4 is part of the only Bible they knew, and it is in terms of the Bible that they sought to present Jesus.

The differences between the striking tale of the resurrection of the Shunammite's son and the resurrection of the dead as envisioned in Judaism and Christianity, however, must not be minimized. The former is a specific episode of limited scope; its subtle and manifold resonances with the larger story of Israel do not suggest (at least not directly) a context of national restoration, a key ingredient in the Jewish expectation of resurrection. Even less does the tale in 2 Kings 4 imply a worldwide judgment and rectification of injustice, key elements in that expectation. There is, to be sure, a sense that the Shunammite couple eventually graced with the unexpected child deserved better than their lot in life. They lacked a child, and thus a future beyond their own lifetimes, and the prophet was to some degree repaying them for their hospitality and their generosity to him and, by implication, to the God who sent him. But the two miracles he wrought for them cannot be construed as a moral judgment on their whole lives, and, even were such the case, there is no contrasting judgment against those whose moral records fall short. And, of course, there is every reason to believe that the child whom Elisha resurrects will eventually die a second and irreversible death, unlike those awakened to "eternal life" in Dan 12:2, for example, or Jesus in the gospels. In short, 2 Kgs 4:8–37 altogether lacks the apocalyptic framework out of which the classic Jewish doctrine grows.

There is, nonetheless, a lesson to be learned from this tale about the Jewish expectation of resurrection that will first appear much later. It is simply that long before the apocalyptic framework came into existence, the resurrection of the dead was thought possible—not according to nature, of course, but through the miraculous intervention of the living God. In the arresting tale about Elisha at Shunem, we see again the collision of the LORD's power to rescue those faithful to him with the hard fact of human mortality, and, significantly, it is again the LORD's power to rescue that triumphs. In the apocalyptic expectation of a resurrection of the dead at the end of history, the experience of deliverance will become general and irreversible in ways that it is obviously not in the tale of the Shunammite couple. But some of its lineaments can already be seen in the little story of miraculous birth, tragic death, and amazing resurrection of a promised son.

Revival in Two Modes

ZION'S CHILDREN RETURN TO THEIR MOTHER

The greatest assault on Israel's existence during the periods documented in the Hebrew Bible was the Babylonian capture of Jerusalem in 586 B.C.E. In short order, the Temple was torched, the house of David was overthrown, and a significant segment of the populace of the southern kingdom Judah was sent into exile (the northern kingdom, Israel, had fallen to the Assyrians 136 years earlier). As we saw in Chapter 5, to the ancient Israelite the Temple was not just another building, if an architecturally impressive one. It was the very House of the LORD. And the house of David was not just the dynasty of the family that had ruled Judah for four centuries. For many, rather, its rule rested on a divine promise to its founding ancestor that he would never lack a descendant on the throne in Jerusalem, just as the possession of the promised land rested on God's promise to Abraham, Isaac, and Jacob. The impact of the bloody Babylonian onslaught in 586 B.C.E. was not just physical or political. It was spiritual, for the fall of Judah and Jerusalem cast some of the most basic tenets of the religion of Israel into profound doubt.

As these things happen, the Babylonians themselves fell nearly half a century later, this time to the Persians, and this aroused great hope among the Judahite exiles in Babylonia. As the Persian conquest of Babylonia and release of the Judahites loomed, an anonymous prophet (whom modern scholars call "Second Isaiah" because his writings have been appended to the book of Isaiah) predicted the restoration of the people Israel to their ancestral land. In soaring poetry, he strove mightily to awaken their faith in the possibility—indeed, the coming reality—of revival and renewal after the long years of misery and ostensible abandonment by their God:

> [1]But now thus said the LORD—
> Who created you, O Jacob,
> Who formed you, O Israel:
> Fear not, for I will redeem you;
> I have singled you out by name,
> You are Mine.
> [2]When you pass through water,
> I will be with you;
> Through streams,
> They shall not overwhelm you.
> When you walk through fire,
> You shall not be scorched;
> Through flame,
> It shall not burn you.
> [3]For I the LORD am your God,
> The Holy One of Israel, your Savior.
> I give Egypt as a ransom for you,
> Ethiopia and Saba in exchange for you.
> [4]Because you are precious to Me,
> And honored, and I love you,
> I give men in exchange for you
> And peoples in your stead.
>
> [5]Fear not, for I am with you:
> I will bring your folk from the East,
> Will gather you out of the West;
> [6]I will say to the North, "Give back!"
> And to the South, "Do not withhold!
> Bring My sons from afar,
> And My daughters from the end of the earth—
> [7]All who are linked to My name,
> Whom I have created,
> Formed, and made for My glory—

[8]Setting free that people,
Blind though it has eyes
And deaf though it has ears." (Isa 43:1–8)

In this oracle, the anonymous prophet brings major themes of Israel's miraculous origins and continuing divine promise together with breathtaking concision and poetic power—their origin in the man Jacob/Israel, the LORD's special relationship with them, and his protection of them in life-threatening waters, probably a recollection of the crossing of the sea after the exodus from Egypt. As usual with Second Isaiah, the past is prologue, and the ancient paradigm of redemption serves as a model for what the LORD—whose love for Israel endures despite all (v 4)—is about to do again. At the center of this new redemption, however, lies an element unprecedented in the exodus narrative but well known, as we have seen, from Genesis and the story of Elisha's resurrection of the Shunammite boy: the return of the lost sons and daughters (v 6). When this occurs, the God of Israel plays the role of Jacob, Job, Naomi, or the nameless Shunammite woman. He becomes the parent who against all odds recovers his children and the promise for futurity and continuation that they represent.

Elsewhere, essentially the same image of redemption recalls most explicitly the promise of posterity given to the fathers of the nation, Abraham, Isaac, and Jacob, as the desiccated nation of the exile comes back to life, renewing their dedication to the LORD and the service that goes with it.

[1]But hear, now, O Jacob My servant,
Israel whom I have chosen!
[2]Thus said the LORD, your Maker,
Your Creator who has helped you since birth:
Fear not, My servant Jacob,
Jeshurun whom I have chosen,
[3]Even as I pour water on thirsty soil,
And rain upon dry ground,
So will I pour My spirit on your offspring,
My blessing upon your posterity.
[4]And they shall sprout like grass,
Like willows by watercourses.
[5]One shall say, "I am the LORD's,"
Another shall use the name of "Jacob,"

Another shall mark his arm "of the LORD"
And adopt the name of "Israel." (Isa 44:1–5)

. . . .

[17]Thus said the LORD your Redeemer,
The Holy One of Israel:
I the LORD am your God,
Instructing you for your own benefit.
Guiding you in the way you should go.
[18]If only you would heed My commands!
Then your prosperity would be like a river,
Your triumph like the waves of the sea.
[19]Your offspring would be as many as the sand,
Their issue as many as its grains.
Their name would never be cut off
Or obliterated from before Me. (Isa 48:17–19)

Whatever the shape, oral or literary, of the earlier traditions to which our nameless prophet had access, the echoes of Genesis in his oracle are still remarkable. The divine blessing on the progeny (or, "seed") of the chosen people about to leave their Mesopotamian captivity for Canaan recalls the initial oracles to Abraham as he leaves his homeland, promising to make him a great nation, to bless him abundantly, and then, after he has entered Canaan, to give the land to his posterity or "seed" (Isa 44:3; Gen 12:1–7). Similarly, the promise above that "Your offspring would be many as the sand" recalls the LORD's promise to Abraham to "make your offspring as the dust of the earth, so that if one can count the dust of the earth, then your offspring too can be counted" (Isa 48:19; Gen 13:16). But it resembles still more closely the divine promise to his grandson Jacob/Israel, the ancestor from whom the nation takes its name, to "make your offspring as the sands of the sea, which are too numerous to count" (Gen 32:13). And the identification of the LORD as Jacob's "Creator . . . since birth" (literally, "from the belly") in Isa 44:2 doubtless derives from the tradition that God already designated Jacob for greatness in the womb (Gen 25:21–23). The revitalization of the downtrodden and despondent people is clearly patterned on the old legends of their having come into being against all odds, historical and natural.

Given the social-familial nature of personal identity in ancient Israel that we explored in Chapter 6, it is hardly surprising that Israel's renewal or restoration is here phrased in ways that suggest fertility and birth. For fertility and birth constitute the prime model of renewal in ancient Israel, a people who thought their supernatural mandate depended upon natural replenishment of lost individuals and that supernatural redemption inevitably involved natural increase.

Alongside the similarities to the patriarchal narratives of Genesis, these images in Second Isaiah exhibit differences that are critical to understanding the exilic and postexilic appropriation of the ancient story of natural origins. We have just examined one nuance of difference in that appropriation, the identification of the community addressed with the patriarch in his anguish, when the promise is still unfulfilled and the existence of the promised great nation still lies in the future. This is not Jacob/Israel in triumph, his hearty brood of tribal ancestors-to-be gathered about him, but Jacob/Israel in distress and fear, comforted with a mere promise of faithful and dedicated posterity yet to be (Isa 44:1–5).

A still more daring reuse of the Genesis themes focuses not on the patriarchs but on their barren or bereaved wives:

[1]Shout, O barren one,
You who bore no child!
Shout aloud for joy,
You who did not travail!
For the children of the wife forlorn
Shall outnumber those of the espoused
　　　　　　—said the LORD.

[2]Enlarge the site of your tent,
Extend the size of your dwelling,
Do not stint!
Lengthen the ropes, and drive the pegs firm.
[3]For you shall spread out to the right and the left;
Your offspring shall dispossess nations
And shall people the desolate towns.

[4]Fear not, you shall not be shamed;
Do not cringe, you shall not be disgraced.

For you shall forget
The reproach of your youth,
And remember no more
The shame of your widowhood.
⁵For He who made you will espouse you—
His name is "Lord of Hosts."
The Holy One of Israel will redeem you—
He is called "God of all the Earth."

⁶The Lord has called you back
As a wife forlorn and forsaken.
Can one cast off the wife of his youth?
　　　　　—said your God.
⁷For a little while I forsook you,
But with vast love I will bring you back.
⁸In slight anger, for a moment,
I hid My face from you;
But with kindness everlasting
I will take you back in love
　　　　　—said the Lord your Redeemer.
⁹For this to Me is like the waters of Noah:
As I swore that the waters of Noah
Nevermore would flood the earth,
So I swear that I will not
Be angry with you or rebuke you.
¹⁰For the mountains may move
And the hills be shaken,
But My loyalty shall never move from you,
Nor My covenant of friendship be shaken
　　　　　—said the Lord, who takes you back in love. (Isa 54:1–10)

The opening address to the "barren one" recalls Abraham's wife Sarah and her long period of infertility—Gen 17:17 reports that she bore Isaac at age ninety—as well as Isaac's wife Rebecca and her twenty years of barrenness (Gen 25:20, 26b). But it especially brings to mind Jacob/Israel's beloved wife Rachel and her years of waiting in frustration until God finally opens her womb (Gen 30:1–8, 22–24).

Like the text of Genesis itself, however, this oracle of restoration after exile does not make a triumphalistic identification of the nation with the husband's preferred wife, but rather offers consolation to the wife who is unloved or bereft. In particular, the prediction that "the children of the wife forlorn / Shall outnumber those of the espoused" draws on the motif (if not the actual story) of Leah, Rachel's highly fertile older sister whose very fertility is the LORD's compensation for her lesser appeal in the eyes of Jacob (Gen 29:31). More distantly, the oracle of Isa 54:1–10 brings to mind the story of Elkanah's barren wife Hannah who conceives Samuel at the LORD's initiative, but only after years of taunting by her fertile co-wife, Peninah (1 Sam 1:1–8, 19b–20). As in the case of Joseph, whom Rachel bears, so with Hannah, it is the single child of the barren wife, and not the many children of the fertile one, who brings about Israel's deliverance. This is, in short, a well-established pattern in the Hebrew Bible. It is also one with great theological meaning.

The stories of Rachel and Hannah resemble the book of Ruth, at least in its current form, in which the child born to Ruth (and, by a legal fiction, to Naomi as well) is identified as the grandfather of David, the founder of the Judahite dynasty and the prototype of the national deliverer (Ruth 4:16–22; see also Mic 5:1–5). In these stories of the unexpected birth of the one who delivers Israel from affliction, we see the conjunction of personal and collective redemption in a particularly poignant statement. In the cases of Rachel and Hannah, two barren women find a personal fulfillment that proves to be the basis of national rescue as well. Rachel's longed-for son, Joseph, rescues Israel from death through famine, just as Samuel, the son for whom Hannah prayed and whom she vowed to the LORD, rescues the nation from Philistine attack, restoring lost territory (1 Sam 7:5–14). And when Joseph has again disappeared—this time not in the form of one young man by that name who is sold into slavery but in the form of the northern tribes collectively carried into exile—a prophet envisions his mother at first distraught and then comforted:

> [15]Thus said the LORD:
> A cry is heard in Ramah—
> Wailing, bitter weeping—
> Rachel weeping for her children.
> She refuses to be comforted

For her children, who are gone.
¹⁶Thus said the LORD:
Restrain your voice from weeping,
Your eyes from shedding tears;
For there is a reward for your labor
   —declares the LORD:
They shall return from the enemy's land.
¹⁷And there is hope for your future
   —declares the LORD:
Your children shall return to their country. (Jer 31:15–17)

Here it is the mother, at least as much as the son, in whom the national story is enacted. We are once again confronted with a tale of loss and mourning that gives way to return and restoration. Not surprisingly, therefore, the resonances of the Joseph story in this oracle in Jeremiah 31 are unmistakable. Like Jacob when he learns of Joseph's (apparent) death, Rachel "refuses to be comforted" (Jer 31:15; compare Gen 37:35). In Hebrew, the mention of her children "who are gone" recalls the evasive words of Joseph's brothers to him (whom they take for the pharaoh's vizier): "one is no more" (*'eynennu,* Jer 31:15; Gen 42:13, 32). But in Jeremiah it is not Jacob who is pictured in deep, inconsolable mourning, nor is it his brothers who bear the painful consequence of the brother who "is no more." Rather, it is Rachel, the beloved but barren wife, who mourns for her lost children. And then, like Jacob in Genesis, she, too, receives them anew— after providence has wondrously intervened.

Other traditions lie in the background of the identification of the people Israel in its miserable demise and joyful restoration with an afflicted woman whose fortune unexpectedly turns for the better. One of these, of course, is the tradition, already old by the time of Jeremiah and Second Isaiah, which sees Israel as the LORD's wife and the relation between the special people and their God as erotic and marital in its essence. Probably the oldest attestation of this metaphor in Israelite literature is found in the first two chapters of the book of the prophet Hosea, who lived in the northern kingdom in the eighth century B.C.E. Here, the wife is at first unfaithful and gives birth to children whose ominous names communicate the termination of the marital relationship of the LORD and Israel, Lo-ruhamah ("Unloved, Unpitied") and Lo-ammi ("Not-My-People"). But then the

corresponding positive names replace the negative ones, the children rebuke their wayward mother, and she, after a painful period of retribution
and reorientation, is restored. The LORD, Israel's God, in fact, woos her
tenderly anew, remarries her in righteousness, justice, goodness, and
mercy—and this time for good. The result is that a covenant of cosmic
peace comes into effect. In Hosea, the remarriage of the LORD and Israel
signifies the redemption not just of the people Israel, but of nature as well.

There is, however, an essential difference between the governing metaphor of Hosea 1–2 and the use of the motif of Israel as matriarch in Jeremiah and Second Isaiah. In Hosea, the sufferings of Israel as wife and
mother are punitive. She deserves her fate because of her breach of
covenant, and her rebetrothal to her divine husband signifies that she has
learned her lesson, concluding, in her own words:

> I will go and return
> To my first husband,
> For then I fared better than now. (Hos 2:9)

In Jeremiah and Second Isaiah, on the other hand, the sufferings of
Rachel, or of Israel itself, imagined as a barren wife or bereaved mother are
undeserved (or no longer deserved), and no new lesson is cited or resolution to repent given. Rather, this rebetrothal and these new births (or the
return of the lost children) are closer in nature to the annunciation to the
matriarchs of Genesis or to Hannah or the birth of a son to Ruth: they are
an unexpected delight and/or a reward for faithful patience during the
time of adversity that is about to come to a surprising end.

This difference makes sense in light of the differing historical circumstances. Hosea prophesies *before* catastrophe, calling for return and renewal. Jeremiah and Second Isaiah prophesy *after* the exile (of the northern and southern tribes, respectively) and announce a new beginning, the
rebirth of the deadened nation, the return of the lost children, an unbelievable renewal of national hope after a long and agonizing eclipse. In a
word, they prophesy life in place of death.

Another source of the metaphor of the barren or bereaved wife as it appears in Second Isaiah comes from the conception of Zion, the Temple
Mount in Jerusalem, as a woman, specifically a princess or matron who
has fallen into contempt and ruin, as we find in this lament over its fall:

Alas!
Lonely sits the city
Once great with people!
She that was great among nations
Is become like a widow;
The princess among states
Is become a thrall. (Lam 1:1)

In the text below, the Temple Mount becomes a name for the sacred city, the capital of the LORD's universal domain, and the mountain and the city, in turn, become synonymous with the consecrated people that worship there—or once did—and for their shifting fate in the tides of history:

^{14} Zion says,
"The LORD has forsaken me,
My Lord has forgotten me."
^{15}Can a woman forget her baby,
Or disown the child of her womb?
Though she might forget,
I never could forget you.
^{16}See, I have engraved you
On the palms of My hands,
Your walls are ever before Me.
^{17}Swiftly your children are coming;
Those who ravaged and ruined you shall leave you.
^{18}Look up all around you and see:
They are all assembled, are come to you!
As I live
                    —declares the LORD—
You shall don them all like jewels,
Deck yourself with them like a bride.
^{19}As for your ruins and desolate places
And your land laid waste—
You shall soon be crowded with settlers,
While destroyers stay far from you.
^{20}The children you thought you had lost
Shall yet say in your hearing,

"The place is too crowded for me;
Make room for me to settle."
[21]And you will say to yourself,
"Who bore these for me
When I was bereaved and barren,
Exiled and disdained—
By whom, then, were these reared?
I was left all alone—
And where have these been?"

[22]Thus said the Lord GOD:
I will raise My hand to nations
And lift up My ensign to peoples;
And they shall bring your sons in their bosoms,
And carry your daughters on their backs.
[23]Kings shall tend your children,
Their queens shall serve you as nurses.
They shall bow to you, face to the ground,
And lick the dust of your feet.
And you shall know that I am the LORD—
Those who trust in Me shall not be shamed.

[24]Can spoil be taken from a warrior,
Or captives retrieved from a victor?
[25]Yet thus said the LORD:
Captives shall be taken from a warrior
And spoil shall be retrieved from a tyrant;
For *I* will contend with your adversaries,
And *I* will deliver your children.
[26]I will make your oppressors eat their own flesh,
They shall be drunk with their own blood as with wine.
And all mankind shall know
That I the LORD am your Savior,
The Mighty One of Jacob, your Redeemer. (Isa 49:14–26)

In this complex oracle, we find a particularly thick weave of the constituent elements of the tradition that we have been exploring: the lasting faithfulness of the God of Israel despite the reality of affliction, the rebe-trothal of the disgraced woman, the return of the lost children, the unex-pected birth of children to the forsaken and barren wife, the Divine War-rior's reliable rescue of his chosen family, and—as befits an oracle to Zion—the reconstruction of ruins and the repopulation of the destroyed areas. Logically, of course, these metaphors are not all consistent one with the other, but strict logic cannot do justice to their incomparable poetic power. The common denominator is the reversal of fate for the better, the victory over the forces of death and destruction, and its corollary, the miraculous appearance of vitality where only recently sterility had held seemingly unassailable sway. The rich interweaving of images for the rela-tionship of God to his people is in the service of the deeper theme of Sec-ond Isaiah—God's stupendous revival and restoration of fallen Israel.

THE WIDOW RE-WED (AND TO THE SAME HUSBAND)

One aspect of that reversal of fate for the better is the reappearance of the vanished husband, without whom, of course, the lost children might return but their new replacements could never be born. Why, precisely, had Israel's divine husband vanished? On occasion, Second Isaiah insists that one obvious possibility, divorce, is not the correct metaphor:

> [1]Thus said the LORD:
> Where is the bill of divorce
> Of your mother whom I dismissed?
> And which of My creditors was it
> To whom I sold you off?
> You were only sold off for your sins,
> And your mother dismissed for your crimes.
> [2]Why, when I came, was no one there,
> Why, when I called, would none respond?
> Is my arm, then, too short to rescue,
> Have I not the power to save?
> With a mere rebuke I dry up the sea,
> And turn rivers into desert.
> Their fish stink from lack of water;
> They lie dead of thirst.

> ^{3}I clothe the skies in blackness
> And make their raiment sackcloth. (Isa 50:1–3)

This passage recalls 2 Kgs 4:1–7 examined in the previous chapter, where the widow fears that creditors will seize her children as debt slaves but Elisha miraculously saves them. In Isa 50:1, however, the LORD insists that he has not literally divorced his audience's mother or sold them to creditors at all. Rather, he has only punished mother and children alike for their misdeeds. His "power to save" remains unlimited, and the painful interruption in the family relationship caused by the sins of the mother and the sons is not final: it is about to end and end happily. The afflictions of Israel—in this case, the agonies and humiliations of defeat and exile—are only temporary, and the legal separation of the LORD and his people will soon be reversed, however unlikely that outcome may seem. God now brings about on the national level the miraculous rescue from the creditors that Elisha brought about on a familial level. In so doing, God restores a damaged and depleted Israel to wholeness and vindicates his own reputation for faithfulness and fairness in the process.

A more radical metaphor for the disappearance of the divine husband is implied a few chapters later, in Isa 54:4–6, a passage we quoted earlier in this chapter. There, God enjoins the woman Zion to "remember no more / The shame of your widowhood" because he will remarry her. Here "widowhood" serves as the functional equivalent of the temporary separation of the spouses in Isa 50:1, and, as was the case there, so here, the temporary condition is about to come to an end as the LORD espouses his bride anew. But, in this case, between widowhood and remarriage lies the resurrection, as it were, of the husband who has died. The qualification "as it were" is important here. For the widowhood of Israel, like the bill of divorce of Isa 50:1, is mostly an illusion. The LORD has not renounced Israel with the finality that the term "divorce" implies; he has only temporarily withdrawn from her in righteous and retributive anger. And he has not died, at least not with all the finality that one associates with death, relegating his wife to the vulnerable status of a widow. Instead, he has but disappeared for a spell, plunging her into justified mourning, before he returns like the loving husband he is. "Can one cast off the wife of his youth?" (Isa 54:6).

To us, it is natural to describe the language of widowhood and remarriage, of the loss of the divine husband and his miraculous, triumphant re-

turn, and of the restoration of the vanished children (or the birth of their replacements) as metaphorical. For Israel or Zion is not literally a wife, their
God does not literally die, and the return from exile and repopulation of
the promised land is not a matter of literal birth. Sometimes, however, this
distinction of the literal and the metaphorical can lead us astray, causing
us to miss the deep interconnections internal to the thinking of ancient Israelites but foreign to us. The sources in the Hebrew Bible have a broader
definition of death and of life than we do. That is why they can see exile, for
example, as death, and repatriation as life, in a sense that seems contrived
(to put it negatively) or artful (to put it positively) to us but probably did not
so seem to the original authors and audiences. In part, this is because the
ancient Israelites, altogether lacking the materialist habit of thought so
powerful in modernity, did not conceive of death and life as purely and exclusively biological phenomena. These things were, rather, *social* in character and could not, therefore, be disengaged from the historical fate of the
people of whom they were predicated. Or, to put it differently, death and
life in the Hebrew Bible are often best seen as relational events and are for
this very reason inseparable from the personal circumstances of those described as living or as dead. To be alive inevitably entailed more than
merely existing in a certain physical state. It also entailed having one's being within a flourishing and continuing kin group that dwelt in a productive and secure association with its land. Conversely, to be widowed, bereaved of children, or in exile was necessarily to experience death. Indeed,
each of these states and others (notably, health or illness) could serve as a
figure to represent the condition brought about by any of the others. None
of them is the master category or bedrock reality for which the other conditions served as mere metaphors.

To almost all the writers represented in the Hebrew Bible, it was inconceivable that the positive condition (which we, following ubiquitous biblical usage, can term "life") could be other than a gift of God or that it could
come into being without a proper relationship to him. Given the thoroughly social and relational character of life and of death in the Hebrew
Bible, the well-being of Israel could never be detached from the relationship of the nation and its tribes and families to its deity. For the evolving national traditions increasingly ascribed the very existence of the nation and
the gift of the land in which the people dwelt to the will of their God. This
is another way of saying that the *natural* state of affairs did not result in that

flourishing kin group living, generation after generation, in a productive and secure association with its land of which we have just spoken. Rather, the death of spouse or children, infertility, exile, famine, and the like were perceived as the common lot from which the God of Israel miraculously and graciously offered redemption. The restorative action of God here does not simply go beyond nature; it opposes the natural course of things. It reverses the pattern of national death and loss by reactivating powers within nature—principally the power to procreate—that had shriveled and virtually disappeared before God's new intervention. This reversal of national death poetically described in Isaiah 40–55 anticipates the idea of an end-time resurrection that appears only later in Jewish history. In passages like those on which we have concentrated here, the redemption takes, not coincidentally, a form that recalls the formation of the people Israel in the beginning—a miraculous birth by an infertile mother, the wondrous return of the lost children, joy replacing grief, all of them brought about by the intervention of the indomitable God who rescues and restores the people with whom he has mysteriously fallen in love. The end time is like the beginning. God's restoration of Israel recalls how he first gave them life.

ISRAEL'S EXODUS FROM THE GRAVE

The best-known text about resurrection in the Hebrew Bible comes from the prophet Ezekiel, who lived during the Babylonian Exile (sixth century B.C.E.). This is the celebrated vision of the valley of the dry bones:

> [1]The hand of the LORD came upon me. He took me out by the spirit of the LORD and set me down in the valley. It was full of bones. [2]He led me all around them; there were very many of them spread over the valley, and they were very dry. [3]He said to me, "O mortal, can these bones live again?" I replied, "O Lord GOD, only You know." [4]And He said to me, "Prophesy over these bones and say to them: O dry bones, hear the word of the LORD! [5]Thus said the Lord GOD to these bones: I will cause breath to enter you and you shall live again. [6]I will lay sinews upon you, and cover you with flesh, and form skin over you. And I will put breath into you, and you shall live again. And you shall know that I am the LORD!"
>
> [7]I prophesied as I had been commanded. And while I was prophesying, suddenly there was a sound of rattling, and the bones came together, bone to

matching bone. [8]I looked, and there were sinews on them, and flesh had grown, and skin had formed over them; but there was no breath in them. [9]Then He said to me, "Prophesy to the breath, prophesy, O mortal! Say to the breath: Thus said the Lord GOD: Come, O breath, from the four winds, and breathe into these slain, that they may live again." [10]I prophesied as He commanded me. The breath entered them, and they came to life and stood up on their feet, a vast multitude.

[11]And He said to me, "O mortal, these bones are the whole House of Israel. They say, 'Our bones are dried up, our hope is gone; we are doomed.' [12]Prophesy, therefore, and say to them: Thus said the Lord GOD: I am going to open your graves and lift you out of the graves, O My people, and bring you to the land of Israel. [13]You shall know, O My people, that I am the LORD, when I have opened your graves and lifted you out of your graves. [14]I will put My breath into you and you shall live again, and I will set you upon your own soil. Then you shall know that I the LORD have spoken and have acted"—declares the LORD. (Ezek 37:1–14)

Verses 11–14 interpret the vision given in the first ten verses. The dead bones are the people Israel, who, living in exile after the great destruction, have given up hope: "Our bones are dried up, our hope is gone; we are doomed." The restoration of those bones to life—the LORD's giving them sinews, then flesh, skin, and finally the breath of life—indicates that God will open the graves of Ezekiel's audience and restore them to the Land of Israel, so that they may once again live upon "[their] own soil." What Ezek 37:1–14 presents, in short, is a vision of resurrection that is then decoded as a prediction of exceedingly improbable historical events that the God of Israel will soon miraculously unfold.

That Ezekiel's experience begins with a vision of desiccated bones readily suggests a connection to Zoroastrianism, an ancient Iranian religion in which the bodies of the dead were left exposed and in which an expectation of a resurrection of the dead figures prominently. Understandably, it has been proposed from time to time that the Israelites borrowed their own expectation from these Iranian sources, and the possibility of Zoroastrian influence remains real. There are, however, some important differences between the Zoroastrian and the Israelite ideas. For our purposes here, the most important of these is that for the Israelites, the burial of the dead was essential (to this day, Jewish law requires burial in the ground and forbids cremation). Ezekiel's conclusion that God will lift the Israelites out of their graves thus fits the Iranian model poorly, though his initial vision of the bones scattered across the valley fits it better. In addition, it seems unlikely that there was strong Zoroastrian influence as early as Ezekiel's time in his venue (Babylonia).

Have we at last found in Ezekiel 37 incontrovertible evidence that a belief in the resurrection of the dead existed in ancient Israel in the Hebrew Bible long before its undeniable presence in late Second Temple Judaism? Against the facile assumption that we have, one might argue that the resurrection in question occurs only in the prophet's imagination. It is not depicted as something that will ever take place on the plane of history, even providential history. Indeed, it is less than clear that Ezekiel thinks that he was ever literally in the valley of the dry bones, to which he was, it must be noted, taken "by the spirit of the LORD" and not necessarily in his ordinary bodily self. The resurrection, too, is symbolic, as the ensuing decipherment makes clear (vv 12–14). Ezekiel's prophesying is more like a message that a prophet acts out rather than the literal means by which an actual historical event takes place. In the vision in the valley of the dry bones, in short, resurrection is not an end in itself, but stands in service to the prophet's real message—that God will bring his chosen people out of the depths of exile and restore them to their land. Even in the prophet's own mind, it could be argued, the revival of the dead in this famous vision is only a figure.

It is also significant that the visionary resurrection does not occur, as we might have expected, in the form of suddenly reanimated individuals rising from their graves. Rather, it is described in stages, as the dry bones acquire first sinews, then flesh, and finally skin before the climactic moment in which God places "breath" and "spirit" in them, finally making them alive anew (vv 6, 9–10). In a recent study, John F. Kutsko has developed an interesting argument that this picture of Israel in the process of its resurrection owes a debt to Mesopotamian rituals in which icons (which the prophets would call "idols") were consecrated and activated, becoming living gods. If he is right, then we must detect here a mode of revival of a devastated people that is markedly different (at least at the level of imagery) from the model centering on remarriage and procreation that we have been examining. In any event, the difference between the two models of the restoration of Israel—the one centering on the replenishment of population and the return of the lost children, the other on the resurrection of the dead nation—must not be minimized. Less naturalistic and more miraculous than those of Second Isaiah, Ezekiel's vision anticipates the later expectation of resurrection much more closely. We seem to be turning a corner.

Kutsko's study also makes the interesting claim that Ezek 37:1–8 "clearly describes the process of revivification using imagery of human creation." He draws attention in particular to the verbal parallels with these verses in Job:

> ⁸Your hands shaped and fashioned me . . .
> ⁹Consider that You fashioned me like clay . . .
> ¹¹You clothed me with skin and flesh
> and wove me of bones and sinews. (Job 10:8, 9, 11)

The prophet's vision of the dead reassembled and revived thus seems to reflect ancient Israelite notions of the stages through which a baby forms in the womb. The visionary resurrection of Ezek 37:1–14 is a kind of re-creation—the creation of the people Israel in a new mode, a mode that entails their recognition of God's power and his action on their behalf (v 14). In a culture in which God's creation of humankind and his gift of life were undisputed, the proposition that he could reassemble his deadened people and bring them back to life was hardly outrageous. Centuries later, a Jew of Talmudic times made the same point in rebuttal of a skeptic's doubt about the doctrine of resurrection: "If those who never existed can come to life, those who once lived—all the more so!"

In its image of redemption as re-creation, Ezek 37:1–14 conforms nicely to the oracles of redemption in the previous chapter of that book, for example:

> ²⁴I will take you from among the nations and gather you from all the countries, and I will bring you back to your own land. ²⁵I will sprinkle clean water upon you, and you shall be clean: I will cleanse you from all your uncleanness and from all your fetishes. ²⁶And I will give you a new heart and put a new spirit into you: I will remove the heart of stone from your body and give you a heart of flesh; ²⁷And I will put My spirit into you. Thus I will cause you to follow My laws and faithfully to observe My rules. ²⁸Then you shall dwell in the land which I gave to your fathers, and you shall be My people and I will be your God. (Ezek 36:24–28)

This oracle reinforces the sense one gets from Ezek 37:1–14 (especially its last verse) that the restored and renewed Israel is also a spiritually and morally transformed Israel. They have become a regenerate people in both senses of the word. Their regeneration, however, is not owing to repentance on their part, but rather to God's intervention, removing their "heart of stone" and replacing it with a "heart of flesh." They are, in other words, not simply restored but *re-created*, transformed from a wicked and idolatrous people into one capable (probably for the first time, in Ezekiel's thinking) of giving the LORD the obedience that is his by right. This re-creation or transformation does not mean that they become "spiritual" in the sense of disembodied or removed from ordinary, historical existence. Nor do the people who undergo it cease to be a natural family. They are still the people Israel, but now they have been reconsecrated in a way that enables them to fulfill their unchanging mandate of faithful obedience to the laws of the one who created them in the first place. Now they will do what they have so long failed to do — to obey their God.

As in the Pentateuch, so here, this ideal state is associated with Israel's restoration to their ancestral and promised land. The verbs that denote God's lifting them out of their graves and bringing them into the Land of Israel immediately recall the promise in Exodus to bring the enslaved Israelites out of the house of bondage and into the land promised to their fathers. The use of the verb "to bring" in connection with the land promise, together with an emphasis on the recognition of the LORD as Israel's God in Ezek 37:12–14, is strikingly reminiscent of an oracle to Moses in Exodus 6:

> [6]Say, therefore, to the Israelite people: I am the LORD. I will free you from the labors of the Egyptians and deliver you from their bondage. I will redeem you with an outstretched arm and through extraordinary chastisements. [7]And I will take you to be My people, and I will be your God. And you shall know that I, the LORD, am your God who freed you from the labors of the Egyptians. [8]I will bring you into the land which I swore to give to Abraham, Isaac, and Jacob, and I will give it to you for a possession, I the LORD." (Exod 6:6–8)

The next verse reports a situation of hopelessness among the victims of Egyptian bondage that is of the same order as that of Ezekiel's interlocutors in chapter 37, who declared that "our hope is gone; we are doomed" (v 11):

But when Moses told this to the Israelites, they would not listen to Moses, their spirits crushed by cruel bondage. (Exod 6:9)

It seems that Ezekiel has reconceived the exodus so as to include death alongside exile and bondage among the conditions from which God redeems Israel—subject, of course, to the limitation of the figurative sense in which the resurrection of Ezekiel 37 functions.

This limitation is, however, actually much less encompassing than it first seems. If resurrection were thought ludicrous, or impossible even for God, then it would be a singularly inappropriate metaphor for the national renewal and restoration that Ezekiel predicts, and the vision in Ezek 37:1–10 could never have succeeded in its goal of overcoming the hopelessness of the audience. "We have as much chance of being restored to our land as dry bones have of being clad in flesh and restored to life," his despondent audience could then have retorted. In short, even as a figure, the vision of resurrection must have carried considerable credibility if it was to do what the prophet intended.

But there is another reason to be leery of categorizing the vision of Ezek 37:1–10 as only figurative. As we noted earlier in this chapter, none of the various conditions from which God was thought to redeem Israel served as the master category of which the others were mere figures. Barrenness, exile, loss of children, abandonment by one's husband (either through divorce or death), estrangement from God, death—all could function as metaphors for others in the list. To these must be added slavery, of course, which often appears in connection with them, especially with death. Thus, it is revealing, as observed in Chapter 3, that Joseph's brothers, seething with resentment over their father's rank favoritism, resolve first to kill the boy and then, having given that nefarious plan up, sell him into slavery instead (Gen 37:18–28). Again, this parallels and foreshadows Pharaoh's efforts to control the rapid growth of Israel's population, which begin with enslavement and graduate to genocide (Exod 1:8–22). Here, too, we see the deep inner connection between slavery and death.

Whether Ezek 37:1–14 presupposes a narrative in which enslavement was the principal affliction of Israel in Egypt is unknown. In chapter 20, the longest and most developed account outside the Pentateuch of Israel's sojourn in Egypt and in the wilderness afterward, Ezekiel betrays no hint of the idea that the Israelites were ever slaves. There the emphasis falls on two items, first, on Israel's perverse penchant for idolatry, which Ezekiel, interestingly, sees as present already during their Egyptian sojourn, and, second, on the LORD's subsequent revelation to them of his laws (especially those governing the Sabbath) in the wilderness. As befits an oracle of judgment (and one dated before the great destruction of 586 B.C.E.), the dominant note of Ezekiel 20 is one of disobedience and punishment. The vision of the dry bones resurrected is, by way of contrast, one of the prophet's oracles of restoration and thus appropriately speaks of Israel's future obedience to the God who has revived them and restored them to their own land (Ezek 37:13–14). To ask whether he restores them from hopelessness, slavery, exile, estrangement from God and his righteous will, or, rather, from death is academic and misses the way Israel conceives these things. Most seriously, it misses the deep inner connection between the substance of the symbol (resurrection from death) and its decoded message (a return to the land, to the knowledge of God, and to obedience to him). That Israel could be fully alive dwelling outside the promised land and lacking the knowledge of God was inconceivable to Ezekiel. Conversely, given Israel's longstanding pattern of disobedience to God's laws (which, in his mind, brought about their national destruction and exile), their undeserved repatriation was surely an exodus from death to life: no one who knows God and has experienced the fulfillment of his promise, it would seem, is dead.

MORTAL ISRAELITES AND IMMORTAL ISRAEL

The vision in the valley of the dry bones in Ezek 37:1–14 is thus the best approximation that we have yet seen to the developed doctrine of a general resurrection that one finds later in Second Temple and rabbinic Judaism and, of course, in early Christianity. What it envisions is, nonetheless, different, and not only for the obvious reason that the vision of resurrection is explicitly decoded as a prediction of national restoration. Unlike the later texts, Ezekiel 37 does not connect the envisioned resurrection with a last judgment such as that in Daniel 12, in which the dead awake "some to eternal life, others to reproaches, to everlasting abhorrence" (v 2). Rather, Ezekiel's is a vision of resurrection *after* judgment has been passed on Israel and on her gentile tormentors as well. Having no sense that the new life into which the nation rises is a *reward*—his pessimism about Israel's character and his uncompromising theology of divine honor do not allow this self-flattering theology—he does not discriminate between classes of Israelites. He makes no separation between the worthy and the unworthy; the entire nation rises, just as the entire nation fell.

Simply put, Ezekiel's vision of resurrection is not a vision of a last judgment. It does not vindicate the innocent nor condemn the guilty. What it vindicates, rather, is the LORD's reputation: he is the absolute sovereign who will fulfill his promises no matter how unlikely they seem to the people of Israel in their despondency.

Did Ezekiel think that those resurrected in his symbolic vision rose "to eternal life," like the fortunate group in Dan 12:2, or did he, instead, expect that they would eventually die a second death? In the opinion of Rabbi Eliezer (a figure active in the Land of Israel in the late first and early second century C.E.), "The dead whom Ezekiel resurrected stood upon their feet, sang a song, and died." The point of the rabbi's statement is not to deny the doctrine of a future resurrection of the dead, which had a venerable history in Judaism and was already normative among the rabbis by the time Rabbi Eliezer taught. The point, rather, is to distinguish between Ezekiel's resurrection, whose effect was only temporary, and the eschatological resurrection, which, as the comments in the Talmud just before Rabbi Eliezer's show, would be irreversible. The very question of whether the people in Ezekiel's vision died again or lived on betrays, however, the influence of the later doctrine. For, as we have seen, Ezekiel's vision focuses exclusively on the nation and not on the individuals who comprise it in any given generation.

There is, therefore, no reason to think that Ezekiel saw the individuals who were resurrected in the valley as now endowed with immortality. What does not die is the people Israel, because God has, despite their grievous failings, honored his unbreakable pledge to their ancestors. *Israelite people* die, like anyone else; the *people Israel* survives and revives because of God's promise, despite the most lethal defeats.

For this reason, although Ezekiel's vision in the valley does not attest to the expectation of resurrection in the later sense, it does constitute a significant step in the direction of the later doctrine. For one thing, its vision of the restored and reconstituted people of Israel differs markedly from the visions of Second Isaiah that we explored earlier in this chapter. There, Israel is restored through *procreation* and the return of the lost children, themes already ancient when those oracles were written. Here in Ezek 37:1–14, by contrast, Israel is restored through the *resurrection* of those long dead. In both cases, we are, of course, dealing with metaphors, but the difference in the metaphors—revival through regeneration and revival through resurrection—is a matter of high significance.

Another fruitful comparison, which also records a striking change, lies with the other highly developed account of a resurrection in the Hebrew Bible, the story of the Shunammite woman and the son whom Elisha revives in 2 Kgs 4:8–37 that we discussed in Chapter 7. In that text, we see both modes of revival that we have been setting forth: procreation when the childless mother bears the promised son and resurrection when the prophet who promised him to her brings him back to life. If we compare this story with Ezekiel's vision in the valley of the dry bones, it immediately becomes evident that in Kings, there is no element of deathlessness at all: no one there corresponds with the people Israel in Ezekiel. Elisha simply honors his original promise to the childless woman by resurrecting the child who he promised would be born to her (see especially v 28). This having been accomplished, the child will eventually go the way of all flesh, though presumably not before he has lived to a respectable age and thus fulfilled his mother's hopes for him. Ezekiel's vision is predicated upon the opposite idea—that the people Israel (as distinguished from the individuals who make it up) shall never go the way of all flesh but shall endure forever. For, as we have seen, Ezekiel's vision is not one simply of revivification, but of transformation and re-creation as well, and the cause of Israel's death—their persistent failure to recognize and heed their God—itself finally vanishes. "[13]'You shall know, O My people, that I am the LORD, when I have opened your graves and lifted you out of your graves.[14] . . . Then you shall know that I the LORD have spoken and have acted'—declares the LORD" (Ezek 37:13–14).

To put the same point differently, the Shunammite woman's fulfillment is a consequence of her immediate situation only. Her pregnancy and the resurrection of the son with whom Elisha has rewarded her are owing to her extraordinary devotion to the "man of God." She attends to his needs first for food, then for shelter, and he responds with the unlikely news of her impending pregnancy (2 Kgs 4:8–10, 16). When the child has died, the prophet makes her whole again—and, not incidentally, demonstrates his own supernatural charisma to all skeptics—by reviving the promised son (vv 32–37). Had the unfortunate mother not demonstrated her devotion, or had she already borne a child at the outset of the tale, the miraculous revival would not have been needed and would never have occurred. Once the resurrection of the lad has taken place, Elisha has discharged his obligation to the Shunammite woman. Although she may be more impressed than ever with his supernatural abilities, there is no sense that she has drawn closer to her God or that the son will have a different spiritual or moral disposition as a result of these events.

The basis for the new resurrection envisioned in Ezek 37:1–14 is, by contrast, the lasting and unshakeable promise of God that Israel shall eventually recognize him, dwell in the land he has given them, and serve him there with undivided loyalty. Far from having deserved this stunning reversal of their fate, Israel in exile are the bearers, according to Ezekiel's theology, of a long and unremitting history of rebellion against their God and immoral behavior and perversion of the lowest order. They have been the rankest of idolaters from early on—even in Egypt—yet their God's commitment to restore and repatriate them remains steadfast. Resting, as it thus does, on an unconditional promise of national restoration, the visionary revival of Israel in Ezek 37:1–14 again foreshadows later notions of the eschatological resurrection, and in ways in which the touching story of the childless Shunammite couple does not. For the Jewish expectation of a resurrection of the dead is always and inextricably associated with the restoration of the people Israel; it is not, in the first instance, focused on individual destiny. The question it answers is not the familiar, self-interested one, "Will I have life after death?" but rather a more profound and encompassing one, "Will God honor his promises to his people?"

Ezekiel's answer to the latter question is a resounding "Yes!" Even a history of the most hideous disobedience and the most obscene idolatry shall not prevent the dry bones that are the whole House of Israel from living again.

"I DEAL DEATH AND GIVE LIFE"

INEVITABLE DEATH AND THE PROMISE OF LIFE

In the second book of Samuel, we hear of a clever effort on the part of King David's general Joab to persuade the king to allow his son Absalom to return and be reconciled with his father. (Absalom had fled from Jerusalem after killing his half-brother Amnon, the rapist of his sister. See 2 Samuel 13). Joab enlisted a wise woman from the town of Tekoa to pretend to be a widow who is in mourning for a son whom another son had killed, just as Absalom had killed his brother Amnon. The community, she says, is demanding that she hand over her sole remaining son to be executed for his murder. "Thus," she tells the king, "they would quench the last ember remaining to me, and leave my husband without name or remnant upon the earth." David promptly promises to issue an order forbidding this sad result. But then comes the surprise. The wise woman goes on gently to accuse the king of doing what he has forbidden in her case: by not bringing back his own homicidal son, Absalom, he is condemning himself to a fate like hers. And should Absalom be killed, as is indeed likely (and does eventually happen), his death can never be reversed. "We must all die," the wise woman of Tekoa tells King David; "we are like water that is poured out on the ground and cannot be gathered up" (2 Sam 14:7, 14).

Some may greet the sad observation of the wise woman of Tekoa with a certain joy. Those holding the characteristic modern skepticism about the traditional doctrines of resurrection, whether in their Jewish or their Christian form, for example, can thus find in the Hebrew Bible a resource for a religious justification for their own naturalism. So interpreted, the Hebrew Bible supports the idea that death is natural, irreversible, and, most importantly, altogether in accordance with God's will—until, that is, the idea of individual resurrection appears very late in the history represented in that book, around the second century B.C.E. Lloyd R. Bailey Sr. states the consensus well when he writes that "mortality as the Creator's design for humans seems to be the basic perspective of the O[ld] T[estament] literature." If so, then the common modern suspicion that resurrection is a vestige of childish, prescientific thinking is not so heterodox after all. For there was a time when the religion of Israel did not know of this now eminently orthodox doctrine. The wise woman of Tekoa was not only wise but ahead of her time as well.

There is, to be sure, a large measure of truth in this, but it is a truth based mostly on the familiar modern phrasing of the question, "Will I have life after death? Will I be resurrected from the grave?" Put that way, the wise woman's observation constitutes the answer most characteristic of the Hebrew Bible: death, sadly, is universal and final. It comes to all of us; it is the last word in our existence. There is, however, a problem with this way of posing the question: it misses another equally characteristic feature of the Hebrew Bible, the highly social and familial construction of personal identity that we explored in Chapter 6. There we saw that in ancient Israel identity tends to be at least as much communal as individual, and the principal community in which the individual was so solidly embedded was the family. When identity continues after death, it does so in the form of descendants, not in the form of the individual. This, revealingly, is what lies behind the wise woman's plea to the king not to leave "[her] husband without name or remnant," that is, without descendants to carry on his identity after he is "poured out" like water, never to be "gathered up" again. By acting to prevent the loss of the Tekoan couple's last surviving son, King David ensures that their individual deaths will not be the last word for them. Here again, as in Israel's national story, the last word lies with life restored, with the return of the doomed child, with the overthrow of certain death.

A similar point can be made about the ubiquitous promise of life as a reward for careful and faithful obedience to God and his will. This appears most memorably in the injunction in Deuteronomy to Israel to "Choose life—if you and your offspring would live—by loving the LORD your God, heeding His commands, and holding fast to Him" (Deut 30:19–20). In

Leviticus, we find an analogous promise: "You shall keep My laws and My rules, by the pursuit of which man shall live: I am the LORD" (Lev 18:5). The theme is especially pronounced in the book of Proverbs, for example:

> ¹My son, do not forget my teaching,
> But let your mind retain my commandments;
> ²For they will bestow on you length of days,
> Years of life and well-being.
>
> . . . .
>
> ¹³Happy is the man who finds wisdom,
> The man who attains understanding.
> ¹⁴Her value in trade is better than silver,
> Her yield, greater than gold.
> ¹⁵She is more precious than rubies;
> All of your goods cannot equal her.
> ¹⁶In her right hand is length of days,
> In her left, riches and honor.
> ¹⁷Her ways are pleasant ways,
> And all her paths, peaceful.
> ¹⁸She is a tree of life to those who grasp her,
> And whoever holds on to her is happy. (Prov 3: 1–2, 13–18)
>
> ²⁰My son, listen to my speech;
> Incline your ear to my words.
> ²¹Do not lose sight of them;
> Keep them in your mind.
> ²²They are life to him who finds them,
> Healing for his whole body. (Prov 4:20–22)

Whatever the idiom, the promise of life to those who observe God's directives suffuses the Hebrew Bible.

Between this offer of life and the equally ubiquitous fact of death, there is, however, a tension. How can the same God who creates human beings mortal and decrees their death also promise them life as a consequence of their obedience to his commands, or even, on occasion, as a gracious gift made despite their failure to obey? By way of answer, let it first be noticed that within its original context, this tension is not so extreme as it seems to us, for "life" has a much wider semantic range in the Hebrew Bible than it does for us. It includes, for example, power, skill, confidence, health, blessing, luck, and joy. Thus, the same Hebrew verb (*chiyya*) can mean both "to bring to life" and "to cure, to make healthy," as we should expect in a culture in which, as we have observed in Chapter 3, the division between sickness and death was less clear than it seems to us and fewer victims of serious illness survived. And so, when ancient Israelite texts speak of life, they usually mean not deathlessness, but a healthy, blessed existence—happiness and "length of days," as the texts from Proverbs quoted above put it. That such an existence must come to its inevitable end in no way implies, therefore, a defeat of God's promise of "life," so understood. The brevity and frailty of human life did, of course, occasion some somber reflections on the human condition and its difference from divinity. One's death, or the death of a loved one, was never a happy prospect; there was no dancing on the grave in ancient Israel. But if God grants the wish to "teach us to count our days rightly," in the words of a psalmist (Ps 90:12), and if the unfailing word of God is favorably fulfilled in one's own life, then one could, like Abraham or Job, die "at a good ripe age, old and contented" (Gen 25:8; Job 42:17). Whatever complaints one had against God could be properly relegated to the past, as long as God graced the end of one's life. This, and only this, could rob death of its sting.

The opposite of "life" in this understanding includes not only weakness, disease, depression, and the like, but also a humiliating death, especially one that is violent or premature. This is the kind of end that in Chapter 4 we called "an unfortunate death." It is this form of death, and not mortality in general, that King Hezekiah, for example, prays that God spare him (Isa 38:1–3), a death in which, as the king puts it, "I must depart in the middle of my days . . . consigned to the gates of Sheol." And when God grants his prayer, Hezekiah quite naturally speaks as one who has been given life and spared "the pit of destruction" to which his sins had doomed him (vv 10, 16–20). That he will still die at the end of his fifteen-year reprieve, symbolized by the miraculous retreat of the shadow on his father's sundial, does not seem to qualify his joy in the least nor to suggest to him that his sins are still working their toxic magic after all. Anyone so favored could die "old and contented," and without recrimination that the fact of death—the inevitable return of the shadow on the sundial—had undermined God's ubiquitous promise of life. The question was not whether one died, but whether one did so within God's favor or outside it. And *this* is a question very far removed from the thinking of modern naturalism.

Further mitigation of the ostensible tension between the inevitability of death and God's promise of life comes from the highly social and familial construction of personal identity that we have been stressing. In a culture in which identity is so deeply embedded in family structures, life is, as we have seen, largely characterized by the emergence of new generations who stand in continuity and deference to the old. Barrenness is here the functional equivalent of death in more individualistic cultures, and the return of fertility functions like resurrection: it replaces death with life. It is thus not surprising that the blessings and curses of covenant offer abundant fertility to those who observe God's commands, but threaten those who violate them with sterility and the death (or loss by other means) of children (see Leviticus 26 and Deuteronomy 28 for copious examples). Note that these blessings and curses are addressed primarily to the entire nation, not to individuals within it. The individual Israelites will all surely die, but without in the slightest impairing the promise of life and fellowship with him that the LORD has extended to the House of Israel. As in Ezekiel's vision in the valley of the dry bones, we are dealing with mortal Israelites and immortal Israel (see Chapter 8). And here again, the fact of death and the promise of life stand in no great tension, for the two move on different planes, the individual and the national, respectively.

Seen within the universe of ancient Israelite belief, then, the promise of life, so prominent throughout the Hebrew Bible, is generally not inconsistent with the brute fact of human mortality equally prominent in the same collection of books. The God of Israel can without contradiction both offer life to his faithful and decree that all shall die.

Still, even within the cultural universe of ancient Israel, a tension between the fact of death and the promise of life can appear. To understand the tension, let us first revisit our crucial point that "life" in biblical Hebrew has a wider semantic range than its English equivalent. If "life" can signify health and well-being, and "to bring to life" can mean simply "to cure, to make healthy," then the promise or offer of life in the Hebrew Bible inevitably comes into contact with another ancient Israelite affirmation, also of high frequency and venerable antiquity. This is the affirmation that the LORD is Israel's healer:

> See, then, that I, I am He;
> There is no god beside Me.
> I deal death and give life;
> I wounded and I will heal:
> None can deliver from My hand. (Deut 32:39)

The rabbis of the early Talmudic period stated the interpretive problem in this verse concisely:

> Our Rabbis taught: "I deal death and give life." One might think that death applies to one individual and life to another, as the world goes its course. Therefore the text reads, "I wounded and I will heal." Just as the wounding and the healing apply to the same individual, so do death and life apply to the same individual. From this, one can derive a refutation to those who say that the resurrection of the dead is not in the Torah.

Within the older understanding of death and life widely found in the Hebrew Bible, however, the position the rabbis want to eliminate has some probability. On that understanding, "I deal death and give life" would mean simply that the LORD alone is the sole source of both death and life, as he is the source of both wounding and healing in the next line ("I wounded and I will heal"). The linchpin of the rabbinic argument—that the wounding and healing must refer to the same person—is not strictly necessary, for one person may suffer an ailment and never recover, whereas another is healed. In each case, the poem is telling us, the omnipotent and inscrutable God is the source of the person's destiny. And just as he decrees both disease and its remedy, he alone decrees both the end and the beginning of life. "I deal death and give life," in other words, need not imply resurrection, as the wording (especially the word order) might imply to today's reader. It may mean simply that deaths and births are ultimately the LORD's doing, as one generation replaces another, "as the world goes its course." If so, the verse in its plain sense cannot be pressed into service in support of the rabbis' own doctrine of resurrection, in which deceased individuals come back to life.

But if life is somehow equivalent to healing, and death to wounding, then why cannot the sole and unchallengeable deity who heals lesser wounds also heal the graver malady that is death? To put it differently, if one use of the term "death" in biblical Hebrew includes both disease and biological cessation, is there any reason—again, strictly within the cultural universe of the text—to think that God could heal disease but could not reverse death? The question is all the more pressing if we recall Aubrey R. Johnson's observation that "death, in the strict sense of the term, is for the Israelite the weakest form of life." If death could be seen as the most severe of illnesses and characterized (in this understanding) not by nonexistence but by debilitation and physical fragility, then the possibility arises that God might heal it, too, just as he heals other diseases and wounds. Not that he heals it in every instance, any more than he heals any other ailment in every instance (as if no one were ever sick), but that he could, in an exception so rare as to call forth exuberant praise, reverse death no less than any other condition.

The Song of Hannah (1 Sam 2:1–10) indicates that this possibility is much more than an abstract logical deduction. The main theme of the poem is how God's victory inverts the ordinary realities of the world:

> [4]The bows of the mighty are broken,
> And the faltering are girded with strength.
> [5]Men once sated must hire out for bread;
> The hungry are fattened on food.
> While the barren woman bears seven,
> The mother of many is forlorn. (1 Sam 2:4–5)

The hymn goes on to speak of God's reversing the status of the rich and the poor, lifting up the "needy" to "seats of honor," and guarding those loyal to him while "the wicked perish in darkness" (1 Sam 2:7–9)—establishing, in other words, a world order quite the reverse of what persists in the familiar world in which God has not yet won, or not yet definitively won, his great victory.

Here we must again turn our attention to an important verse, one we have already discussed toward the end of Chapter 3:

> The LORD deals death and gives life,
> Casts down into Sheol and raises up. (1 Sam 2:6)

Our point now is the light the verse sheds on Deut 32:39. The first half-line of 1 Sam 2:6 closely resembles the affirmation of Deut 32:39 that the LORD "deal[s] death and give[s] life"; only the person of the verb varies, with a first person in Deuteronomy and a third in Samuel. The second half of the verse from the Song of Hannah, however, does not permit the view that it affirms only the LORD's control of the change of generations, as Deuteronomy 32 did. That he "raises up" from Sheol can mean only that he reverses death, returning the deceased from the netherworld just as he reverses other tragic or unjust conditions in the hymn. The injustice that resulted in the dispatch of some individuals to Sheol will be reversed when the LORD establishes the reign of justice that the hymn celebrates throughout. The Song of Hannah does not regard the netherworld as beyond his power; it suggests that the similar language in Deuteronomy 32 did not either.

If we return to our question of the relationship of the fact of death to the promise of life, we are compelled to say that the Song of Hannah upholds both—and not only for families, let it be noted, but for individuals as well. God brings death upon all human beings, casting at least some down to Sheol, but he also brings up afterward a subset of the latter group—context suggests they are those who arrived there unjustly—or will do so when he establishes his reign of justice in what both these texts regard as an earth-shaking and world-transforming victory.

This is not to deny that some texts in the Hebrew Bible tacitly assume the accuracy of the wise woman of Tekoa's observation that "we must all die; we are like water that is poured out on the ground and cannot be gathered up" (2 Sam 14:14). The affirmations in Deuteronomy 32 and the Song of Hannah alert us, however, to the presence of another perspective, one in which death, or at least unjust death, will be miraculously reversed. There are psalms, for example, that praise the LORD for bringing the psalmist up from Sheol (see Ps 30:4). For in the psalmists' mind, the adversity they had experienced—illness, false accusation, enemy attack—had truly brought them into the domain of death, from which their God's faithfulness and justice rescued them. The psalmists' ecstasy makes more sense if we remember that such rescues from death were thought to be exceedingly rare. For the wise woman of Tekoa's observation is the rule, not the exception; deliverance from death was deemed an act of God, a miracle, and thus defies the regularity of nature. Even rarer are those instances in the Hebrew Bible in which someone who is "really" dead returns to life, as does the boy whom Elisha resurrects in 2 Kings 4 (see Chapter 7). Were resurrections not thought to be rare, were they, that is, the ordinary course of things, the mother of the child whom Elisha's predecessor Elijah resurrects in a strikingly parallel story would hardly have had occasion to affirm, as she does in the last words of the narrative, "Now I know that you are a man of God and that the word of the LORD is truly in your mouth" (1 Kgs 17:24).

This line of reasoning gives us another insight into the relationship between the fact of death, on the one hand, and the promise or offer of life, on the other. We saw above that these are not in logical contradiction in the Hebrew Bible after all, because "life" there can mean simply a long life span or one that ends in peaceful and honorable circumstances, which bespeak God's approval of the person. The association of death with disease suggests another way of understanding the simultaneous acceptance of these two seeming opposites. Death is the ordinary human fate, and it is ordinarily irreversible, just as serious disease in the ancient world was ordinarily incurable. For in an age before antibiotics, steroids, and effective surgery, few people recovered from illnesses that are today readily curable, or at least controllable. Consider Naaman, the leprous Aramean general whom Elisha, the Israelite man of God, cures in the chapter that appears — instructively — just after the one that tells of the Shunammite resurrection that we analyzed in Chapter 7. Surely Naaman had visited the best healers in Damascus in a futile quest of a cure for his affliction (which was probably not what modern clinicians classify as leprosy). His response when the man of God has healed him is strikingly reminiscent of the response of the mother of the boy whom Elijah had resurrected: "Now I know that there is no God in the whole world except in Israel!" (2 Kgs 5:15).

Indeed, within the tale of Naaman itself there is a basis for connecting healing with resurrection. It lies in the answer of the king of Israel to the letter in which the king of Aram asks that he cure his ailing general: "Am I God, to deal death and give life, that this fellow writes to me to cure a man of leprosy?" (2 Kgs 5:7). The close resemblance here in language and thought to both Deut 32:39 and 1 Sam 2:6 is obvious, as is the implication that to heal the leper would be a miracle on the order of resurrecting the dead. In the ordinary course of events, lepers remain lepers, and the dead remain dead. But the God who "heals all your diseases" and "redeems your life from the Pit," as a psalmist says (Ps 103:3–4), is not constrained by the ordinary course of events, and the exceptional case is still a reality with which to reckon. What is more, its very status as a rare exception commends it to the Israelite mind as an act of God, a supernatural intervention into the dreary course of nature, marked as it is by incurable disease and irreversible death.

The worldview of the texts in the Hebrew Bible of which we have been speaking is, to be sure, different from the worldview of those later Jews and Christians who held a doctrine of the resurrection of the dead. It does not, however, do justice to the difference to say, as many do, that in the earlier period, death was thought to be irreversible, appropriate, and in accordance with God's will, whereas in the later period (among those who believed in resurrection) God was thought to rescue from death. A better way of stating the point, we would maintain, is to say that what had been a rare exception in the early period became the basis for a general expectation in the late one. This is the apocalyptic expectation of a universal resurrection in a coming dispensation in which all of God's potentials would be activated in a grand finale of stupendous miracles very much at odds with the natural course of history. One central aspect of the eschatological inversion is that the previous exception becomes the norm, as even the most formidable opposition to God's saving power melts before his might —death emphatically included. It is not that human nature becomes invulnerable to death, spontaneously and on its own. Rather, God would at long last grant the rescue from adversity for which Israelites had always prayed, delivering those who, against all hope, had placed their hope in him.

"HE SHALL TURN BACK FROM HIS WAYS AND LIVE"

We have now seen that the understanding of the promise of life in texts that presuppose a covenant between God and the people Israel does not imply that any individual Israelite will escape death or be resurrected after it occurs. For it is the people of Israel and not individual Israelites who are granted the eternal covenant that, among other things, prevents their annihilation, fertility thus being the rough functional equivalent of resurrection in a more individualistic culture. The promise of a bright future after affliction, therefore, in no way implies that any given individual will have a future beyond his or her appointed life span. The promised future finds its fulfillment in the later generations of the chosen people.

In one key text, the shift of generations comes to be telescoped into the life of one individual, and in the process a death sentence is revoked and replaced with an affirmation of life. The text is Ezekiel 18, the chapter in which the great prophet of the early sixth century B.C.E. protests against the notion of inherited guilt, epitomized in the popular saying, "Parents eat sour grapes and their children's teeth are blunted" (v 2). Ezekiel's retort— "The person who sins, only he shall die" (v 4)—is often taken as a denunciation of the idea of collective guilt and a decisive advance for the opposing notion of moral and spiritual individualism. The prophet's focus, however, is not on contemporaneous individuals at all, but on *generations*, and his principal point is that the guilt of the ancestors which caused the recent destruction of the kingdom at the hands of the Babylonians and the ensuing exile does not condemn their current descendants to unending misery. A righteous man, one who abstains from abuses like robbery or sexual relations with a menstruating woman, "shall live," the prophet assures his hearers (vv 5–9). Should he have a son who engages in such flagrant sins, however, "He shall not live!" Ezekiel insists. "If he has committed any of these abominations, he shall die; he has forfeited his life" (vv 10–13). But his own son, if he "has taken heed and has not imitated" his father's abuses, "shall not die for the iniquity of his father . . . he shall live!" (vv 14–19). The message is obvious:

> The person who sins, he alone shall die. A child shall not share the burden of a parent's guilt, nor shall a parent share the burden of a child's guilt; the righteousness of the righteous shall be accounted to him alone, and the wickedness of the wicked shall be accounted to him alone. (Ezek 18:20)

The upshot of this would seem to be that in God's moral calculus, each moment carries equal weight. No one generation can condemn its descendants, or acquit them. It bears mentioning that Ezekiel's preaching is in opposition not only to the popular proverb he cites, but also to some sources in the Hebrew Bible itself. The affirmation in the Decalogue that God "visit[s] the guilt of the parents upon the children" (Exod 20:5; Deut 5:9) springs to mind immediately. More relevant to Ezekiel's situation, however, is the claim that the destruction of the kingdom of Judah and the Jerusalem Temple in the prophet's own time is owing to King Manasseh's sin two generations earlier (2 Kgs 21:11–15; 24:3–4).

For our purposes, two points about Ezekiel 18 are especially interesting. One is that the language of God's approval or disapproval of a person's actions is the language of life and death, respectively. The righteous shall live; the wicked shall surely die. What Ezekiel is reporting is not case law or guidance for human courts, but God's ultimate verdict—a judgment of life and death, with no intermediate points. (How, if at all, that judgment is realized in human affairs and procedures is not the prophet's concern.)

The more important point for our discussion lies in the scenario the prophet sketches after having laid out his scenario of the righteous father with the wicked son and the righteous grandson and stated the conclusion cited above. Now Ezekiel moves away from the problem of generations that has occupied his attention throughout the chapter and speaks, instead, of two moments in the life of one person:

> ²¹Moreover, if the wicked one repents of all the sins that he committed and keeps all My laws and does what is just and right, he shall live; he shall not die. ²²None of the transgressions he committed shall be remembered against him; because of the righteousness he has practiced, he shall live. ²³Is it my desire that a wicked person shall die?—says the Lord GOD. It is rather that he shall turn back from his ways and live. (Ezek 18:21–23)

The reverse, the prophet then goes on to say, is also the case. The treachery a once righteous person now commits condemns him: "he shall die" (v 24). In each situation, the national has become personal. The two *generations* have been consolidated into two *moments in one life*, a life once imperiled by sin but always graced by God's preference for life and by the availability of repentance.

We must not overlook the consequence of this consolidation. The idea that Israel, condemned to a sentence of death, can, by the grace of God, recover in a future generation uncontaminated by the ancestors' violations has been transformed into the notion that an analogous recovery can occur in one individual's lifetime. In a certain sense, the parent and the child have been telescoped into one person, a former sinner who has now repented, and just as the child's status was determinative in the intergenerational scenario, so now it is the new person, the penitent, whose moral status is determinative. The national or familial history has been transformed into biography, and, as a result, the new lease on life offered to the innocent second generation applies to the repentant individual as well. The condemned person can escape a death sentence by returning to God and his commandments. One who faced certain death can find life.

But how shall we take this happy verdict, "he shall live" (Ezek 18:28)? Does Ezekiel really believe that the righteous and the repentant will never know death's sting, that returning to God invariably removes the prospect of individual death? Does he not know that eventually there comes a time when even repentance (or good deeds or faith) is powerless to stave off death? It would seem more likely, rather, that Ezekiel 18 understands "life" the way the verses from Proverbs 3 discussed above understand "length of days"—as a prosperous and healthy life that is of normal or above-normal length and ends peacefully and in dignity. Biological cessation terminates such a life but does not constitute "death" in the highly freighted theological and forensic sense that Ezekiel intends when he pronounces the words "he shall die!" We cannot be certain of this, of course, because the whole question of the ultimate fate of individuals, however pressing it is to us, is simply not on Ezekiel's mind. It is tempting, nonetheless, to speculate on how he would have reacted if it had been. Would he have turned away from the unqualified, forensic idiom, "he shall live!" and "he shall die!" that dominates Ezekiel 18 and made it explicit that all he means is "length of days" and premature death, respectively? Or would he have continued to elect the promise of life over the fact of death, upholding without compromise his insistence that God does not want the wicked to die but only to abandon evil deeds and to return to him—and thus to life (Ezek 18:23)? Were the latter the option he chose, Ezekiel would have had to connect repentance with some vision of personal immortality or individual resurrection, thus embarking on the course that develops fully only in a later form of Judaism and in Christianity and Islam as well. As it is, he stops short of that, leaving the ambiguities of his rhetoric unresolved.

FROM DEATH TO LIFE

How, then, shall we think of the teaching of most of the Hebrew Bible—the Hebrew Bible before an expectation of resurrection appeared—about death and life? With the exception of a very few special individuals like Elijah and perhaps Enoch, whom God takes directly to himself (2 Kgs 2:6–12; Gen 5:21–24), death is universal and inevitable in this literature. And with the exception again of a very few individuals—the special sons whom Elijah and Elisha revive, a man who comes back to life when his body touches the latter's bones (1 Kgs 17:17–24; 2 Kgs 4:8–37; 13:20–21)—death is never reversed. This is not just an empirical observation about the narratives in the Hebrew Bible. Some texts therein articulate the point explicitly and offer theological explanations of how humanity rightly lost the opportunity for the immortality for which they long and how they came to have their life span limited (for example, Ps 49:6–13; Gen 2:25–3:24; 6:1–4). This being the case, it is no cause for wonderment that those who identify Judaism with the Hebrew Bible are surprised to find that belief in resurrection occupies a prominent and central place in classical Jewish literature and theology and becomes, in fact, a normative and obligatory aspect of the tradition.

But we have been at pains to argue that the inevitability and irreversibility of death in the Hebrew Bible is only part of the story. The other part is the ubiquitous promise of life, sometimes conditional, sometimes not, offered by a God who enjoins his people, in the words of Deut 30:19, to "Choose life." Especially in the foundational texts in Genesis and Exodus, the survival of that people is continually under attack by infertility and genocide. And yet just as continually—and often miraculously—new life appears, and God's promise overcomes the power of death that had seemed invincible. That God has the power to heal the most hopeless of diseases and even to bring people up from Sheol, restoring their vitality, is also a well-attested affirmation of the hymns and laments of the Hebrew Bible. The revival of the recently deceased individuals who come into contact with Elijah or Elisha provides suggestive narrative examples of this theology at work. Ezekiel's vision in the valley of the bones (Ezek 37:1–14) comes somewhat closer to the idea of resurrection, however, for the people revived there have long been dead; their bones are dry.

We face, in sum, a more complicated situation than scholars of the Hebrew Bible have usually taken to be the case. Death is indeed universal therein and seldom reversed, but God is frequently said to offer and prefer life and to save his chosen people from annihilation. He even saves some individuals (in rare and therefore especially noteworthy circumstances) from a death that is impending or one that has already occurred. When a full-fledged doctrine of the resurrection of the dead appears, it reflects certain key features that have long been part of the deep structure of the theology of Israel. For this is a theology in which the fact of death and the promise of life, each of them of capital importance, stand in a relationship of tension. That tension, or more precisely, the eagerness to uphold its two poles, will contribute to the Jewish expectation of resurrection. The expectation of a future general resurrection (the subject of our next chapter) does not arise around the early second century B.C.E. solely out of the needs of the moment. Contrary to what is almost always claimed, it is not primarily an answer to the challenge to God's justice that the death of those martyred in the persecutions of that period posed, though that problem doubtless contributed to its diffusion and acceptance. Instead, the resurrection of the dead is best seen not as a solution to a problem at all, still less as the way out of a logical embarrassment. It is best seen, rather, as another statement of the continuing Jewish need to uphold both the fact of death and the promise of life, while expecting and celebrating the victory of the God who can defeat death and who promises life.

THE GREAT AWAKENING

THE REVERSAL

The great reversal of death of which poets had long sung becomes an explicit prophecy in Dan 12:1–3, the first transparent and indisputable prediction of the resurrection of the dead in the Hebrew Bible:

> ¹At that time, the great prince, Michael, who stands beside the sons of your people, will appear. It will be a time of trouble, the like of which has never been since the nation came into being. At that time, your people will be rescued, all who are found inscribed in the book. ²Many of those that sleep in the dust of the earth will awake, some to eternal life, others to reproaches, to everlasting abhorrence. ³And the wise will be radiant like the bright expanse of sky, and those who lead the many to righteousness will be like the stars forever and ever.

The passage comes toward the end of a long narrative in which an angelic figure ("one who looked like a man," Dan 10:16) gives an exceedingly detailed, and maddeningly opaque, account of future events on the international plane. These events have, of course, vast implications for the Jewish people. The penultimate stage centers on "a contemptible man," a violent king who, in his godlessness and arrogance, will be determined to do harm to "the holy covenant," "desecrate the temple," and "set up the appalling abomination"—an idol in the most sacred place on earth. Contrary to what one might expect, the foreign king's assaults on the traditional order meet with a mixed response in the Jewish community. The angelic figure's own sympathies, however, are hardly divided:

[32]He will flatter with smooth words those who act wickedly toward the covenant, but the people devoted to their God will stand firm. [33]The wise among the people will make the many understand; and for a while they shall fall by sword and flame, suffer captivity and spoliation. [34]In defeat, they will receive a little help, and many will join them insincerely. [35]Some of the wise will fall, that they may be refined and purged and whitened until the time of the end, for an interval still remains until the appointed time. (Dan 11:32–35)

The key division is between "those who act wickedly toward the covenant," on the one hand, and "the people devoted to their God," on the other (v 32). The latter receive their sacred and invaluable knowledge from a smaller group, termed "the wise" (*maskilim*), who impart understanding to the masses (*yavinu larabbim*). The wisdom of this group, however, cannot deter death, and some of these "wise" will die, for the consummative moment will not yet have arrived. Here, death remains real and tragic, and no immediate restoration into life, no magical reversal, nullifies its reality and its tragedy. But it is, in the mysterious divine economy, also temporary.

Meanwhile, our prophecy tells us, the evil "king will do as he pleases," continuing on his course of unrestrained blasphemy, failing to honor even "the god of his ancestors" (Dan 11:36–37). Finally, after many a victory and having plundered richly, "he will pitch his royal pavilion between the sea and the beautiful holy mountain"—the Temple Mount in Jerusalem—"and he will meet his doom with no one to help him" (v 45). At long last, death will vanquish the victor.

If this text had come during an earlier period in the history of ancient Israel, it could well have stopped there, with the defeat of the arrogant idolater, perhaps with a codicil noting the escape of Israel, or some subset of Israelites, from his clutches. In Daniel, however, a question remains open and the traditional structure cannot adequately answer it. That question is the fate of the "wise" who have fallen by "sword and flame" or suffered "captivity and spoliation." Their demise, it will be recalled, is to be but temporary, lasting only "an interval . . . until the appointed time" (Dan 11:33, 35). It is the events at the other end of that painful interval, the events of the eschatological "appointed time," that occupy this first clear and indubitable text about resurrection in the Hebrew Bible.

In Dan 12:1–3, the victims seem to be both the nation as a whole and those individuals within it deemed worthy of resurrection. "Your people will be rescued," the manlike being prophesies to Daniel, but also—or is it exclusively?—"all who are found inscribed in the book," especially the "wise" (vv 1, 3). The national dimension here recalls earlier texts about "a time of trouble" from which the chosen people are likewise delivered (for instance, Jer 30:5–7). In Dan 12:1–3, however, the traditional affirmation that "[the] people will be rescued" and their oppressors doomed is complicated by that division between those "who act wickedly toward the covenant" and those who are "devoted to their God" (Dan 11:32). Presumably, only the latter shall benefit from the predicted resurrection, as the covenant-breakers share the ignominious fate of the foreign invaders with whom they have cast their lot, politically and religiously. How "[the] people will be rescued" when some of them are, in fact, doomed is less mysterious in the cultural world of ancient Judaism than in ours. For membership in the "people" was both ascribed and achieved, a matter of birth but also of behavior, in particular the observance of the moral and ritual norms that one born a Jew was charged to obey. As this passage would have it, those who disobey—especially through rank idolatry—have excluded themselves from the national identity and thus from the expected redemption as well. If so, then "all who are found inscribed in the book" (Dan 12:1) do not comprise a subset of "the people." Rather, the traditionalists *are* the people. The other party has unwisely removed itself from the category of Jews who will participate in the national restoration that their God has promised.

The notion of a "book" in which destinies are inscribed appears only a few times in the Hebrew Bible. Perhaps the most memorable is in Moses' demand upon the LORD in the wake of another great act of defection and idolatry, the episode of the golden calf: "Now, if You will forgive their sin [well and good]; but if not, erase me from the record [or "book," Hebrew *sepher*] which You have written!" To which the LORD responds in words with a clear affinity to our passage, perhaps even an influence upon it: "He who has sinned against Me, him only will I erase from My record [*sepher*]" (Exod 32:32–33). In Psalm 69, the mysterious book exhibits a name familiar from rabbinic tradition, especially the liturgy of the High Holy Days: "the book of life." In this the psalmist believes the righteous are inscribed but hopes that his sadistic persecutors will not be (v 29). Similarly, in another anticipation of our passage in Daniel, an oracle in Isaiah speaks of a remnant "who are inscribed for life in Jerusalem" (Isa 4:3). Here, of course, there is every reason to believe that the remnant escapes death. They do not undergo it and return to life, as the remnant in Daniel 12 does. Eventually, the remnant in Isaiah 4 will experience a death from which there is no return to life, but which does not contradict the fact that their rescue shows that they have been inscribed for life and not death.

These resonances in Daniel of older texts suggest that the language and symbolism of resurrection were present and available, perhaps even abundant, long before the literal expectation. Modern historians, researching the origin of the Jewish idea of resurrection, understandably think of it as an innovation and seek a situation of keen discontinuity in which it arose. This is not altogether wrong, but it does underestimate the verbal particularity and the textual character of its appearance—points of great significance to the ancient Jewish culture itself. Given the rich intertextual connections and dependence in which it is enveloped, the resurrection of the dead in Dan 12:1–3 may have seemed (at least to some sectors) much less innovative than it does to those who, ignoring its linguistic embedding, think of it as an *idea*. Much is lost when the resurrection of the dead is treated as a free-floating concept whose essence remains constant no matter what the culture in which it appears or to which it migrates. For a religious tradition is like a game of chess: every item stands in a systemic relation to every other and cannot be detached and examined on its own without serious damage to its organic function (and thus to our capacity to understand its nature). In the case of Judaism from the Second Temple period onward, religious affirmations (even new ones) are so deeply embedded in the particularity of the scriptural language that efforts to disregard the allusions in order to penetrate back to a core "idea" only lead us into grave misunderstanding.

Other than the statement that those destined for resurrection "sleep in the dust of the earth" (Dan 12:2), our text gives no indication of their location—Sheol, Gehinnom, or elsewhere—and we should be wise to respect its reticence on this point. First Enoch, a roughly contemporaneous Jewish book that is not part of the Jewish canon today, evidences a belief that the dead are in the netherworld, though in different chambers in accordance with their different moral characters; not all of them currently dwell in the place of torment to which the wicked will finally be dispatched (1 Enoch 22). In comparison, Daniel 12 is remarkably restrained, giving no indication that those about to be resurrected, whatever their ultimate destinies, are sleeping in a netherworld.

The familiar identification of sleep with death that Dan 12:2 makes is by no means universal. It has been pointed out, for example, that Zoroastrianism (the Iranian religion from whom the Jews have often been said to have gotten the belief in resurrection) did not make the same equation. Here again, the book of Daniel exhibits its thoroughgoing indebtedness to the culture and scriptures of what already in its own time could have been justly termed "ancient Israel." It will be recalled that when Gehazi fails to restore the Shunammite woman's dead son, he tells Elisha, "The boy has not awakened" (2 Kgs 4:31). Similarly, Jeremiah predicts that when God exacts his punishment on the Babylonians, who have destroyed Jerusalem and its Temple and exiled the Judahites, those punished will "sleep an endless sleep, / Never to awake" (Jer 51:39, 57), using the same two verbs as in Dan 12:2. Perhaps most memorable are Job's sarcastic words in one of his laments over the finality of death:

> So man lies down never to rise;
> He will awake only when the heavens are no more,
> Only then be aroused from his sleep. (Job 14:12)

We must remember that sleep in the Hebrew Bible is not characterized primarily by refreshment and renewal. It is, rather, a dangerous and uncertain state. It is no wonder that momentous events, like the creation of woman and the first prediction of the enslavement in Egypt and the ensuing exodus, occur when the subject is asleep (Gen 2:21; 15:12). Nor is it a wonder that a psalmist likens waking after lying down to the LORD's answering from his sacred mountain when he calls out for aid against the attacks of foes who outnumber him (Ps 3:6). Sleep, in short, is a mini-death, or, as an anonymous passage in the Talmud puts it, "sleep is one-sixtieth of death." In the Hebrew Bible, however, it would be more precise to say that sleep is a death that is—or one devoutly hopes will be—temporary. With this in mind, we can more readily understand as well the Christian apostle Paul when he writes, "Christ has been raised from the dead, the first fruits of those who have died," or, literally, "fallen asleep" (1 Cor 15:20).

Even now, the traditional Jewish daily prayers begin with thanks to God (recited while still in bed) for compassionately returning one's soul. This is not to say that ancient Israel, or its Second Temple, Christian, and rabbinic successors, could not distinguish sleep from death, or waking up from being resurrected. It is to say, however, that the vocabulary in which the belief in resurrection is couched builds on an already ancient perception that sleep is a mortal threat and waking life something miraculous, a testimony to God's special care for his faithful. Israelite literature attests to a belief that God restores the worshiper's soul (or, more precisely, the life force) well before a belief in the general resurrection of the dead appeared, and when it does appear, it finds a rich preparation in the older literature of the Hebrew Bible.

One element that truly is novel in Dan 12:1–3 is, however, signaled by an expression that, for all its frequency in later Jewish literature, occurs nowhere else in the Hebrew Bible, "eternal life" (v 2). In it we can detect the outstanding difference between the beneficiaries of this resurrection and those brought back to life in the few places that speak of a similar restoration, such as the tale of Elisha's resurrection of the Shunammite woman's little boy that we examined in Chapter 7. The difference, in a word, is finality. Dan 12:1–3 envisions no second death for those resurrected, only "eternal life" for the faithful and "everlasting abhorrence" for the desecrators of the covenant. At long last, the periodic alternation of death and life comes to a dynamic halt. The granting of "eternal life" thus corresponds to, indeed it is inseparable from, the prediction earlier in Daniel that

> the God of Heaven will establish a kingdom that shall never be destroyed, a kingdom that shall not be transferred to another people. It will crush and wipe out all these kingdoms, but shall itself last forever. (Dan 2:44)

The irreversible triumph of life is of a piece with the establishment of the kingdom of heaven and the decisive and definitive victory of justice over the injustice that has, in the author's view, characterized all of human history to date.

The precise identity of the "wise" (*maskilim*) who are the prime beneficiaries of the apocalyptic transformation remains unclear. The term is common in the book of Proverbs and in this context recalls the promise of abundant life and avoidance of Sheol made to those who tread steadfastly on the path of the wise (for example, Prov 3:13–18; 15:24). But biblical scholars have long recognized that the choice of this particular term has been dictated to some degree by a famous passage about the so-called suffering servant prominent in Isaiah 40–55. This is the first of three influential antecedents of Dan 12:1–3 that will concern us here. The passage from Isaiah begins:

> [13]Indeed, My servant shall prosper [*yaskil*],
> Be exalted and raised to great heights.
> [14]Just as the many [*rabbim*] were appalled at him—
> So marred was his appearance, unlike that of man,
> His form, beyond human semblance—
> [15]Just so he shall startle many nations.
> Kings shall be silenced because of him,
> For they shall see what has not been told them,
> Shall behold what they never have heard. (Isa 52:13–15)

The passage goes on to detail the man's humiliation—his ugliness, his suffering and disease, his repudiation and rejection by those who thought themselves his moral superiors but actually fell far short of him. All this he bore submissively, "like a sheep being led to slaughter," until he was taken away in defiance of justice, "cut off from the land of the living." As a result, though he was a man of justice and truth, "his grave was set among the wicked" (Isa 53:7–9). Not least among the murky questions this enigmatic and ambiguous passage poses is the postmortem fate of the servant. For the text goes on to say that all this happened, at least in part, so that "he might see offspring" (Isa 53:10). Shall we, then, add Isa 52:13–53:12 to the small list of pre-Danielic texts that speak of the resurrection of the dead? This depends, in part, on a more basic and equally murky question: whether the servant is an individual (in which case the restoration and vindication occurs after his death) or the people Israel (in which case the offspring and long life that follow his death need not be taken as a resurrection in the later and more individualistic sense of the term). Either way, of course, the God of life triumphs over death in this passage; either way, hope survives death, and the power of God at last becomes manifest for all to see.

For our purposes, it is not necessary to resolve these points of longstanding contention among scholars. For it is clear that whatever Isaiah 53 understands to be the nature of the servant's vindication, Daniel 12 interprets it to apply to its own vision of resurrection. As has often been noted, the announcement in Dan 12:3 that "the wise . . . lead the many to righteousness" (*matzdiqé harabbim*) similarly echoes the prediction that the once suffering and now vindicated servant "makes the many righteous" (*yatzdiq larabbim*, Isa 53:11). The "wise" have taken on the identity of the servant, afflicted and mocked in life, vindicated and exalted after death.

The language of Dan 12:1–3 thus leaves it beyond doubt that the postmortem fate of the righteous is one of resurrection—the reanimation of corpses rather than merely vindication in the heavenly realm with a conferral of life (as may be the case in Isaiah 53). But it would be a mistake to imagine that the "eternal life" the deserving receive is simply a restoration to their old and familiar reality, only without the pain and injustice. To "be radiant like the bright expanse of sky" (Dan 12:3) is light-years away from having to reinhabit one's old body for all eternity. This is worth noting because scholars often present the issue as if the only alternatives are immortality of the soul, on the one hand, and resurrection of the body, on the other. To do so is to neglect the key fact that resurrection was thought to yield a transformed and perfected form of bodily existence and thus a state of being both like and unlike any we can know. To glance ahead to later historical periods, one thinks, for example, of Paul's comment on the resurrection of the dead: "It is sown a physical body [*soma psuchikon*]; it is raised a spiritual body [*soma pneumatikon*]" (1 Cor 15:44). Or, to give a Jewish analogy from a century and a half or so after Paul, the early third-century Talmudic sage Rav contrasts this world and the World-to-Come in these words: "In the World-to-Come, there is neither eating nor drinking nor sexual relations nor business transactions nor jealousy nor hatred nor rivalry. Rather, the righteous sit with their crowns on their heads and enjoy the radiance of the Divine Presence [*ziv ha-shekinah*]." This is not to imply an easy equivalence of Paul's resurrection existence with the rabbinic World-to-Come. Both do, however, imply embodiedness—Rav's righteous have heads on which to put crowns, after all—though in some transfigured mode that is hard to visualize and can be conveyed only symbolically. In both cases, the beneficiaries of the new way of being are not disembodied spirits, but neither are they ordinary human beings who, amazingly, were once dead. In both the Christian and the rabbinic cases, postmortem existence is a radical transformation, and not the indefinite prolongation, of earthly life.

The ultimate fate of those unfortunates who, in the words of Dan 12:2, "awake . . . to reproaches, to everlasting abhorrence" is less clear. If we are to take postmortem experience as the opposite of the "eternal life" granted their fortunate counterparts, then perhaps we should imagine a second death following the public humiliation to which they awaken. Alternatively, "eternal life" may refer to quality more than to duration, so that each group survives in perpetuity, the one in blissful vindication, the other in wretched disgrace. An intermediate position—death that never ends—appears in a passage whose influence on Dan 12:1–3 is patent:

> 22For as the new heaven and the new earth
> Which I will make
> Shall endure by My will
> > —declares the LORD—
> So shall your seed and your name endure.
> 23And new moon after new moon,
> And sabbath after sabbath,
> All flesh shall come to worship Me
> > —said the LORD.
>
> 24They shall go out and gaze
> On the corpses of the men who rebelled against Me:
> Their worms shall not die,
> Nor their fire be quenched;
> They shall be a horror
> To all flesh. (Isa 66:22–24)

Here, the rebels seem to endure forever, though, to be sure, not in life but in the disgraceful mode of unburied corpses whose putrefaction and consumption in flame shall never end. Rather than arguing rationalistically and prosaically for this or that view of the postmortem fate of the condemned in these highly poetic and visionary texts, we should do better to note that in both Daniel 12 and its antecedents in Isaiah, the fates of the two groups are linked. The main point in each case is not afterlife; it is *vindication through the power of God*, the vindication of the just against the rebels or defectors who had of late triumphed over them and disgraced God. In short, in these texts the resurrection of the dead is best conceived as a reversal, not primarily of death but of condition and status. God intervenes to make the downtrodden and the triumphant exchange places, in the process vindicating his own honor and sovereignty. In stark contrast to recent experience, the faithful traditionalists will live (and the "wise" among them will shine radiantly), but the desecrators of the covenant will either die or endure an unending ignominy.

WHY RESURRECTION? A FALSE ANSWER

One of the most secure and long-lived contributions of modern biblical studies is the dating of Daniel to the time of the Seleucid persecution of 167–164 B.C.E., which makes it one of the latest texts in the Hebrew Bible. The "contemptible man" who "rag[es] against the holy covenant" and instigates the desecration of the Temple, the abolition of the daily offering, and the setting up of the idolatrous "appalling abomination" in that most sacred precinct (Dan 11:21–31) is none other than Antiochus IV, the Hellenistic monarch against whom the Maccabees would rise in resistance and win a victory that Jews celebrate to this day in the festival of Chanukkah. Although Jewish traditionalists over the centuries have stereotypically spoken of this confrontation as one of the evil foreign oppressor versus faithful innocent Jews, it is clear that many Jews were more sympathetic to the new Hellenistic culture than to the old ways of their ancestral Torah. The conflict, in other words, was internal and not just external, and it is this split between traditionalists and innovators among Jews that the book of Daniel reflects when it contrasts "those who act wickedly toward the covenant" with "the people devoted to their God" (11:32). More importantly for our purposes, it reflects the same split when it contrasts those who awake "to eternal life" with those who awake "to reproaches, to everlasting abhorrence" (12:2).

Another commonplace among scholars draws a causal connection between this concern for retributive justice—that all should receive what they deserve—and the emergence of the belief in resurrection itself. Reflecting on the differing fates of the faithful traditionalists and the more cosmopolitan innovators during this period, George W. E. Nickelsburg puts it well. "Thus piety caused death, and disobedience led to life," he writes. "Clearly this confounded the standard Israelite canons of justice and retribution. Resurrection to life, on the one hand, and to punishment, on the other, was the answer to this problem."

Whatever theologians or philosophers may think of this common line of reasoning, as an explanation for the emergence of a belief in resurrection it fails drastically. For one thing, the notion that the pious may experience death (even as a consequence of their piety) and the disobedient may experience life (even as a consequence of their disobedience) was hardly a discovery of Second Temple Judaism. Nickelsburg's conception of "the standard Israelite canons of justice and retribution" is, though widely shared, much too simple. Consider, for example, the narrative of Cain and Abel (Gen 4:1–16), already ancient by the time of the book of Daniel. Abel loses his life because God "paid heed to . . . his offering," but not to Cain's (vv 4–5), and Cain, unable to control his jealousy and rage, commits the first murder, a cold-blooded fratricide at that. Yet Abel is not revived nor is Cain condemned to death, as Israelite law requires (Exod 21:12). Quite the reverse: "the LORD put a mark on Cain, lest anyone who met him should kill him" (Gen 4:15). In sum, when the tale ends, the innocent victim, whose favor in God's eyes led to his demise, is still dead, and his murderer is still alive, protected by the mysterious grace that had once provoked the murderer's own lethal rage. This is not to say that the theme of judgment and vindication that we saw behind Dan 12:1–3 and in Isa 52:13–53:12 is absent here. On the contrary, God confronts Cain directly: "What have you done? Hark, your brother's blood cries out to Me from the ground!" As a consequence, the ground "shall no longer yield its strength to you," and Cain the farmer must become a "restless wanderer on earth" (vv 10, 12, 14). But the indictment of Cain and the vindication of Abel in no way reverse the former's survival or the latter's death. More importantly, the narrator does not seem bothered by the grave theological problem that modern scholars (and hardly they alone) perceive in this. He recognizes the injustice of Abel's death but feels no need to predict his resurrection. Justice is served when the malefactor is confronted and punished. Vindication of the devout and innocent victim does not require his resurrection.

Similar things can be said for a host of other texts, all of them earlier than the deaths of Jewish martyrs in the second century B.C.E. One thinks, for example, of the murderous assaults of Jezebel and her husband, King Ahab, in the ninth century B.C.E., which resulted in the deaths of many of "the prophets of the LORD" (1 Kgs 18:13). A particularly telling text focuses on their mistreatment and murder of the innocent traditionalist Naboth, who refused to cede his ancestral holding to the palace: "The LORD forbid that I should give up to you what I have inherited from my fathers!" (1 Kgs 21:3). Here, too, the vindication of the righteous victim arrives, when Elijah first discredits and then slaughters Jezebel's prophets of Baal and when, just as the prophet predicted, the queen dies an ignominious death: the horses trample her body and the dogs devour her remains. As for Ahab, though the justice of the LORD tarries, come it surely does. Hearing the verdict upon him, Ahab "humbled himself" before the LORD, and as a result the LORD brings the predicted disaster not in his lifetime, but in his son's (1 Kgs 18:20–40; 2 Kgs 9:30–37; 1 Kgs 21:27–29). In this case also, the vindication of the LORD's justice and his prophets takes place purely and exclusively on the plane of history (whether the narrated events happened or not): the innocent victims remain dead, and death in disgrace exhausts the punishment on their murderers or of their descendants who inherit their guilt. Neither victim nor victimizer awakens to a further judgment.

Consideration of texts like these impels us to but one conclusion: the possibility that the innocent might die and the guilty continue to live was indeed recognized early in the history of Israel and, more importantly, was not necessarily thought to impugn God's justice. For vindication of the oppressed could be realized after the latter's death, quite without objection (however inadequate this may seem to us). The opposing view, that people receive in their own lifetimes only and exactly what their deeds warrant, is in the nature of an intellectualistic and schematic formula useful (then as now) for moral exhortation but hardly the unanimous view of the culture. The narratives of the Hebrew Bible are generally subtler, more lifelike, and more cognizant of tragedy than the mechanistic view of deed and consequence that so many scholars (and not a few laypeople) take to constitute "the standard Israelite canons of justice and retribution." Cases like those of Abel, the prophets of the LORD in Elijah's time, and Naboth all demonstrate that in pre-exilic narratives, the righteous will of God could triumph, justice could be done, and the hapless victim vindicated, all without the need for the dead to be compensated or revived.

To be sure, the question of the suffering of the righteous and the prosperity of the wicked came to attract increasing attention over the centuries. The book of Job, for example, deals with an innocent sufferer whose experience dramatically refutes the mechanistic theology that holds that one always and only gets what one deserves. Similarly, the book of Qohelet (or Ecclesiastes), one of the latest books in the Hebrew Bible, is troubled by the fact that "the same fate is in store for all: for the righteous, and for the wicked; for the good and pure, and for the impure" (Qoh 9:2). In the case of Job, however, it is surely relevant that the restoration occurs before death — or, to be more precise, before Job's own death, since, as we saw in Chapter 6, the seven sons and three daughters who die in the prologue never come back but are only replaced in the epilogue by new children in the same numbers (Job 1; 42:13–15). In general, what Job seems to want, even in the poetic dialogues, is not so much a new lease on life, as vindication — a divine act of justice that will clear his record (for example, Job 23:2–7). In this, the underlying assumption is not so far from those of the narratives about Abel and Naboth that we have examined.

The same cannot be said for the book of Qohelet, which casts into grave doubt the belief in a personal and just God who providentially directs the destinies of nations and individuals and who restores innocent sufferers like Job. For Qohelet, rather, "God" refers to an inexorable and ultimate fate unresponsive to human action and thus human merit. This is indeed a frontal assault on the previous thinking, but it should not go missed that Qohelet has a resolution of his own to the problem. What he counsels is not the abandonment of religious norms or a life of unreflective hedonism, as one might expect. Instead, he thinks that a happy life is possible even with all the limitations that follow from the absence of a personal, intervening deity, including the greatest limitation of them all, the finiteness of human existence evidenced in the certainty and inexorability of death (for example, Qoh 11:9–12:8). We have no real basis on which to claim that Qohelet influenced Judaism during the period in which the belief in resurrection was emerging to any significant degree. But even were we to grant that the book of Qohelet exerted great influence on the literature of its time, we should still have to wonder why its challenge had to be answered but its own resolution of it rejected.

If the authors of Job and Qohelet could do without an expectation of resurrection, why should we assume that they made it impossible for Jews of later times to do so?

Finally, we must note one other logical difficulty with the claim that the theological problem posed by innocent victims and triumphant victimizers is the mother of the belief in resurrection. If the inner logic of Jewish theology necessitated the belief, why did so many Jews at the time not accept it? For example, as is well known, the Sadducees rejected it outright:

and as we shall see in the next chapter, early rabbinic Judaism condemned without ambiguity those who denied it or denied that it would be found in the Torah, obviously indicating that a group large enough to draw the condemnation existed. It is, of course, often difficult in the extreme to reconstruct the thinking of those branded as heretical, since it is their opponents who have usually left the descriptions of them, but it does seem likely that in this case they continued to adhere to the older and supposedly discredited theology. In that theology, God's promises are reliable and his justice sure, but, as we have explored in previous chapters, they apply to groups (especially families) and to history rather than to individuals and their personal destinies.

One finds no better example of the survival of the older model into the period when an expectation of resurrection is first clearly attested than in the Wisdom of Joshua Ben Sira (also known as Sirach or Ecclesiasticus), a Jewish composition from the early second century B.C.E. that nowadays is part of the Roman Catholic and Eastern Orthodox Bibles but not the Jewish Bible. Ben Sira's counsel is that we neither give up the expectation of retribution nor expect it to occur postmortem, except in the destinies of the descendants (for example, Sir 11:26–28). Given this familial orientation, we should not be surprised to find that for Ben Sira, retribution is not only for the individual, but also for the nation:

> [23]May he give us gladness of heart,
>> and may there be peace in our days
>> in Israel, as in the days of old.
> [24]May he entrust to us his mercy,
>> and may he deliver us in our days! (Sir 50:23–24)

Like the book of Daniel, Ben Sira harbors a hope for the restoration of Israel. Indeed, the verses that follow express contempt for three traditional enemies of the Jews (Sir 50:25–26), beginning with the Edomites, whose downfall has eschatological connotations in the Hebrew Bible. Yet here, too, there is no sense that God's intervention involves any resurrection whatsoever. The older pattern survives.

What cases like Ben Sira indicate is that it is a mistake to attribute the emergence of an expectation of resurrection to a logical problem that only the new belief could solve. On the contrary, however unpersuasive the older theology represented (with some new twists) by Ben Sira may seem today, it continued to hold the allegiance of many then. There was nothing inevitable about the rise of the expectation of resurrection.

"OH, LET YOUR DEAD REVIVE!"

We have been examining the formidable logical obstacles to the idea that the martyrdom of faithful traditionalists under Antiochus IV in the years 167–164 B.C.E. accounts for the expectation of resurrection. Had we only Dan 12:1–3, which has been securely dated to that period and reflects its salient events, the explanation would, to be sure, have a certain historical plausibility. Even then, however, one would have to pay attention to the longstanding tradition that the God of Israel is a God of life, not death; nothing historical emerges in a vacuum. When we go outside the current Jewish canon, however, we find that predictions of resurrection and a last judgment already appear in literature that is generally thought to predate those events. The reports of some of the cosmic journeys of the ancient sage and visionary Enoch are relevant here, for example, his journey to the high mountain in which "the spirits of the souls of the dead should assemble . . . until the date of their judgment" (1 Enoch 22:3–4). As in Daniel, so here, the context of resurrection is forensic. It is one of judgment and vindication, in which the wicked and the righteous finally receive their just deserts, of which they were apparently deprived in their lifetimes. Here again, there is continuity between the envisioned resurrection, a relatively new phenomenon, and the older and well-attested concern for a posthumous vindication of the innocent and punishment of the wicked.

Although Dan 12:1–3 was surely the first passage in what is now the canonical Bible to speak unambiguously of a judgment on those raised from the dead, the idea was already present in apocalyptic Jewish circles beforehand and cannot be attributed to the immediate situation of the martyrs in Antiochus' persecutions of 167–164 B.C.E.

In the case of Daniel, the resurrection and judgment occur within the framework of the eschatological restoration of Israel: "At that time, your people will be rescued" (Dan 12:1). The different verdicts rendered to the righteous and the evil hardly constitute a new idea: that "the LORD watches over all who love Him, / but all the wicked He will destroy" (Ps 145:20) is a principle ubiquitous in Israelite literature of various periods and genres. Dan 12:1–3, in common with much Second Temple literature, applies the same principle to the restoration of Israel. The "people will be rescued," but the wicked among them — those who have not acted as the Jewish people ideally acts — will awaken to disgrace, and not to life everlasting. The double resurrection may be relatively new, but the duality of divine judgment is not.

Even the idea of national resurrection is not quite so new in the second century B.C.E. as is often claimed. Apart from Ezekiel's vision of the dry bones (which we examined at length in Chapter 8), one finds an anticipation of Dan 12:1–3 in a text from Isaiah on which the latter manifestly depends:

> Oh, let Your dead revive [*yichyu*]!
> As a corpse they shall arise [*yequmun*]
> Awake [*haqitzu*] and shout for joy,
> You who dwell in the dust ['*aphar*]! —
> For Your dew is like the dew on fresh growth;
> You make it fall on the land of the shades [*repha'im*]. (Isa 26:19)

The verse occurs in a section of the book of Isaiah (chaps. 24–27) that is widely and reasonably believed to date from a relatively late period, surely in the time of the Second Temple. The focus of these chapters, called the "Isaianic Apocalypse," is thoroughly eschatological, fixed firmly on the frightening yet (for some) joyous events about to dawn. As Brevard S. Childs puts it, Isaiah 26 "offers a great variety of conventional forms, but in the end it results in a highly theological presentation directed to the faithful, who testify to the effect of God's victory, yet still experience the full weight of divine and human judgment." Thus, a few verses before ours, the poet can speak of the final, irreversible punishment of masters other than his own, and in language that anticipates our verse. The coming revival of the dead is the mirror image of the fate of the idolatrous lords whom the true Lord has dispatched:

> ¹³O LORD our God!
> Lords other than You possessed us,
> But only Your name shall we utter.
> ¹⁴They are dead, they can never live [*yichyu*]:
> Shades [*repha'im*], they can never rise [yaqumu];
> Of a truth, You have dealt with them and wiped them out,
> Have put an end to all mention of them. (Isa 26:13–14)

Yet just afterwards, the poet can liken his community to a woman "writhing and screaming in her pangs"; it is "as though we had given birth to wind [and] won no victory on earth" (Isa 26:17–18). As is generally the case in apocalyptic literature, the era of affliction and tribulation—though still in force—is not ultimate. The last word of the God of life is not death and sterility at all, but revival and "fresh growth," the awakening of the dead to new life on analogy to the new life that dew brings forth in the fields. The end of the chapter nicely captures the complex temporal situation:

> [20]Go, my people, enter your chambers,
> And lock your doors behind you.
> Hide but a little moment,
> Until the indignation passes.
> [21]For lo!
> The LORD shall come forth from His place
> To punish the dwellers of the earth
> For their iniquity;
> And the earth shall disclose its bloodshed
> And shall no longer conceal its slain. (Isa 26:20–21)

The connections of these three passages in the book of Isaiah to the prediction of resurrection in Dan 12:1–3 are obvious. Like the latter passage, Isa 26:19 speaks about an awakening (*heqitz*) to life (*chayah*) of those in the dust (*'aphar*). If one reads the verse in conjunction with Isa 26:13–14, the second passage above, then it, too, depicts a judgment, contrasting those who rise to live again with those whom God has wiped out so that "they can never live." To be sure, Isaiah 26 gives no indication that this latter group will "awake" to punishment, but the notion of contrasting verdicts and a revival of the faithful is prominent therein nonetheless. It accords well with the stirring words of the same section of the book of Isaiah about the fate of death itself:

> He will destroy death forever.
> My Lord GOD will wipe the tears away
> From all faces
> And will put an end to the reproach of His people
> Over all the earth—
> For it is the LORD who has spoken. (Isa 25:8)

The mention of "the reproach of His people" demonstrates the historically particular circumstance to which the oracle speaks. But that alone does not require us to read the allusion to the destruction of death as only metaphorical. Rather, it would seem that death (which here quite possibly refers to a Canaanite god by that name, Mot) is one of the enemies, or even the ultimate enemy, of the people of God, and no victory of that God can be complete until this lethal foe is finally eliminated. The ultimate victory of the God of life, which is also the definitive manifestation of his power, requires the elimination of his great foe, death.

Scholars have debated whether the revival described in Isaiah 24–27 is a true resurrection of the sort that Jews and Christians later anticipated or, instead, only a metaphor for national recovery, the restoration of the humbled and afflicted people Israel. Do the same individuals come back to life, as in Dan 12:1–3, or do these texts simply predict a miraculous change in the historical fortune of the nation, as in Ezek 37:1–14? Our judgment is that the cry "Oh, let Your dead revive [*yichyu*]!" in Isa 26:19 suggests something closer to the image in Daniel, but the texts are ambiguous and the argument will just as surely continue. What is not ambiguous is that Dan 12:1–3 echoes and reuses these texts—texts that give every sign of being earlier than the persecution of the martyrs at the hands of Antiochus IV—in its own prediction of the great reversal to come. The rhetoric and the image of resurrection and a last judgment existed in Jewish culture well before that persecution, and the date at which an expectation of an eschatological resurrection and judgment first appeared remains shrouded in mystery. The likelihood is that the expectation of a resurrection of the dead did not appear suddenly and in response to a particular crisis. Rather, it grew slowly over the centuries, nourished by the power of earlier biblical texts of the sort we have been discussing.

THE DEEPER ROOTS OF RESURRECTION

We have now established that the first universally acknowledged reference to a general resurrection of the dead in the Hebrew Bible (Dan 12:1–3) is itself a passage rich in allusions to earlier texts. However new the belief may have been in the second century B.C.E., when that passage was written, its phrasing looks back to multiple scriptural antecedents. One important antecedent lies in Isa 52:13–53:12, which speaks of the vindication and restoration of the servant of the LORD, so despised in his life, so humiliated in his death. Another lies in the Isaianic Apocalypse (Isaiah 24–27), which speaks of violent changes about to occur, specifically the resurrection of the dead when the season of national affliction finally passes and the yearned-for resurrection comes about (Isa 26:19). Historians of biblical literature tend to date both these texts to a relatively late period, the end of the Babylonian Exile (about 540 B.C.E.) or the early Second Temple period (late sixth or early fifth centuries B.C.E.).

In fact, we can push back further than the immediate antecedents of Dan 12:1–3, tracing the antecedents of the antecedents, as it were. In the case of Isa 26:19, the most revealing source lies in Hosea 13–14. The British scholar John Day has identified fully eight parallels between this verse (or its surroundings in the Isaianic Apocalypse) and these chapters. More pertinent to our discussion are the passages in Hosea 13–14 that speak of a redemption from death, such as 13:14:

> From Sheol itself I will save them,
> Redeem them from very Death.
> Where, O Death, are your plagues?
> Your pestilence where, O Sheol?
> Revenge shall be far from My thoughts.

In idea, though not in wording, this famous verse recalls the affirmation of (or prayer for) resurrection in Isa 26:19, which drew our attention above and in which the revivifying role of dew ("For Your dew is like the dew on fresh growth; / You make it fall on the land of the shades") recalls, in turn, another nearby text in Hosea:

> [5]I will heal their affliction,
> Generously will I take them back in love;
> For My anger has turned away from them.
> [6]I will be to Israel like dew;
> He shall blossom like the lily,
> He shall strike root like a Lebanon tree. (Hos 14:5–6)

The opposite of this healing, life-giving substance is a "blast, a wind of the LORD" that, as Hosea puts it, "shall come blowing up from the wilderness," parching Ephraim's fountain, drying up his spring, and plundering his treasures (Hos 13:15). Similarly, the Isaianic Apocalypse speaks of "His pitiless blast [that] bore them off / On a day of gale" (Isa 27:8). In each case, Day points out, the imagery of the "destructive east wind [is] symbolic of exile."

The representations of redemption in the two texts also display a remarkable resemblance, in Day's view. For example, the imagery of "Israel blossoming and like a vineyard" appears prominently in both (Hos 14:2–9; Isa 27:2–6). Of the eight parallels between Hosea 13–14 and Isaiah 26–27 that John Day develops, some are surely more compelling than others. But whatever the weakness of some of Day's parallels taken individually, the sheer density of them in a delimited corpus is highly curious and suggests that Hosea 13–14 has indeed had an influence to one degree or another on Isaiah 26–27.

The theme of death and resurrection, it turns out, is much more prominent in Hosea than these parallels with Isaiah 26–27 would indicate. Day makes a strong case for the influence of two earlier chapters in Hosea (chaps. 5–6) on chapters 13–14, in turn, and these are replete with images of death and resurrection into life. Many scholars have argued, to be sure, that the pertinent texts in Hosea 5–6 refer not to resurrection, but only to recovery from illness. God does not revive here; he only heals. If so, then Hosea 13–14, too, can hardly be put onto a trajectory that results in the Jewish belief in a resurrection at the end of days. In the ancient context, however, the difference between those actions, reviving and healing, is not so great. As we had occasion to note in Chapter 3, death in the ancient Near Eastern world was often conceived as a disease — the most serious disease, to be sure, and seldom, if ever, curable — but a disease nonetheless. Michael Barré has put it well: "For the ancient Semites, life and death were not contradictory categories, but simply the opposite ends of a continuum; hence, to bring a dead person back to life would represent only a further step to healing a gravely ill person." In defense of the notion that Hosea 5–6, and therefore chapters 13–14 as well, speak of the healing of death rather than of a lesser disorder, Day draws attention to two key verbs — "revive" and "raise up" in English — in Hos 6:2:

> In two days He will revive us [*yechayyenu*]
> On the third day He will raise us up [*yeqimenu*],
> And we shall live [*nichyeh*] in His presence.

"All the other places in the Old Testament where these two verbs (*chayah* and *qwm*) appear as word pairs," he maintains, "the meaning clearly relates to resurrection, not simply healing." Furthermore, the image Hosea uses for God's action in inflicting the malady to be reversed is clearly one of nothing less than killing: "I, I will attack and stride away, / Carrying the prey that no one can rescue"; "[I] have slain them with the words of My mouth" (Hos 5:14; 6:5).

In short, Hosea's addressees are dead, and the healing for which they pray and that God ultimately promises to grant them is a restoration into life — deliverance from Sheol, redemption from death.

To us, of course, they are not really dead at all. If they were, how could they say, in Hosea's hearing, that "in two days He will revive us"? Once again we confront a key difference between ancient and modern perceptions of the basic categories of life and death. Our modern conception of death as totally discontinuous with life impels us to understand the community's condition as one of grave affliction and debility only, and thus to interpret the unmistakable language of resurrection as thoroughly metaphorical. If so, it is, however, still a metaphor founded on the conviction that the literal referent is, however miraculous, indeed possible in the hands of God. What in Hosea's experience could have generated that conviction? Perhaps it stemmed from traditional affirmations of the LORD's unlimited power, which, precisely because it is unlimited, extends to death as to life (for example, Deut 32:39; 1 Sam 2:6). Why, after all, should almighty God be able to heal all illnesses but death? Or perhaps Hosea's conviction stemmed from folklore of the sort represented by the three resurrections that came about through his fellow northern prophets, Elijah and Elisha (see Chapter 7). In truth, we need not choose between these alternatives (and others that can be suggested), for all of them attest to the possibility that death might indeed be reversed, and its victims miraculously revived. That the dead in question are the Israelite community, not the separate and distinct individuals within it, means less in context than we first think.

The claim that Hosea's use of death and resurrection is metaphorical is thus only partly true. For in the prophet's understanding, Israel sinning has indeed died, losing fertility and vitality along with its identity as the loyal covenant partner of the LORD. If the subject is the Israelites as atomized individuals, the language of resurrection is highly metaphorical. If the subject is the people Israel in their collective, national life on their land, it is less so. And, once again, if death encompasses such phenomena as drought, infertility, famine, and defeat, and life encompasses their opposites, then the language of death and resurrection in the book of Hosea is not metaphorical at all.

THE VICTORY OF THE DIVINE WARRIOR

The dichotomy of death and new life is actually widely attested in the Hebrew Bible. It is best known from a pattern that has come to be called that of the "Divine Warrior." In this pattern, God marches out to battle against a formidable foe, and, in Frank Moore Cross's words, "Nature convulses (writhes) and languishes when the Warrior manifests his wrath." When he has won his victory and has been gloriously enthroned on his holy mountain, however, "Nature again responds. The heavens fertilize the earth, animals writhe giving birth, and men and mountains whirl in dancing and festive glee." The natural order, in other words, reflects and manifests the mode of divine activity. When God is angry, it loses its vitality and fertility, dying for a season, as it were. When God has triumphed and received the glory that is his due as universal king, the natural order again responds, this time with new life, fertility, and luxuriance. Contrary to a common stereotype, the religion of Israel did not effect a radical separation between history and nature or pit the God of history against nature. Quite the opposite: the order that we call "nature" (a term with no counterpart in biblical Hebrew) is closely bound up with God's action in history, and when his kingship, so often challenged in history, is finally secure, nature flourishes richly along with the human community that does his will:

> [11]Let the heavens rejoice and the earth exult;
> let the sea and all within it thunder,
> [12]the fields and everything in them exult;
> then shall all the trees of the forest shout for joy
> [13]at the presence of the LORD, for He is coming,
> for He is coming to rule the earth;
> He will rule the world justly,
> and its peoples in faithfulness. (Ps 96:11–13)

What we (but not the ancient Israelites) dichotomize as history and nature are simply two dimensions of the same reality, a reality that answers to the mode of divine activity at the moment—the mode of anger and death or the mode of deliverance and life. But in the Divine Warrior these two modes are more closely related, and the inner life of the deity less dichotomous than first seems the case. For the anger of the Divine Warrior is often a righteous anger, a reaction, that is, to injustice, and thus a sign of imminent deliverance to its victims.

The term "Divine Warrior" is misunderstood if it first calls to mind the all-too-familiar world of violent religious fanaticism, in which believers kill for the greater glory of their God (and a better chance to enjoy the sensory delights of paradise). For the focus of the literature about the Divine Warrior in the Hebrew Bible does not lie primarily on the destruction of the enemy. It lies, rather, on the enthronement of God in righteousness and justice, the longed-for arrival of the one who "will rule the world justly / and its peoples in faithfulness." In the Hebrew Bible, and more generally in the ancient Near East, the just rule of the king is inseparable from his deliverance of the weak and victimized from the stronger hand of the oppressor. In the "festive glee" with which human beings and nature alike respond together to the Divine Warrior's victory, one can thus usually detect a markedly ethical dimension. Indeed, few things are more characteristic of the Israelite idea of the Divine Warrior than the confidence of the beleaguered and oppressed loyalists that their divine patron will not prove impotent in the face of the challenge and allow his justice and his power to be discredited. When at last he manifests his long-acclaimed power, the effects are felt not only in the social realm (with the establishment of justice) but also in the natural realm in which desiccation and languishing yield to revitalization and health.

We find the same language of desiccation and languishing, on the one hand, and vitality and flourishing, on the other, in some passages that contrast the faithless and idolatrous person with the opposite, the one who trusts the LORD above all:

> 5Thus said the LORD:
> Cursed is he who trusts in man,
> Who makes mere flesh his strength,
> And turns his thoughts from the LORD.
> 6He shall be like a bush in the desert,
> Which does not sense the coming of good:
> It is set in the scorched places of the wilderness,

In a barren land without inhabitant.
⁷Blessed is he who trusts in the LORD,
Whose trust is the LORD alone.
⁸He shall be like a tree planted by waters,
Sending forth its roots by a stream:
It does not sense the coming of heat,
Its leaves are ever fresh;
It has no care in a year of drought,
It does not cease to yield fruit. (Jer 17:5–8; compare Psalm 1)

Here we must cite the important observation of Leonard J. Greenspoon: "the state of the wicked is precisely that of nature at the time the Divine Warrior marches off to combat his foes. The righteous man, on the other hand, is like an ever-verdant tree firmly established and continuously nourished by waters which stand as the source of life against any onslaught that threatens the vitality and growth of nature. . . . The return of the Divine Warrior brought just such fertility and blossoming forth throughout nature."

In this case, we must reckon with a whole set of interlocking dualities: the Divine Warrior challenged/the Divine Warrior victorious; nature dying/nature revitalized; the wicked and faithless individual/the ethical and loyal individual. Inasmuch as the campaign of the Divine Warrior in Israelite religion is, in large part, in the service of justice and righteousness, we should hardly be surprised that those who practice that same ethic and put God first in their lives (which are really the same thing) experience the fruits of his victory in their own individual destinies, unfazed by the heat that destroys the faithless.

In Jer 17:5–8, enhanced or diminished vitality—one either flourishes like a luxuriant tree or atrophies before the force of the elements like a bush in the desert—depends upon the quality of one's life. Jeremiah does not, of course, envision a resurrection or a last judgment and different verdicts for the righteous and the evil, to be sure. His vision suggests, instead, something more akin to the perpetual youthfulness and fertility of those who have tasted of the Tree of Life. The biological character of his metaphor is striking: "Its leaves are ever fresh . . . It does not cease to yield fruit." But the moral dimension must not be missed, for Jeremiah's vision does render different judgments on the worthy and the unworthy, and it is life with which the worthy are rewarded.

If we take into account the complex of images that has come to be known as the Divine Warrior, this difference between enhanced vitality and resurrection into eternal life (and, for that matter, between diminished vitality and everlasting humiliation) contracts markedly, though it does not disappear. It will be recalled that when the Divine Warrior marches forth in wrath against the oppressive forces of chaos and death, nature languishes, and when he returns enthroned in victory and justice, nature flourishes and luxuriates. A good example of this pattern appears in Isaiah 34–35, each chapter of which represents one of these two moments. In chapter 35, which represents the flourishing of nature in response to the LORD's deliverance, we read not only of the blooming of the desert and the like (vv 1–2), but also, and more importantly for our purposes, of the miraculous reversal of human infirmities:

> 5Then the eyes of the blind shall be opened,
> And the ears of the deaf shall be unstopped.
> 6Then the lame shall leap like a deer,
> And the tongue of the dumb shall shout aloud;
> For waters shall burst forth in the desert,
> Streams in the wilderness.
> 7Torrid earth shall become a pool;
> Parched land, fountains of water;
> The home of jackals, a pasture;
> The abode [of ostriches], reeds and rushes. (Isa 35:5–7)

Here, we see not just the transformation of uncultivated territory hostile to human habitation into well-watered farmland, but also a kindred and equally miraculous healing of human disabilities. The blind shall see, the deaf hear, the lame leap, and the mute sing. In a world like ours, which has witnessed advances in surgery and medication that would have been classified as science fiction only a few decades ago (think of gene therapy), these transformations doubtless seem less amazing than they did to the prophet's original audience. Similarly, the experience of the past two centuries may cause us to underrate the impact of the transformation of the desert into a blossoming garden and the appearance of a highway in it for the ransomed to traverse on their return to Zion (Isa 35:1–2, 8–10). We can too easily forget that the fertilizers and pesticides that have vastly increased agricultural production, and the explosives and other engineering advances that have enabled mountains to be leveled and huge canals to be built did not exist in the prophet's world. For him and his audience, all these transformations were equally miraculous, equally inconceivable apart from the triumphal advent of God.

What is missing in Isaiah 35 is the healing of another disorder, the greatest of all—death. We term it a "disorder" because, as we have seen and many scholars have remarked, the ancient Israelites generally conceived death as a disease. To us, who have as yet found no way to reverse death, the omission comes as no surprise. Surely this is the one disease that is intractable! It is highly unlikely, however, that the ancient Israelites saw the matter in such a naturalistic manner. To them, all these transformations, whether of deserts or mountains or unjust fates or human disabilities, were equally impossible and equally exceptional. Or, to put the point positively, all of these reversals were equally exceptional: if they were to take place at all, they would have to take place by the special intervention of the Divine Warrior, for whom (so the liturgies affirmed) no obstacle was too great, no exception impossible to accomplish. The ancients saw the blind recovering their sight, the deaf their hearing, the lame their ability to leap like a deer, and the mute their ability to sing as often as we have seen the dead recover their lives. Such was the state of medicine at the time. All of these reversals are the rarest of exceptions (on that ancient and modern can agree); to those of little faith, they are mere fantasies and impossibilities. But within the complex of ideas associated with the Divine Warrior, they were all equally to be expected when the omnipotent redeemer at long last comes in justice and victory. If this is so, then the absence of mention of resurrection in Isaiah 35 is not so important, and the presence of resurrection in the related texts of Isaiah 24–27 is not so unparalleled, as first seems the case. That the all-powerful God of deliverance "will destroy death forever" and revive the dead, to revert to texts we have already examined (Isa 25:8; 26:19), is readily understandable in the context of stupendous reversals that characterized the victory of the Divine Warrior. Within this scenario of exceptions, resurrection was hardly exceptional.

SUMMARY: OLD AND NEW IN RESURRECTION

Having traced the antecedents of the expectation of a general resurrection of the dead in the form in which it appears in Dan 12:1–3, we are now in a position to summarize the results and draw conclusions. The central concern of Dan 12:1–3 is twofold: the rescue of the Jewish people from their oppression and the vindication of those who held fast to the tradition against those who cast their lot with the foreign tormentors. The notion of a full vindication that takes place after death was already ancient, and in no sense strange, at the time this text appeared. What was new (relatively speaking) is the participation of the deceased righteous in their own posthumous vindication and, correlatively, of the wicked in their posthumous condemnation.

Both groups (or representative samples of them) now rise from the dust in which they have been "sleeping" to confront either eternal life or unending disgrace, as befits their conduct while alive. The vindication of righteous individuals no longer takes place only in a historical reversal in which they, now deceased, cannot participate, nor does it come about solely in the lives of their future descendants. Indeed, in the apocalyptic thinking that is the immediate matrix of the belief in resurrection, the old notion of a fortunate death, which we developed in Chapter 4, has no place. The condemnation of the wicked no longer involves their simply ceasing to exist or their being dispatched to Sheol, never to rise from there. Now both groups awake from death, but to different verdicts.

Among the immediate antecedents of Dan 12:1–3 is Isa 52:13–53:12, which seems to speak (admittedly with considerable obscurity) not only of the postmortem vindication and exaltation of a faithful but mistreated servant of the LORD but also of his being awarded new life in the process. It is evident that the vision in Daniel identifies the righteous of its own time of persecution with the servant of that text and sees the language of healing and restoration after death therein as references to resurrection. The vindication of the servant takes place against the denigration and mistreatment of him by others, to be sure, but the latter do not rise from death to face any punishment (indeed, their death forms no part of Isa 52:13–53:12 at all). Rather, the servant, like the "wise" of Daniel 12, "makes the many righteous" (Isa 53:11; compare Dan 12:3), changing their behavior by some unspecified process, perhaps prophetic preaching.

The interaction of individuals and the community is, in fact, essential to the expectation of resurrection as it appears in Daniel 12 and in subsequent Judaism as well. For resurrection is part of a larger scenario of national deliverance in which God at long last makes good on his promises to his people Israel. It is, in short, inherently historical and communal in character, and little or no light is shed on it if it is subsumed under the familiar, self-interested question, "How can I attain life after death?" This historical and communal dimension appears in bold relief in the dependence of Dan 12:1–3 on passages from the Isaianic Apocalypse (Isaiah 24–27), especially Isa 26:19, which speaks of those "who dwell in the dust" awakening with shouts of joy when God finally redeems them from their longstanding suffering and despair. This happy event, in turn, follows upon the LORD's astonishing victory over his foes, including death itself, which he destroys "forever," wiping away tears and "put[ting] an end to the reproach of His people" (Isa 25:8). It is possible, of course, to interpret this language of the joyful awakening of the dead and the destruction of death as only metaphorical for the restoration of Israel and the establishment of its collective security. Even so, one has to concede that Daniel 12 did not so interpret it, and if the author or authors of Isaiah 24–27 thought resurrection literally impossible, their choice of it as a metaphor for the national resurrection that they fully expected was highly inappropriate and self-defeating.

In the background of this application of resurrection language to Jewish national restoration lies the idea that the advent and presence of God not only brings about deliverance for his people; it also revitalizes nature, bringing life-giving moisture to desiccated land and fertility to dwindling flocks and herds. But, as we have noted, the dichotomy of history versus nature is alien to the Israelite worldview and productive of much modern confusion. Thus, a prophet like Hosea (whose oracles influenced Isaiah 24–27) can describe Israel after its revival in terms of luxuriant nature. In response to the LORD's life-giving dew, the people blossom like the lily and strike root like a great tree, giving forth a fine fragrance (Hos 14:2–9). The new life is a correlate of the renewed relationship between God and his people that human repentance and divine grace conjointly bring about. The flourishing of nature (including human vitality) is the normal state of affairs when Israel is faithful to the LORD's covenant with them.

Behind all these older biblical antecedents of the prediction of resurrection in Dan 12:1–3 lies, in turn, the momentous Israelite transformation of the myth of the Canaanite god, Baal. In the Canaanite version, Baal dies, a victim of deified Death (Mot), in the hot, dry summer; nature dies with him. But Death is, in turn, killed; Baal lives anew; and nature flourishes and luxuriates in response. Israelite culture (at least as reflected in the Hebrew Bible) adapts this model to a theology centered on the LORD's relation to the people Israel in history. He is the living God and never dies, but Israel's own fortunes dwindle and revive in relation to their distance from or nearness to him. When they are distant from him, or he from them, they sicken and perish. When they reapproach him in repentance, or he returns to them in deliverance, they revive and flourish. In the vision of texts like Dan 12:1–3, when at last the victorious king arrives to "rule the world justly" (Ps 96:13), the victims of the era of injustice will surely receive their due. But the origin of the idea of God's dramatic intervention and its inversion of the standing world order does not lie simply in the embarrassment caused by the deaths of the Jews martyred by the Seleucid king Antiochus IV at the time the book of Daniel was composed.

Each of the several elements that appear in Dan 12:1–3 existed, at least germinally, in earlier stages of the religion of Israel, though their combination and fusion are relatively new and distinctive. They point forward to the Pharisaic and rabbinic doctrine of resurrection (and to their Christian counterpart) as much as they recall their ancient forebears. In addition, however, some scholars have long argued that Zoroastrianism, the religion of the Persian Empire, played a key role in the development of the idea of a resurrection of the dead in Second Temple Judaism. For Zoroastrian theology also spoke of an eschatological victory of truth over falsehood, of light over darkness, and of life over death, the last, importantly, involving a literal reviving of dead bodies. This eschatology has obvious and striking connections with Jewish apocalyptic in general, and with the expectation of resurrection as it appears in books like Enoch and Daniel in particular. Indeed, since the Persians controlled the Land of Israel from their defeat of the neo-Babylonian Empire in 539 B.C.E. until their own demise at the hands of Alexander the Great two centuries later, it is hard to believe that they exerted no influence at all on Judaism of the period.

In the case of resurrection, however, any such influence seems to have been quite distant, a matter of milieu rather than of direct borrowing. For, as John Day points out, the idea that the dead shall awaken from their graves is hard to square with the fact that the Zoroastrians neither buried their dead nor spoke of resurrection in the language of waking. These practices, Day stresses, are found in Canaanite tradition, however. It would seem that at most the force of Zoroastrian eschatology nudged Judaism along in its movement toward a belief in the future resurrection of the dead. If Jewish apocalyptic is the parent of the expectation of a general resurrection, then Zoroastrian theology (which probably influenced the development of apocalyptic in Jewish circles) is at best the grandparent. If, however, our argument that the notion of the Divine Warrior is the most important influence on the expectation in question, it would be better to describe Zoroastrian theology as at most a collateral relation whose influence is indirect.

When the belief in resurrection finally makes an unambiguous appearance in Judaism, it is thus both an innovation and a restatement of a tension that had pervaded the religion of Israel from the beginning—the tension between the LORD's promise of life, on the one hand, and the reality of death, on the other. In the case of resurrection the last word once again lies not with death—undeniably grievous though it is—but with life. Given the reality and potency ascribed to death throughout the Hebrew Bible, what overcomes it is nothing short of the most astonishing miracle, the Divine Warrior's eschatological victory.

THE LEAST KNOWN TEACHING
IN JUDAISM

"POWERFUL TO SAVE"

In the hands of the figures who shaped rabbinic Judaism in the first few centuries of the common era, the expectation of resurrection that had made its first unambiguous biblical appearance in Daniel 12 became a defining doctrine of Judaism. A highly liturgical religion, whose forms of worship are regulated by religious law, rabbinic Judaism early on gave the doctrine of resurrection a central place in its daily worship. Consider the second benediction in the prayer known variously as the *Amidah* ("The Standing Prayer"), the *Tefilla* ("The Prayer," par excellence), or the *Shemoneh Esreh* ("The Eighteen Benedictions"):

You are mighty forever, my Lord. You are the one who revives the dead, powerful to save.

(You make the wind blow and the rain fall.)

He sustains the living with kindness and revives the dead with great mercy, supports the falling, heals the sick, releases captives, and keeps faith with those who sleep in the dust.

Who is like You, Lord of power? And who can compare to You, O King who brings about death and restores life and makes salvation sprout?

Faithful You are to revive the dead. Blessed are You, LORD, who revive the dead.

According to rabbinic law, this ancient prayer is to be said three times each weekday; four times on Sabbaths, new moons, and festivals; and five times on the Day of Atonement. There is never a day—never a morning, never an afternoon, never an evening—without it. The prayer is thus as authoritative a summary of rabbinic theology as one can find, and its second benediction endorses the idea of resurrection repeatedly and emphatically: "revives the dead" (four times), "keeps faith with those who sleep in the dust," "brings about death and restores life." Known as *Gevurot* ("Power"), the benediction sees in God's revival of the dead the outstanding and incomparable instance of his might. It is the definitive proof of God's power. The other affirmations of his assistance to those in need—his support of the falling, his healing of the sick, and his release of prisoners—are enclosed within an envelope-like structure that begins and ends with an address to the God of Israel as the one who resurrects.

When precisely the resurrection takes place the benediction does not specify. The mention of God's power "to save" and especially the phrase "makes salvation sprout" suggests that the miraculous revival forms part of an eschatological scenario. Later on, following a precedent from the Hebrew Bible (for example, Jer 33:15), the fifteenth benediction of the same prayer will use the language of "sprouting" to refer to the expected messianic king, "the Branch of David"—an unmistakable allusion to the end-time restoration of the people Israel after their long degradation. We cannot say, however, that Gevurot asserts that God's assistance to the falling, ailing, and imprisoned is a constant and reliable reality in the present order of things. Surely, its authors, like the authors of the scriptural texts from which they draw their language, knew that some who fall do not rise, illnesses are often progressively debilitating and ultimately fatal, and many who are incarcerated will never leave prison alive. The likelihood, therefore, is that the atemporal language of the benediction (which speaks in participles rather than finite verbs) affirms that God's deliverance may occasionally be witnessed in the present dispensation but will become fully manifest and unassailable only at or after the messianic consummation. What it affirms, in other words, is not that we can rely upon God to prevent our falling, illness, imprisonment, and death but that he has the power to reverse these painful conditions and will eventually prove faithful to his promise to do so.

That God has, in fact, made a promise to the dead and can be trusted to keep it becomes evident from the two instances of the root *'mn* (used of words indicating faithfulness or trust, such as *'amen*) in the benediction.

The first, reflecting the language of the eschatological resurrection predicted in Dan 12:1–3, speaks of God's "faith with those who sleep in the dust." What is new here, over against the scriptural base, is the affirmation of God's faithfulness (*'emunato*). Here, the reference is not to the believer's faith in God, but to God's faithfulness to raise to life those who, as Dan 12:2 puts it, "sleep in the dust of the earth." The same idea appears in the penultimate affirmation that "Faithful (*ne'eman*) You are to revive the dead." Here again, the people praying are only indirectly affirming their own faith that the omnipotent deity will perform an act of resurrection. That which they directly affirm is God's fidelity or faithfulness to do so. God can be trusted to keep faith even with the dead.

In sum, Gevurot, the second benediction of the Amidah, affirms simultaneously the cold, hard, unavoidable reality of death and the unshakable trust that God will revive the dead in the eschatological future. It thus stands among the multitude of texts in the Hebrew Bible (whose language it continually adopts) that maintain that although bad things do indeed happen to good people, they are not the last word. The last word, rather, is a good thing—in this case God's miraculous intervention into history to grant the dead of all generations new life as he finally secures his triumph over evil and suffering and establishes on earth the kingdom over which he already reigns in the higher realm.

In this view of things, death does not lose its reality or its grimness but only its finality. Its continued existence constitutes a standing reproach to the God who "keeps faith with those who sleep in the dust" and yet allows them to do so, having (to all appearances) quite forgotten his promise of life. In this way, death must be seen as an opponent of the living God whose faithfulness to his promises will not be self-evident until death is vanquished and eliminated. Yet the theology that underlies Gevurot is far from dualistic. For the same God who is "powerful to save" and "faithful to revive the dead" is also the "king who brings about death"—in other words, death's own author, the One who gives life but also withdraws it. Death, no less than life, is part of God's plan, but it is—or can be made into—only one stage of the plan, and not the last. The gracious king who gives and withdraws life will give it again.

Gevurot leaves open a question that readily occurs to us. What is the fate of the dead before they are resurrected? The identification of them as "those who sleep in the dust" tempts us to say that they are not really dead at all, but only asleep, enfolded in God's protective grace until they are at last revived. The temptation is best resisted. For neither in the Hebrew Bible nor in rabbinic literature is sleep seen as such a benign state. It is more than occasionally associated with death, as it is here, just as waking up is associated (in both literatures) with resurrection. And "dust," not a pleasant place to sleep under the best of circumstances, recalls the LORD's sentence upon Adam that he shall

> . . . return to the ground—
> For from it you were taken.
> For dust you are,
> And to dust you shall return. (Gen 3:19)

But we also should not conclude that the Gevurot benediction relegates the dead to oblivion until the day of their restoration into life. For they do still exist at least in the mind of the God who faithfully remembers his promises to them and will bring about their redemption, and nothing in Gevurot should be taken to imply that the dead lack souls that survive the demise of their bodies. The point, rather, is that neither the soul alone nor the body alone constitutes a full person. As we have argued in Chapter 5, a stark dichotomy between the resurrection of the dead and the immortality of the soul is overdone. A firm belief in the resurrection of the dead does not at all entail a disbelief in the immortality of some aspect of the person or in the notion that the departed righteous even now enjoy a blissful communion with God. The point is, rather, that whatever notions of the soul circulated in ancient Judaism, in rabbinic theology God was not thought to have fulfilled his promises until the whole person returned, body included. Like death, a disembodied existence was deemed to be other than the last word, for the person is not "the ghost in the machine" (that is, the body) but rather a unity of body and soul. A parable in the Talmud makes the point brilliantly:

> Antoninus [a Roman emperor] said to Rabbi [Judah the Patriarch]: The body and the soul can both exempt themselves from judgment. How? The body can say, "The soul sinned. For from the day it separated itself from me, I lie like a mute stone in the grave." And the soul can say, "The body sinned. For from the day I separated from it, look, I am flying in the air like a bird."
> He [Rabbi] said to him: I'll give you a parable. What does this resemble? A

human king who had a beautiful orchard that had beautiful figs in it. He appointed two watchmen, one lame and the other blind. The lame man said to the blind man, "I see beautiful figs in the orchard. Come, lift me up on your shoulder so that we can get them to eat." The lame man mounted onto the blind man, and they got the figs and ate them. After some days, the owner of the orchard came and said to them, "The beautiful figs—where are they?" Said the lame man to him, "Do I have feet to walk with?" Said the blind man to him, "Do I have eyes to see with?" What did he do? He lifted the lame man onto the blind man and judged them together. Thus will the Holy One (blessed be He!) bring the soul and put it into the body and judge them together, as it is said:

> He shall summon the heavens above
> and the earth, to the judgment of His people (Ps 50:4).

"He shall summon the heavens above"—this is the soul. "And the earth, to the judgment of His people"—this is the body.

The parable asserts that the person can indeed be resolved into two components, body and soul, but with one major qualification: separated, body and soul are each defective, handicapped, as it were, and if the person is to be fully human, they must be reunited. Another rabbinic text views the separation and reunification of the two components as a daily occurrence. This is a prayer that the Talmud ordains a Jew recite upon waking:

> My God, the soul You placed within me is pure. You created it in me, You breathed it into me, You preserve it within me, and You will eventually take it from me and put it back into me in the Time-to-Come. So long as the soul is in me, I give thanks to You, LORD, my God and God of my fathers, Master of all worlds and Lord of all souls. Blessed are You, LORD, who puts souls back into dead bodies.

Here, sleep is seen as an anticipation of death, and people pre-enact daily the awakening into life that awaits the righteous in the end time when the God who "keeps faith with those who sleep in the dust" restores them to life.

It is important to remember that the duality of body and soul that pervades rabbinic literature is actually something of a departure from the way the Hebrew Bible habitually views the matter. In the Hebrew Bible, the word *neshamah,* translated in the parable and the prayer above as "soul," usually means "breath." The notion of a soul that survives the death of the person and awaits its reentry into his or her body is quite foreign to the Hebrew Bible (it does not, for example, appear even in the prediction of resurrection in Dan 12:1–3). It does, however, have strong affinities with the thinking about the soul (*psuché, anima*) in the Greco-Roman cultural world in which the early rabbis lived. Here again, we must note an important qualification: the Greek and Roman discussion of life after death did not focus on a restoration of the body but only on the immortality of the soul. The idea of a reunion of body and soul testifies to the influence of Greco-Roman thought on the rabbis but also and equally to the rabbis' fidelity to their biblical heritage.

AN OBLIGATION, NOT AN OPTION

The Mishnah, the great law code of rabbinic Judaism (compiled about 200 C.E.), defines belief in the resurrection of the dead as a requirement of Judaism:

All Israelites have a share in the World-to-Come, as it is written:

> And your people, all of them righteous,
> Shall possess the land for all time;
> They are the shoot that I planted,
> My handiwork in which I glory. (Isa 60:21)

And these are the ones who do not have a share in the World-to-Come: He who says that the resurrection of the dead is not in the Torah, [he who says] that the Torah is not from Heaven, and the skeptic.

Rabbi Akiva says: Also he who reads in the outside books, and he who utters an incantation over a wound, saying, "I will not bring upon you any of the diseases that I brought upon the Egyptians, for I the LORD am your healer" (Exod 15:26).

Abba Saul says: Also he who pronounces the Name according to its letters.

This mishnah begins on an inclusive note, promising all Jews a place in the World-to-Come. The prooftext, Isa 60:21, is highly appropriate here because it speaks of the people as "all of them righteous" and thus eligible for survival, and its language of inheriting the land can, in the rabbinic mind, easily suggest taking rightful possession of the future world. The mishnah's inclusive language must not, however, be taken as an indication that the rabbis affirmed no standards for admission to it or failed to link behavior to salvation. Like any genuine inclusiveness, the position of the mishnah can be distinguished from relativism or cheap universalism by its specification of a control on the inclusion. And certain positions do indeed exclude a Jew from the World-to-Come. Those listed are the position that denies that the resurrection of the dead can be found in the Torah; the one that denies that the Torah is of divine origin; and that of the "skeptic" ('*apiqoros*), an umbrella term that seems to indicate one who denies the basic elements of rabbinic belief, most centrally the belief in divine providence and justice. To those guilty of these offenses, Rabbi Akiva adds those who read "the outside books," almost certainly noncanonical Jewish works (perhaps liturgically) and those who use a text from the Torah as a medical incantation. Another rabbi, Abba Saul, adds those who pronounce the four-letter name of God according to its written form, instead of substituting a euphemism, as rabbinic law requires.

A Tanna (that is, an early rabbi) found it eminently fitting that the first exception to the rule that "all Israelites have a share in the World-to-Come" should be "he who says that the resurrection of the dead is not in the Torah":

> And why so much? A Tanna taught: He denied the resurrection of the dead. Therefore he shall have no share in the resurrection of the dead. For all the measures [of retribution] of the Holy One (blessed be He!) operate on the principle that the consequence fits the deed.

As phrased in the mishnaic text, however, the heretic in question did not deny the resurrection of the dead at all, but only its presence in the Torah. In fact, in some versions the word "in the Torah" is missing, and surely this latter version is the one that the Tanna quoted above presupposes. The wording that adds the phrase "in the Torah" has a somewhat different focus. It seems to be directed against two positions that were associated with the Sadducees, who were in opposition to the Pharisees, the group out of whose traditions it is widely believed rabbinic Judaism eventually developed. According to the Acts of the Apostles in the New Testament, "the Sadducees say that there is no resurrection, or angel, or spirit; but the Pharisees acknowledge all three" (Acts 23:8). Early rabbinic literature says much the same thing about the Sadducees but also speaks of their rejection of the Oral Torah transmitted by the rabbis themselves. By branding as heretical anyone who "says that the resurrection of the dead is not in the Torah," the Mishnah challenges the Sadducees (or some later group with the same theology) on their own turf. The argument thus rests not on oral tradition, but on the text of the Torah. The challenge that remained for the rabbis — and a formidable challenge it was indeed — was to find allusions to the resurrection of the dead in the Torah.

One strategy they employed was to give a future interpretation to verses that seem at first glance to speak of past events. What results, to put it kindly, is some highly imaginative exegesis. For example, the preface to the Song of the Sea reads:

> Then ['*az*] Moses and the Israelites sang [*yashir*] this song to the LORD. (Exod 15:1a)

The *Mekilta de-Rabbi Ishmael*, an early midrash collection on parts of Exodus, observing correctly that "sometimes the word 'then' ['*az*] refers to the past and sometimes to the future age," places our verse in the former category: at that moment, having crossed the sea, Moses and the Israelites sang the ensuing celebratory hymn. Rabbi Judah the Patriarch, redactor of the Mishnah, dissents:

> "Then Moses sang [*shar*]" is not written here, but rather "Then Moses will sing [*yashir*]." Thus we are instructed that the resurrection of the dead can be derived from the Torah.

Rabbi Judah the Patriarch's dissent is premised upon an understanding of a particular point of Hebrew grammar, one that changed in the transition from the biblical language to the rabbinic. One need not know Hebrew to understand the gist of his interpretation. In rabbinic Hebrew, the form of the verb in question would not be used to indicate the past tense. In biblical Hebrew, in contrast, the matter was more complicated, and after certain words, '*az* ("then") being one of them, that same form often (but not always) did refer to the past. The rabbi's point is that if the Torah wanted us to understand Moses' singing as having already occurred, it would have used the form that in his time serves as the regular form for past-tense narration. But it did not, and the singing in question thus must refer to the future—to a time, that is, after Moses had already died and, if the verse is to be proven true, had already been resurrected as well!

This interpretation makes for exceedingly bad philology, to be sure, but also for rich and powerful theology. For it places the celebratory hymn in the eschatological future, and in so doing, it presents the resurrection of the dead as a radical reversal of the sort attested in the other verses that use "then" (*'az*) in an eschatological sense listed in the *Mekilta*. These verses speak of Israel seeing and "glowing" as the wealth of nations passes to them and their Temple (Isa 60:5); of the light of redemption bursting upon them, as the LORD comes to their rescue and vindication (58:8); of the lame leaping like a deer (35:6); of the eyes of the blind being opened and the ears of the deaf unstopped (35:5); of maidens dancing gaily when God has turned "mourning to joy" (Jer 31:13); and of Israel's mouth being filled with laughter and the nations saying, "The LORD has done great things for them!" (Ps 126:2).

In short, Rabbi Judah the Patriarch's interpretation places the resurrection of the dead squarely in the context of the restoration of Israel in the end time. Whereas a plain-sense reading of the Song of the Sea views it as a celebration of Israel's redemption from Egypt, vindication over their oppressors, and miraculous passage through the sea, in his reading, it celebrates an even greater redemption, an even greater vindication, and an even greater and more miraculous passage: the redemption of the dead, the vindication of the righteous, and the passage from death to life. The exodus has become a prototype of ultimate redemption, and historical liberation has become a partial anticipation of eschatological liberation, a token, perhaps the token of things to come. What God did in the biblical past has been transformed into a sign of the still greater things he will do in the future consummation—a consummation that moves the Jews not merely from slavery to freedom, but quite literally from death to life as well.

Beneath this last transformation lies a conviction that the classical forms of both Judaism and Christianity hold passionately. As long as human beings are subject to death, they are not altogether free. A liberation that results only in social and political betterment is, in this view, sadly inade-

quate. Resurrection is not only the ultimate liberation; it is the only liberation that is complete.

To moderns given to historical thinking, Rabbi Judah the Patriarch's
reading of Exod 15:1a represents a thoroughgoing reinterpretation of the
biblical text and testifies to the change that the introduction of the doctrine
of resurrection brought about in Judaism, a change so great that it required
a reinterpretation of the Hebrew Bible itself. To the rabbi, however, his
reading involves no reinterpretation and no recognition of historical development. He claims the grammar of the verse supports his interpretation of
it as proof that the Torah testifies to the resurrection of the dead. This example, connecting as it does with several deep themes in Jewish thought,
involves more theological profundity than most, but it is only one of several
attempts in rabbinic literature to show that the Torah endorses resurrection, or, to put it differently, that resurrection is not a sectarian tenet of the
rabbinic party (or their Pharisaic predecessors), but an intrinsic element of
the Mosaic legacy of the whole House of Israel.

The Talmud, too, asks the question, "How do we know that the resurrection of the dead can be derived from the Torah?" One answer:

> From the verse, "and from them you shall bring the gift for the LORD to
> Aaron the priest" (Num 18:28). Did Aaron exist forever? Was it not the case
> that he never entered the Land of Israel; and yet the gift should be rendered
> to him? Rather, it teaches that he will be resurrected and Israel will give him
> the gift. Hence, resurrection of the dead can be derived from the Torah.

Aaron, it will be recalled, was the older brother of Moses and the ancestor of the hereditary Jewish priesthood (*kohanim*). Here, the point is simply
that an enduring commandment to bring sacrificial offerings to Aaron
makes no sense after Aaron's death, which took place even before the Temple was built. Thus, the text in Numbers, if it is to apply at all today, must
predict his return from the dead. This, of course, leaves open the question
of just who is to receive those gifts in the interim. Thus, it is not surprising
that immediately after this proof we find the comment of the School of
Rabbi Ishmael that "'to Aaron' means 'like Aaron,'" that is, to a priest with
certain qualifications, of whom Aaron, the ancestor of all priests, is the
Torah's paradigm.

The same objection can be raised against another proof on the same
page in the Talmud:

Rabbi Simai says: How do we know that the resurrection of the dead can be derived from the Torah? From the verse, "I also established My covenant with them [that is, Abraham, Isaac, and Jacob], to give them the land of Canaan" (Exod 6:4). "To you" is not written but "to them." Hence, resurrection of the dead can be derived from the Torah.

It is striking that the gospels of Matthew, Mark, and Luke report that Jesus used the same appeal to the patriarchs to argue for the resurrection of the dead against the Sadducaic opponents of the doctrine:

[31]And as for the resurrection of the dead, have you not read what was said to you by God, [32] "I am the God of Abraham, the God of Isaac, and the God of Jacob"? He is the God not of the dead, but of the living. (Matt 22:31–32, quoting a version of Exod 3:6. Compare Mark 12:26–27 and Luke 20:37)

This, along with other pieces of evidence that we need not develop here, suggests that Jesus had close affinities with the Pharisaic Jewish sect, which emphatically endorsed the doctrine of resurrection, as did the rabbis after them. The idea that Jesus' faithful followers would rise from the dead may seem odd to those who identify Judaism with the Hebrew Bible/Old Testament. For that set of books, as we have seen, did not in the main endorse a belief in individual resurrection at all—if, that is, one reads them according to their simplest and plainest sense. But if one reads them according to the Jewish conventions of interpretation of the time, one can easily see how even the book of Exodus could be seen to support the controversial doctrine of resurrection.

How can God fulfill his covenantal promise to give the land to the patriarchs if they have already died? Only, Jesus and Rabbi Simai maintain, by raising them from the dead. Here, the exegesis is vulnerable to the same point that the School of Rabbi Ishmael scored about the use of "Aaron" in Num 18:28. The covenantal promise was made to Abraham, Isaac, and Jacob but will be fulfilled only to those who are like them, that is, to their descendants, who bear their name and continue their identity. This interpretation, in fact, accords well with the original promise of land to Abraham in Genesis: "I will assign this land to your offspring" (Gen 12:7). As far as the Hebrew Bible goes, it would be most unwise to make a sharp division between Abraham and his descendants as the recipient of the promise.

In silently presuming exactly such a division, Rabbi Simai, for all his rooting in ancient exegetical practice, is thus in one important way more modern than biblical. For, as we saw at length in Chapter 6, the Hebrew Bible is comfortable in describing national history as biography in ways that are baffling to the modern mind (including even modern religious traditionalists). Given this biblical concept of the self, Rabbi Simai's logic fails. God can surely give the promised land to Abraham, Isaac, and Jacob after they are dead without resurrecting them, for the people that carries their blood, bears their name, and reenacts their experience (in part) still lives and is still able to experience the fulfillment of the promise.

How then shall we take the rabbinic insistence that a doctrine of general resurrection appears in the Torah? The interpretations on which the rabbis base this insistence are surely forced. But here we must remember that we are dealing with midrash, a form of biblical interpretation that does not hold the plain sense highest but rather aims for a more imaginative—and, to the rabbis, a more spiritually profound—sense of the scriptural verses. Given the playfulness of midrash and the joy it takes in multiple meanings, it would be dangerous to assume Rabbi Judah the Patriarch, Rabbi Simai, or others who propounded similar interpretations intended their readings to be exhaustive and exclusive. It is difficult to imagine, for example, that Rabbi Judah the Patriarch thought that the Song of the Sea had actually not been sung after the miraculous crossing at all, but would only be sung after Moses and the Israelites of his generation were resurrected at the end of time. The likelier interpretation is that he understood and accepted the plain-sense reading of Exod 15:1a (that is, the reading that accords with the biblical verbal system) but saw in the verb *yashir* (sang/will sing) a hint of another, more encompassing meaning, one focused on the future rather than on the past redemption. The plain-sense interpretation proved less worthy of comment, not only for the obvious reason that it is the plain sense, but also for the more important reason that it lacked the capacity to advance the rabbinic case in the argument against the Sadducees or others who denied that God would revive the dead.

In sum, the rabbis defined the expectation of resurrection that they inherited from their Second Temple predecessors as an obligatory item of Jewish belief and required that it be reaffirmed in prayer every day, repeatedly. Like their contemporaries, the church fathers whom we shall discuss in the next chapter, the rabbis saw in the future resurrection of the dead proof positive of the power of God and his faithfulness to his promises.

However unlikely it may seem now, they insisted, the Lord of power would prove faithful to revive the dead when he at long last fulfilled his promises to the Jewish people and redeemed the world.

DOUBTS AND REFORMS

For many centuries, the prominent place that the affirmation of an eschatological resurrection held in the classical Jewish liturgy ensured that the doctrine would be known among Jews with even the most minimal acquaintance with their religion. The fact that almost all Jewish communities lived under Christendom or Islam, two traditions that also affirmed resurrection in the end time, further lessened the chance that the traditional Jewish doctrine would be challenged.

The challenge that did appear, such as it was, came from philosophy. Philosophers, at least from the time of the ancient Athenian Plato, had long been concerned with the nature of the soul, with the question of what in the human was immortal and what was not. Resurrection of the dead derives from a different family of concepts. It comes, as we have seen, not from philosophy but from scripture; resurrection will occur, so the religious traditions that affirm it teach, by the act of a personal God miraculously redeeming and transforming the world, including human nature. It was perhaps inevitable that there would be some clash between what we might call (with all due caution) the Hebraic and the Hellenic, or the biblical and the philosophical dimensions of the Jewish heritage, and this became acute for the first time in the Middle Ages. In particular, the great twelfth-century Sephardic philosopher and legal authority Maimonides advanced the idea that the part of the person that survives death is the acquired intellect. For only this dimension of the self is not dependent upon the body in any way but instead comes directly from God. The absolutely incorporeal deity, in other words, has created an equally incorporeal dimension of the human self that is, or can become, invulnerable to the forces that bring about bodily death.

The implications are as clear as they are heterodox: the hereafter is indeed real, but it is a matter of the intellect alone and thus utterly devoid of any bodily dimension. Thus, Maimonides wrote, "In the World-to-Come, there is no body or corporeality, but only the souls of the righteous without bodies, like the ministering angels." And he interpreted the Talmudic claim that the righteous will there "enjoy the radiance of the Divine Presence" to mean "that they know and apprehend something of the truth of the Holy One (blessed be He!) that they do not know when they are in their murky and lowly bodies." Here we see a great Jewish authority endorsing not only the high estimation in which some Platonic philosophers had long held the mind and the soul but also the low estimation in which they held the body. In the minds of some of his contemporaries, Maimonides had strayed into heresy.

In his response to his critics, the *Treatise on Resurrection*, Maimonides insisted that they had badly misunderstood him. He had never denied the resurrection of the dead, "for such a denial . . . leads to the denial of all miracles (chronicled in the Bible) and the denial of miracles is equivalent to denying the existence of God and abandonment of our faith." His point, he claimed, was that resurrection is only the penultimate stage in the attainment of everlasting felicity. "Those individuals whose souls return to their bodies (after death) will eat and drink and engage in sexual intercourse and sire children and die after an extremely long life like the life that will exist during the days of the Messiah." Those resurrected, in other words, will undergo a second death, from which they will never rise in bodily form. Rather, they will then and only then enter into the complete felicity of the World-to-Come, transfigured into angel-like beings capable at last of comprehending divine truths in ways they never could when they were embodied.

The effect of Maimonides' doctrine of a second death was to uphold the traditional belief in resurrection while at the same time rendering it superfluous. To be sure, his affirmation is consonant with rabbinic theology on the face of the matter: God resurrects the dead because he promised he would, and anyone who denies that he can accomplish this miracle doubts the power of God. The problem, however, is that once accomplished, the miracle is undone, as the beneficiaries return eventually to the dust anyway, with only their intellectual faculty surviving for all eternity. This is not only a drastic departure from the traditional rabbinic doctrine, as Maimonides' critics pointedly noted. It is also a contrived and uneconomical scenario that gives the appearance of being devised simply to free its inventor of the suspicion of heresy. Some have even wondered whether Maimonides fully believed it himself. For our purposes, the key point is that he had to issue the clarification, and affirm bodily resurrection, at all. His doing so testifies to the enormous power of the rabbinic teaching, and of the rabbinic liturgy in which it is so central, over the Jewish people in the Middle Ages.

So why does the idea that Judaism once insisted on the resurrection of the dead come as a surprise today even to many committed Jews? What has changed in modern times?

The major change has been widespread skepticism about the one who performs the expected resurrection—the personal, supernatural God, the God of Abraham, Isaac, and Jacob, who intervenes in the course of human and natural events and brings about results that are otherwise impossible. The tendency among many modern people, certainly including modern Jews, has been either to doubt all claims of the existence of God or to redefine God so that the word refers to human ideals and feelings alone and not to the source of miraculous acts and providential guidance. In short, in the modern world, the idea of a God who does things has become highly problematic. And whatever else one may say about a God who does not do anything, one thing is sure: he does not resurrect the dead. To Jews who subscribe to this modern transformation of the understanding of God (not all modern Jews do or ever did, of course), the wording of the Gevurot benediction of the Amidah is, of course, a major challenge. In Maimonides' day, the text of the traditional prayer book was sacrosanct, protected by Jewish law (*halakhah*), as it still is for Orthodox Jews. But beginning about two hundred years ago, some Jews called for revising the prayers in order to make them reflect modern ideas and sensibilities, and, predictably, the traditional affirmation of resurrection was a prime candidate for revision.

Neil Gillman identifies "three possible [Jewish] strategies for handling a liturgy that no longer reflects your theology: replace the Hebrew with a more palatable alternative; keep the Hebrew text and shade the translation to accommodate your new interpretation of the doctrine; or provide options which allow the worshipper to choose a text that reflects his or her particular belief." Gillman points out that the great scholar and early exponent of Reform Judaism Abraham Geiger (1810–74) explicitly wrote that the concepts of afterlife appropriate to modern Jews "should not be expressed in terms which suggest a future revival, a resurrection of the body; rather they must stress the immortality of the human soul"—a view widely held in his time. In consequence, Geiger's own German translation of the close of Gevurot rendered it, "who bestows life here and there"—"a vaguely-worded promise of eternal life," as Gillman puts it, and hardly an affirmation of resurrection.

Later Reform prayerbooks have tended to follow the lead of another important figure in early Reform Judaism, David Einhorn (1809–79), who served the movement first in Germany and then in the United States. Advocating the "replac[ement of] the doctrine of resurrection with 'the idea of a purely spiritual immortality,'" Einhorn closed his Hebrew version of the Gevurot not with the classical expression, "[You] who revive the dead," but with another traditional liturgical affirmation, the benediction that closes with the words, "Who has planted immortal life within us." This both removes the scandal of resurrection and transfers the focus of immortality from Torah to something ostensibly more universal, creation itself. This upholds God's miraculous power—for what could be more miraculous, more contrary to biology, than "immortal life"?—but it relegates the miracle safely to the primordial past and removes any expectation that something analogous to it will occur in the eschatological future.

The best-known and longest-lasting Reform prayerbook, *The Union Prayerbook* (1895), pursued several strategies to affirm the continued existence of the dead while sidestepping the rabbinic expectation that they will be miraculously revived. "Only the body has died and has been laid in the dust," reads one of its prayers. "The spirit lives in the shelter of God's love and mercy." Here, immortality of the soul is affirmed along with the implication that the body will stay in the dust. Not only is resurrection nowhere to be found, but even immortality has, in comparison with the classical rabbinic ideas, been massively redefined and drastically curtailed. It lacks a crucial element in the classical vision of God's postmortem involvement with human beings—the element of reward and punishment, which secures in the future life the justice of God so often and so mysteriously absent in this one. In sum, this formulation not only excludes the element of the re-creation of the whole person, body and soul; it also excludes the exercise of divine mercy and judgment upon the dead. As we have seen, all of these points had been central to the classical rabbinic teaching.

The *Union Prayerbook* followed Einhorn's lead in altering the Hebrew as well as the English translation of resurrection so as to vitiate the unpalatable doctrine without openly negating it. Instead of "You are the one who revives the dead" (*mechayyeh metim 'attah*), for example, it substitutes "Thou preservest all" (*mechayyeh hakkol*), thus retaining but also retranslating the Hebrew verb and changing its object as well. The wording leaves open the possibility that God's preservation extends beyond the grave but stops well short of affirming that it does. Even if this possibility is accepted, however, the substitution of "preserve" for "revive, give life to" makes it difficult to conceive the afterlife in question as the result of God's supernatural intervention to reverse death and establish his longed-for justice. The image, instead, is one of a smooth and uneventful continuation of the this-worldly scenario in which God "sustains the living." Death makes so little difference it can be safely left out. Things continue almost as if it does not happen. In fact, the two movements evident in this text from the *Union Prayerbook* are implications of each other. Since death is no great source of grief—divine sustenance continues whether it happens or not—its reversal in the joy of resurrection or immortality can be safely minimized as well.

Gillman points out that the successor to the *Union Prayerbook*, the *Gates of Prayer* (5735/1975), "adopts the more recent practice of providing several options for the evening and morning service," only one of which, however, retains the traditional Hebrew formulation, *mechayyeh metim*, "Who revive the dead." Even this it renders, however, in a very strange way indeed:

> We pray . . . for love through which we may all blossom into persons who have gained power over our own lives."

This wording subordinates the traditional affirmation of resurrection at the beginning of Gevurot to the affirmation immediately preceding it that God "sustains the living with kindness." The objectionable Hebrew phrase, though retained, is now reinterpreted to refer to God's role in aiding human self-empowerment. The dead have disappeared altogether, and resurrection has been redefined as "power over [one's] own life." The inversion is striking: an ancient acclamation of divine power in the face of ultimate and inescapable human defeat has been transformed into a thoroughly modern prayer for enhanced personal autonomy.

At the end of the same blessing, the blurring of the Hebrew is even more thoroughgoing:

> Praised be the God whose gift is life, whose cleansing rains let parched men and women flower toward the sun.

In this metaphor, the dead are "parched men and women" who are like vegetation in need of watering, resurrection is rainfall, and the new life that follows is a flowering in the presence not of God, but of the sun. Whatever poetic resonance this English prayer possesses (or lacks), it continues the older Reform strategy of evading the affirmation of the resurrection of the dead, though in the more moderate form that retains the very Hebrew that the English evades. In this case, however, the English does not seem to substitute immortality, as earlier Reform translations did, but defines God's action in strictly this-worldly terms—as directed toward human self-empowerment and refreshment, metaphorically conveyed by reference to the revival of plants that, unlike the people about whom the ancient blessing spoke, have not died.

The implication of these various Reform adaptations of the classic rabbinic liturgy—that Judaism in the aggregate is agnostic on the question of the resurrection of the dead—is one that the rabbis who authored Gevurot would have abhorred. One can affirm it or one can deny it, without loss. The choice is one of personal preference. A similar equivocation to those in the Reform prayer books can be found in the versions associated with the Conservative movement. Speaking of one influential volume, Gillman (himself an exponent of Conservative Judaism) notes the "predilection for the second strategy for handling troublesome liturgical passages: wherever possible, retain the Hebrew but shade the English translation to reflect a more modern sensibility." Thus, the *Sabbath and Festival Prayer Book* (1946), which dominated Conservative worship for nearly four decades, defends its translation this way: "The rendering of the phrase *mehayyai hameitem* 'who calls the dead to life everlasting' is linguistically sound and rich in meaning for those who cherish the faith in human immortality, as much as for those who maintain the belief in resurrection." *Siddur Sim Shalom*, which replaced the *Sabbath and Festival Prayer Book* and is now widely used in Conservative services, follows a similar tack when it renders the closing words of Gevurot as "Master of [or over] life and death." "Puzzling enough," Gillman remarks, "the phrase immediately preceding the closing benediction is translated as 'Faithful are You in bringing the dead to life again,' or as 'Faithful are You in giving life to the dead.'" The solution to the puzzle most likely lies in one of two places: ambivalence in the translators themselves or disagreement among them. Either way, the easiest approach was to allow both options to stand.

Whereas in Maimonides' time the wording of the ancient prayers protected the vulnerable doctrine of resurrection and set limits on how far it could be reinterpreted, in modern times the prayers themselves have been changed so as to weaken the suspect doctrine. Gevurot, long the testimony par excellence to the infinite power of God, has become evidence for modern doubts about the whole idea of an all-powerful deity.

As a result of this move, Judaism once again appears agnostic on the issue of whether the mode of existence in the afterlife is one of a disembodied spirit or of a restoration of the full person, body and soul. What had been a central affirmation and defining doctrine of the community has become a personal choice. Jews seeking guidance from the prayer book (the most general and familiar source of instruction in Jewish belief) on how to choose wisely are thrown back upon their own lights. In the modern cultural environment of secularity and in the absence of the countervailing force of religious teaching, their own lights are overwhelmingly likely to lead them to doubt or neglect the resurrection of the dead and, ultimately, to think that Judaism never taught such a thing. And that, in fact, is precisely the situation that now prevails.

This loss of contrast between Judaism and secularity is complemented by a heightened, but spurious, contrast between Judaism and Christianity on the issue of resurrection. Given the central place of the reports of Jesus' resurrection in Christian theology, especially its classical creeds (see Chapter 1), it is harder for Christians than for Jews to minimize or neglect resurrection. Continued Christian belief in resurrection has often served in Jewish minds to fuel a contrast between an other-worldly and superstitious Christianity, on the one hand, and a this-worldly, socially responsible, and progressive Judaism, on the other. In short, in modern times, some Jewish apologists have sought to position Judaism as the more modern and thus the more desirable of the two religions, further strengthening the erroneous claim that the Jewish tradition has no important teaching about the resurrection of the dead.

Christians who think such a teaching to be indispensable can, in turn, find in this very claim evidence for the theological and spiritual shallowness of Judaism, a religion that cannot reckon with the most profound dimension of the human condition. Or, believing, as Christians traditionally have, that the hope for resurrection depends upon faith in Jesus, they take the putative absence of resurrection as empirical proof of their own theology. And so it goes . . .

In this book, we have sought to counter such old apologetics and polemics and to replace them with a more accurate description of the role of the resurrection of the dead in Judaism and Christianity in antiquity. Christianity inherited its expectation of a future resurrection from certain forms of Judaism, as we have seen, and in the early centuries of the common era, groups that would have enormous influence over the subsequent shape of the traditions sought to define that expectation as a necessary affirmation. In this chapter, we have seen how the early rabbis did so; in the next chapter, we shall examine their Christian counterparts and contemporaries.

WHAT WAS WRONG
WITH THE GNOSTIC GOSPEL?

SKEPTICS AND HERETICS

At the same time the early rabbis were defining the resurrection of the dead as an indispensable requirement of Judaism, Christian teachers were doing the same thing for their own tradition. As we saw in Chapter 2, as early as the time of Paul some Christians doubted the reality, or even the possibility, of resurrection. That doubt persisted within some Christian communities at least until the time the Gospel of John was written (around 100 C.E.). We know this because, in that gospel, one of the apostles, Thomas, is depicted as doubting the claim of the other apostles that Jesus had risen and had appeared to them (Thomas was absent at the time of the initial appearance). Only if he were able to see and feel the crucifixion wounds, Thomas said, would he believe that Jesus had risen with visible, tangible postmortem flesh. Only with the second appearance of Christ to the apostles and the invitation to Thomas to touch the wounds of Christ (as well as Jesus' admonition to "stop doubting") could "Doubting Thomas" be brought to believe (John 20:24–29).

Whatever the historical truth of this story, John put it into his gospel in order to affirm belief in the bodily resurrection of Jesus. He directed it against those who doubted. Our best guess is that those who doubted were a community, the "Thomas Community," that produced, among other things, the Gospel of Thomas, an early Christian book that is not part of the Bible of the church. We know little about this community. It seems clear, however, that they doubted that Jesus rose in the flesh. John uses

Thomas in order to speak to this community and to persuade them to surrender their doubts. One of his cleverest moves was to put the proclamation of belief in the physical resurrection on the lips of Thomas, the very apostle around whom the opposed (and, he thought, wayward) community was formed. For that community, no higher apostolic authority could be imagined. The author of the fourth gospel hoped that Thomas' declaration of faith in the physical resurrection would cause them to move, as had Thomas, from skepticism to belief.

The so-called Thomas Community was likely a part of a larger movement in the early church whose views on the nature of Christ, both before and after his resurrection, are sometimes called "docetic." Their name deriving from a Greek work meaning "to seem" or "to appear," docetic Christians believed that matter and spirit could not coexist. In this view, it only *seemed* as if Christ's humanity were real. Indeed, in this view it would have been impossible for the heavenly Son of God to have taken on flesh, either at his birth or after his death. Docetic Christians usually assumed that the heavenly Christ merely inhabited or used the body of the man Jesus, or that his flesh was simply an optical illusion. In either case, they could not imagine that a heavenly emissary could truly have united himself to flesh.

As we move into the second and third centuries, this docetic view of Christ was absorbed as a central article of belief by a loosely related group of teachers and their churches usually described by the shorthand word "Gnostic." (The "Gospel of Judas," which has received so much coverage in the media recently, was in all probability produced by and for a Gnostic group.) Until fairly recently, it was difficult to say much about these teachers and groups. A collection of their writings was, however, discovered in 1946 in Nag Hammadi in Egypt, and after making its way through the market in antiquities, it has been analyzed very closely. These documents, when compared and synthesized with documents produced by the emerging orthodox wing of Christianity, can tell us quite a lot about Gnosticism and its teachers.

DUALISM

There is no single representative Gnostic teacher or school. It is not certain how many people whom modern scholars call Gnostics would have embraced the term. Nonetheless, those called Gnostics by contemporaries and modern scholars were fairly well represented and influential in certain parts of the ancient world, and their teachings did often contain common elements. For our purposes, it is important only to observe that, in almost all cases, Gnostic teachers emphasized the incompatibility of matter (including flesh) and spirit. For this reason, they are sometimes called "dualists." Matter they regarded as the creation of a lower, malevolent deity, whom they typically associated with the God of the Jews; spirit they associated with a higher deity, the God of Jesus Christ. The point of the "knowledge" imparted by Gnostic teaching (for *gnosis* is simply the Greek word for knowledge)—for Christian Gnostics by Jesus Christ, the apostles, or one of their teachers—is to show the elect how to escape the evil material creation for their heavenly, spiritual home. Given this devaluation of the physical world, it will come as no surprise that no Gnostic is known to have proclaimed a physical resurrection. Basilides, a Gnostic teacher from Egypt active early in the second century, is reported to have asserted, "Salvation belongs to the soul alone" (Irenaeus, *Contre les heresies* [*Adversus Haereses, AH*] 1.19.3). Similarly, a Roman Gnostic, Valentinus, is supposed to have declared, "it is impossible that material substance should partake of salvation" (*AH* 1.1.11). Indeed, dualist teachers and adherents regarded such a proclamation as the product of an overly literal mind and scorned Christian believers in it. Valentinus apparently called such believers, for their supposedly crude simplicity, "animal men," "utterly contemptible and ignorant" (*AH* 1.1.11–12). Generally confirming the orthodox reports, Gnostic sources themselves regard with contempt the ignorant Christians who believe in the physical resurrection. The Gnostic Gospel of Philip, found at Nag Hammadi, says: "Those who say they will die first and then rise are in error." Most Gnostic texts also rejected the future dimension of the resurrection. In *The Treatise on Resurrection*, an anonymous document also discovered at Nag Hammadi, "resurrection" is imagined as a present experience, a "disclosure," or moment of enlightenment. In addition, this was a secret, esoteric experience only available to a few, as Valentinus pointedly maintained. Salvation, then, for the Gnostic devotee consisted in the liberation of the spiritual, immortal soul from the evil material realm, including the body. There was emphatically no future, bodily dimension involved.

One second-century figure who fell under the influence of dualistic and docetic modes of thought was a man named Marcion (who lived, roughly,

110–160). In his career as an ecclesiastical organizer, theologian, and agitator, Marcion generated a lot of heat and many opponents, as well as many sympathizers. A wealthy man, he developed something like a parallel church of his own in the Mediterranean (after having been excommunicated twice, once by his father in Asia Minor and once by the church of Rome).

Marcion attracted the ire of the orthodox for several reasons. He drew an especially sharp distinction between the teachings of the Hebrew Bible and those of Christ. In his work *The Antitheses*, he juxtaposed, as his title suggests, what he took to be the contradictory propositions of each of the two testaments of the Christian Bible. He was determined to prove that the Law was discontinuous with the gospel and that, taken together, they revealed a duality of deities. In his mind, one, the God of the Old Testament, represented justice and justice alone; the God of Jesus Christ, on the other hand, was a God of mercy.

In order to justify this (again dualistic) theology, Marcion rejected almost all of the books that finally made it into the New Testament. He would accept as authentic only the Gospel of Luke and ten of what he took to be the authentic letters of Paul. Even these he edited heavily, for they of course presumed continuity between the story of Israel and that of the church. He dismissed such a presumption as the interpolating work of "Judaizers" or the apostles, who failed to understand that Jesus was not the promised Jewish messiah. Thus he purged these passages when drawing up his own biblical books and canon. Anything that alluded to, resonated with, or was expressly invoked to connect to the grand story of the Hebrew Bible he simply expunged. Given his views on the incompatibility of flesh and spirit, he simply cut out most of the beginning of Luke, which places Jesus' birth in the context of Israelite salvation history and most certainly sees Jesus as an embodied, fleshly being. Not surprisingly, Marcion also omitted the accounts of Jesus' resurrection. Thus, to the docetism and dualism of the wider Gnostic movement, he added an explicitly anti-Jewish element. The orthodox church could not accept any of these three, and in fact explicitly rejected them not simply as erroneous or false but as heretical and dangerous.

For writers in the emerging orthodox Christian tradition, the Gnostic message in fact constituted a profound threat to the proclamation of the gospel. If Christ had not truly taken on a body, he had not redeemed embodied human beings. As they commonly observed, what Christ had not assumed, he could not heal or save. Accordingly, bodies would not be redeemed if Christ did not assume true flesh. In addition, orthodox Christians could not accept the separation that the Gnostics posited between the "Jewish" creator God and the redeeming God of Jesus. Sharing the account of creation in Genesis with its Jewish authors (and with the Jewish people), Christians identified the creator of the world as the Jewish God who had graciously brought the cosmos into existence — and made it good. Against the theological dualism of the Gnostics, the emerging Christian orthodoxy also identified that same God, the one God, as the God of Jesus Christ. The God of Jesus was no less the God of Abraham, Isaac, and Jacob. The God of the Christians was the God of the Jews, and to assume otherwise, as Gnostics of Marcion's sort did, was defined as a heresy.

The God of creation and the God of redemption were not two different Gods, one Jewish and one Christian. Rather, Christians recognized in this one God two modes of divine activity, creation and redemption, both of which were undertaken by the one God of Judaism and Christianity. The history of salvation that he inaugurated was one continuous history — the history of God's power to save Jews and Christians. In this sense, the history of Israel and of the young church were inextricably linked and their narratives continuous with one another. To distinguish between Gods, to shear the grand story of salvation in two, to repudiate (even scoff at) understandings of resurrection common to Jews (including Jesus) and early Christians was, in the minds of the emerging orthodox church, outrageously inconsistent with the natural sense of scripture and the truths of the young faith.

The goodness of creation and the hope of the resurrection of the flesh were central to the truths the early church proclaimed in its creeds. When these were composed, the Gnostic groups and their teachers must be understood as standing in the background as silent interlocutors. It was also against the Gnostic gospel and the threat it posed to the orthodox message of salvation and to the theological and historical unity of Jews and Christians that orthodox Christian writers wrote their polemical treatises. We know this to be true in part because these writers often explicitly name their opponents — Gnostic or semi-Gnostic teachers like Marcion, Basilides, Valentinus, and their followers, or "heretics" in general.

A second, non-Christian group against whom Christian writers directed their treatises on resurrection were pagan skeptics — those whom one early

Christian opponent, Tertullian, dubbed "the deriding crowd" (*De resurrectione [DR]* 1). Unlike the Gnostics, who claimed Jesus as their savior and called themselves Christian, these cultured despisers felt only aversion and even hatred for Christianity and revulsion for the message of resurrection. By the late second century, caricatures of Christianity and Christians were commonplace. Pagan critics of Christianity ridiculed it for ignorance, superstitious beliefs, lower-class social status, and a rejection of contemporary social life and culture (this last claim was not entirely off target, as the Christian community itself would have observed with satisfaction). Connected both to the historically false assumption that Christians were drawn only from the uneducated lower orders and to the real possibility of martyrdom in the second century C.E., pagan critics claimed that Christians credited the "myth" of resurrection belief because the poor and potential martyrs needed such belief for consolation in the face of the harsh conditions of life or a violent death at the hands of the Romans. It was their lack of education, these critics taunted, that caused them to accept old wives' tales such as the resurrection of Jesus and his followers.

One critic named Celsus, who wrote in Greek around the year 180 in Alexandria or Rome, also argued that the resurrection of the dead was simply impossible, given the mutability of the flesh and of all matter. All matter changes over time; once dissolved, it could not, he thought, be restored. Moreover, were the divine to raise up a body dissolved by change and death, he would in effect be violating the very laws of nature he had established. In addition, the proclamation of the resurrection filled the pagan critic with horror and disgust: "Who," Celsus asks, "would want a rotted body back?" (Origen, *Contra Celsum* 5.14). Christian apologists, convinced that their bodies would be healed and restored by the power of God, would address this question, as well as the entire battery of objections enunciated by critics like Celsus, when taking up their pens to vindicate the doctrine, inherited from Judaism, of the resurrection of the flesh. Along with the Gnostics, pagan critics mocked Christians into defending (and thus into refining) their views on bodily resurrection.

Two second-century orthodox writers, Irenaeus (who died around 200) and Tertullian (died in 225), are famous for having taken on the challenges posed by both secular critics and, especially, Gnostic disbelievers in the physical resurrection. The later orthodox doctrine of the physical resurrection of the dead was laid on the foundation they put down. Irenaeus became bishop of Lyons after a persecution in Gaul took the life of the presiding bishop there. His most influential book, *Against the Heresies,* was for a long time one of our major sources of Gnosticism, and it is in this work that he lays out his views on the wrongness of Gnostic views of resurrection. A North African convert to Christianity, Tertullian became one of its foremost apologists and one of its most eloquent, prolific, and pungent prose stylists. He wrote voluminously against Marcion, the Gnostics, and other heretics. Unlike Irenaeus, however, he left a treatise specifically on resurrection. The title indicates its emphasis: *On the Resurrection of the Flesh.*

Both Irenaeus and Tertullian heartily agreed with Paul's observation in 1 Cor 11:19 that "there have to be factions" or heresies in order to clarify the true faith. We will concentrate on their writings here because they both summarize the main lines of second-century thought on the resurrection and serve as the foundation for all future reflection on the resurrection, including the belief in resurrection that is proclaimed in churches around the world in our own time.

DRY BONES, RESTORATION, AND RESURRECTION

Ancient Christian writers found bodily resurrection of the dead ubiquitously prophesied in the Hebrew Bible. Nonetheless, they spent much time on Ezekiel 37, which held pride of place among the scriptural prophecies of resurrection. As we saw in Chapter 8, Ezekiel's vision of the valley of the dry bones expresses the certainty that God will bring Israel out of exile and miraculously restore the people to their land. The bones that God reassembles seem not to be individuals but a people that he would restore and re-create, as the allusions to the exodus from bondage suggest.

In Chapter 8, we made the point that the vision of Ezekiel was not merely figurative, and it remains important that the message of restoration is coded in the language of resurrection. To distinguish meanings sharply here — was it exile or death from which God had restored Israel? — is to introduce a question not native to ancient Israelite religion or to the thought of the Hebrew Bible.

Fortunately, ancient Christian writers were well aware of both potential meanings. Indeed, they could be remarkably sensitive to the interwoven meanings—restoration and resurrection—in the original text. For several Christian writers of the second century, the two meanings of the text were intimately linked. The crucial image, discussed at length by all, is the metaphor of God's miraculously stitching together the bones. For Tertullian, it is obvious that the reincorporation and recompacting of bones symbolizes the "restoration of the Jewish state," "tribe to tribe, people to people"—for the text itself supplies its own interpretation. Thus, for Tertullian the text predicts that the sinews of power and the nerves of royalty were to be brought out of their sepulchers—that is, out of the miserable and degraded abodes of captivity to breathe afresh, restored, in the land of Judah.

Yet, Tertullian argues, seeming to recognize something truly native to the text and to the culture of the Hebrew Bible, "the image itself still possesses a truth of its own" (DR 30). Tertullian, too, is reluctant to reduce the text to either its figurative or contextual meaning. The second "truth" the image possesses is, he writes, that God will eschatologically reassemble dry bones and raise dead bodies. For Tertullian, this is the literal meaning of Ezekiel's vision. Whatever the intent of Ezekiel, Tertullian argues that the prophet gave expression to the doctrine of the resurrection of the dead. But he acknowledges that the text also figuratively expresses the restoration of Israel, its delivery from harassment, and its repatriation in the renewed state (DR 29–30). Yet, in the last analysis, Tertullian seems indifferent to the careful theoretical correlation of senses and meanings: "What does it matter to me, so long as there will be a resurrection of the body, just as there is a restoration of the Jewish state?" (DR 30). What matters to him is that *both* meanings are present, both meanings expressed, or implied, by Ezekiel and both understood by his readers—especially those who would deny the resurrection of the flesh.

Arguing specifically against the Gnostics who regard the resurrection of the dead as a metaphor for the flight of the soul from the body, Tertullian insists that there is a literal meaning of resurrection language, on which all secondary meanings depend (DR 20). Nor is it true, as the heretics would have it, that the resurrection has already occurred; nor can it be understood metaphorically as a symbol for a renewed life (DR 20). In line with Second Temple and early rabbinic Judaism, Tertullian insists that resurrection is an eschatological event (DR 22).

In his discussion of the text, Irenaeus seizes upon the image of God's life-giving breath in Ezekiel: "Thus said the Lord GOD to these bones: I will cause breath to enter you and you shall live again" (Ezek 37:5). For Irenaeus, the entire history of salvation is organized around chronologically distant but metaphorically symmetrical and harmonious moments of divine grace. In Ezekiel 37 God is presented as revivifying dead bodies with his breath in order to recall the way in which he had primordially breathed life into Adam: "the LORD God formed man from the dust of the earth. He blew into his nostrils the breath of life, and man became a living being" (Gen 2:7). In Ezekiel, Irenaeus observes, God graciously breathes life into the dead at the end of creation. This is the way God works. In the beginning, God's action, figured in the metaphor of breathing, gives life to creatures who would be lost or nonexistent except for his loving desire to create from nothing or restore from death. God's desire is always to bring things to, or back to, life (*AH* 5.15.1–2). Thus in creating, God had breathed into Adam and had given life to those who had no life, and could have no life, apart from the vitalizing, animating act of a gracious creator. In the end, he enlivens those who, without his saving breath, would have lain forever inert.

We can have faith in the resurrecting God of Ezekiel, Irenaeus implies, because we know the creating God of Genesis. To sever the Christian message from the Jewish scriptures, he equally implies, is to distort and corrupt the gospel.

RESURRECTION AND THE POWER OF GOD

The identity of the God of creation with the God of resurrection is underscored virtually everywhere in early Christian writings on the resurrection of the dead. Practically all second-century Christian writers, with the exception of the Gnostics, defended the doctrine of the miraculous resurrection of the dead by grounding it in the power God demonstrated in creation. Tertullian, for example, observes that God will surely be able to re-create the flesh that had fallen into nothing. Why? Because he has already demonstrated the power to create out of nothing. This was an ancient idea, again inherited from Judaism: "Therefore the Creator of the world, who shaped the beginning of humankind and devised the origin of all things, will in his mercy give life and breath back to you again" (2 Macc 7:23) — a favorite text from the Old Testament among the early martyrs of the church and one used in at least one ancient hymn dedicated to them. Indeed, it is a much more difficult thing, Tertullian maintains, to create than to re-create, harder to fashion than to preserve. "On this principle," Tertullian concludes, "you may be quite sure that the restoration of the flesh is easier than its first formation" (DR 11). As Irenaeus puts it: "Surely it is much more difficult and incredible, from non-existent bones, and nerves, and veins, and the rest of man's organization, to bring it about that all this should be, and to make man an animated and rational creature, than to re-integrate again that which had been created and then afterwards decomposed into earth" (AH 5.3.2). The God of the resurrection, he reminds us, is the all-powerful creator of life. For Tertullian, too, the lesser miracle of raising dead flesh is both promised and prophesied by the awesome primordial victory over chaos and death and the principal miracle of the creation of life (DR 11). God's final activity is foreshadowed in his first; in both he gives life.

In attempting to persuade the "deriding crowd" of the truth or possibility of resurrection, early Christian writers also put forward arguments based, not on scripture or tradition, but on reason and "nature." The idea was to step on opponents' turf, play by their rules, and demonstrate the truth of Jewish and Christian revelation within the arena, so to speak, of secular truth and reasoning. As Tertullian observes: "Now it is possible even on the basis of popular ideas to be knowledgeable in the things of God . . . For some things are known even by nature, as is the immortality of the soul among many people and as is our God among all" (DR 3). He will, in other words, use pagan wisdom (as he would put it) to assert Christian truth.

Thus it was that many apologists began by inspecting the natural world for evidences that point to the possibility of the general resurrection. Each day, Tertullian observes, the glory of the world is enshrouded in darkness, even in death. Yet each morning, death is slain, and life is renewed. Seeds and fruits disappear only to rise again. Even the phoenix, an animated being, passes out of existence and then back into life. And so Tertullian is moved to ask, mocking the cultured despisers of resurrection and alluding to Jesus' comments about men being infinitely more valuable than sparrows (Matt 10:31), "So men might die, while birds in Arabia are sure of a resurrection?" (DR 13).

Tertullian's comments on each of these illustrations are based on a comprehensive theory of the nature of creation that he thinks his secular opponents can accept. For Tertullian, creation carries within itself the seeds of its own regeneration. "All creation," he writes, "has an instinct for renewal" (*DR* 12). All of creation is part of a revolving order of things; things come to their end only for the purpose of coming once again to existence and to restoration. This self-generating order is, of course, created and sustained by God and serves to bear witness to the resurrection of the dead.

Tertullian and Irenaeus both also accept a view of the cosmic order that holds to the principle, which had wider currency in the non-Christian philosophical culture, that "what falls must rise." Indeed, Tertullian, a brilliant Latin rhetorician, observes that the word for dead body, *cadaver*, derives etymologically from the Latin word for falling (*cadendo*). As Tertullian puts it, "nothing can be expected to rise again, unless it has first been prostrated" (*DR* 18). Indeed, the very term "resurrection" expresses the notion that what once fell will rise again. For what is resurrection, Tertullian asks, but a rising again from sleep, a restoration to a prior state, a revival from the condition of decay and disuse, a restitution of that which appeared to be lost or defunct? (*DR* 18). For Tertullian and Irenaeus, then, resurrection is, so to speak, built into the structure and nature of the cosmos. Jesus' resurrection and the general resurrection of the dead are special instances of the general principle that all repose, each fall, every succumbing is temporary and that nature's destiny is re-creation and restitution. Again, note that these early Christian writers make their arguments (at least some of them) from first principles—what falls must rise—derived from the wider secular culture.

THE FLESH

Tertullian makes the important observation that most doubts about the resurrection begin with complaints about the flesh itself. Of the Gnostics, he writes: "Their great burden is . . . everywhere an invective against the flesh: against its origins, its substance, against the casualties and the invariable end which await it; unclean from its first formation from the dregs of the ground, uncleaner afterwards from the mire of its own seminal transmission; worthless, weak, covered with guilt, laden with misery, full of trouble, and after all this record of its degradation dropping into its original earth and the appellation of a corpse and destined to dwindle away even from this loathsome name" (*DR* 4).

Tertullian's response arises from the intuition that the flesh derives its dignity not from its intrinsic properties but from being the work of God. It is God's molding and selection of the flesh that make it worthy. Thus it is both the dignity and the skill of the maker that give the flesh nobility and splendor. So artistically is humankind created that it becomes impossible to distinguish flesh and spirit. Drawing on Christological language about the relation of the divine and human in the incarnate Christ, Tertullian observes of humanity: "so intimate is the union, that it may be deemed to be uncertain whether the flesh bears about the soul, or the soul the flesh; whether the flesh acts as servant to the soul, or the soul to the flesh" (*DR* 7). Besides, had not both testaments of the scriptures magnified the flesh? Had not Isaiah declared, "all flesh, as one, shall behold [the Presence of the LORD]" (Isa 40:5)? Had not Paul called our bodies temples of the Lord, members of Christ? (1 Cor 6:19). In their argument that the material creation cannot be redeemed, the Gnostics typically use Paul's point that "flesh and blood cannot inherit the kingdom of God" (1 Cor 15:50), as Irenaeus points out (*AH* 5.9.1). But Tertullian argues, it is not the substance of the flesh that Paul railed against, but its actions. What is more, if flesh were not raised, would not death have preserved victory over that which God had created and hallowed? Soul and body had acted coordinately in sinning and in doing good, and, for justice to prevail, they must be judged together at the end of time, as both Jews (excepting Sadducees, Tertullian notes) and Christians believe (*DR* 14–17). At the end of time, the body will be changed; it will be incorruptible. But it will be a fleshly body that will rise (*DR* 55). For Irenaeus the proof of this is in the raising of Jesus with the body that preserved the nail wounds, proof that we, too, would be raised in our bodies (*AH* 5.7.1).

For orthodox writers like Tertullian and Irenaeus, it is the Gnostics and not the gospel of Jesus Christ that is negative regarding the body. The Gnostic dismissal of the fleshly resurrection of the dead is but one symptom, though perhaps the most important one, of their inability to appreciate God's handiwork.

These second-century Christian writers are well aware that some of the scriptures, such as Colossians and parts of the letters of John, speak of the resurrection as a present reality, rather than an event of the end time. These were particularly popular texts among the Gnostics. But both Tertullian and Irenaeus use the same texts against the Gnostics in order to emphasize that there is a future, and bodily, dimension to resurrection. Thus Tertullian quotes 1 John 3:2: "Beloved, we are God's children now; what we will be has not yet been revealed." He quotes other texts to the same effect (*DR* 23–24). John and Paul also speak of a future bodily resurrection. Does not Paul say, "He will transform the body of our humiliation that it may be conformed to the body of his glory, by the power that also enables him to make all things subject to himself" (Phil 3:21)? Although our flesh will undergo change, in other words, its substance will be preserved (*DR* 55). The notion that resurrection would be purely spiritual was wrongheaded and based on a misunderstanding of the scriptures, particularly Paul. When Paul spoke of the human as a temple of the spirit, he was not referring to souls only but simply to the notion that it was an integral human being, body and soul, who became such a dwelling place for God.

Both Tertullian and Irenaeus go to some pains to argue against a view of salvation that is understood strictly in terms of the survival or salvation of the soul. Again, the Gnostic message is in the background. Both the Gnostics and the orthodox agreed that the soul would be "safe" after death, that is, that by virtue of its intrinsic immortality, it would survive and be saved. What was at issue was whether that which *was* subject to decay and destruction—the flesh—would similarly be saved. The Gnostics denied it would. But the orthodox Christian view of God's creation, of human nature, and of justice could not allow for this partial understanding of salvation. As the orthodox saw it, the texture of humanity was a seamless, indivisible work of art, composed of flesh and soul—very much like the view of the rabbis we examined in the previous chapter. God will reward the blessed, body and soul. "How could we be blessed," Tertullian asks, "if any part of us were to perish?" (*DR* 34). Only if the *whole* person, both elements of which were created by God, were raised could humanity be redeemed and justice achieved. Also crucial, again, is the presumption of God's stupendous power. As Irenaeus sums up the case, "For if He does not vivify what is mortal, and does not bring back the corruptible to incorruption, He is not a God of power" (*AH* 3). Had the Gnostics not read Paul? God would, in the end, clothe our perishable bodies in imperishability, our mortal bodies in immortality, and death would be swallowed up in victory (1 Cor 15:54).

RESURRECTION, TRUTH, AND POWER

It is important to stress that, for thinkers such as Tertullian and Irenaeus, these were cardinal ideas, central building blocks in the Christian's faith. As Tertullian put it, with powerful sincerity: "For if the resurrection of the flesh be denied, the prime article of the faith is shaken; if it is asserted, the faith is established" (*DR* 4). They were not ideas harnessed, as is sometimes suggested, in order to concentrate ecclesiastical power in the hands of a few bishops. Life and death depended on their truthfulness; the issue was not simply one of politics. Tertullian and Irenaeus firmly believed that if the Gnostic notions of the body and resurrection were true, this meant that Christians had not really been saved. The stakes were that high. To suggest that such men were really more interested in securing their own comfortable existence or power is to misrepresent or misunderstand them woefully, to present them falsely, and to obscure how seriously and conscientiously such thinkers wrestled with the truth of the claim that Christ had been raised and that all of his followers would be raised on the last day. As the distinguished historian Caroline Walker Bynum has observed, the argument that anti-Gnostic treatises were really about the assertion of male hierarchical power "is a problematic one" that "does not really work." The reason it does not work is that Tertullian and Irenaeus, not to mention their Gnostic interlocutors, were primarily interested in the content of the religious idea of resurrection, not its political function, nor its effects upon women.

Both Tertullian and Irenaeus agreed with Paul: had Christ not risen, then their faith and all their catechesis and writing were in vain (1 Cor 15:14). For these men, to claim, as the Gnostics had, that the bodily resurrection was impossible was also to sever a key bond to the grand story of Israel: a narrative without which the new Israel that was the church could not be understood or justify itself. These stalwart defenders against Gnosticism were not prepared to jettison the expectant hope that the God of Abraham, Isaac, and Jacob, who was also the God of Jesus Christ, the one God, would raise all his faithful at the end of days.

THE REDEEMED LIFE—
IN THE HERE AND NOW

CHRISTIANS AND JEWS

It is conventional to say that Christianity is the child of Judaism and cannot be understood apart from its parent religion, for Jesus and all his disciples were Jews and references to the Jewish scriptures pervade the New Testament. This is, of course, true, as far as it goes, but it misses the point that the form of Judaism from which the religious traditions of modern Jews descend took shape in the early centuries of the common era, that is to say, at the same time, and to a significant degree, in the same places as the church was taking shape. So it would be more accurate to say that rabbinic Judaism and Christianity are not parent and child but siblings, sister religions whose parent was Second Temple Judaism and whose more distant ancestors were still earlier phases of the religion of Israel. During the period on which we have been concentrating over the past two chapters, the two communities were contemporaries.

Awareness of the sibling relationship of Christianity and Judaism requires that members of both communities adjust the way they think of themselves. Whereas Christians have traditionally affirmed a theology in which their religion replaced Judaism, this was never the case historically. Judaism continued to live, to develop, and to spread long after Christianity appeared, and it survives, often flourishing, to this day. Moreover, Christians can acquire an accurate view of the way their religion originated in Judaism only if they familiarize themselves with the rich Jewish literature of the late Second Temple and early rabbinic periods of Jewish history.

They must not rely only on their Old Testament, whose last composition was probably written more than two centuries before the earliest parts of the New Testament. It is a commonplace in Christian circles to say that one cannot understand the New Testament apart from the Old. This is quite true (and still underappreciated), but one also cannot adequately understand the New Testament apart from the Jewish literature of its own time, broadly conceived. And when Christians read the New Testament and other early Christian literature in this context, they become keenly aware that the familiar claims of the radical distinctiveness of Christianity over against Judaism are at least overdrawn and often downright wrong.

The same points carry important implications for Jews as well. Once one becomes aware of the variety and fluidity of Judaism during this period, one cannot simply describe Christianity as having "broken off" from Judaism. Rather, both traditions were in a state of formation and attempted consolidation in late antiquity. Almost all rabbinic literature dates, in fact, from *after* the time of Jesus and Paul, not before. For Jews, too, honest study of early Christianity must soften or destroy claims of radical uniqueness.

Given this relationship, it is not surprising to find that the church fathers and the rabbis faced similar opposition and fought similar battles on behalf of the belief in an eschatological resurrection of the dead that they inherited from the same streams in Second Temple Judaism. Against the consensus of the Greco-Roman world in which they lived (and to which they were also indebted), they strove to uphold faith in a God who transcends nature and can overcome it, even bringing back the whole person, body and soul, a God who acts in history, fulfilling his amazing promises to his people. In the early centuries of the common era, the notion that God had a special relationship with the church or with the Jewish people seemed absurd to many, since both groups suffered dire persecutions at the hands of the Roman Empire. Yet members of each persevered in their commitment, even at the cost of their lives.

Against members of their own communities who interpreted their respective scriptures, with varying degrees of plausibility, as endorsing only the immortality of the disembodied soul, the church fathers and the rabbis insisted that the body, too, would be a locus of redemption—that redemption did not mean disembodiment. Indeed, as we shall see in this chapter, they insisted that the redeemed life began in the here and now, with the life of discipleship (Christians) or the life of Torah (Jews), and would come to its spiritual fulfillment with the general resurrection and the eternal life that resurrection would inaugurate.

THE NEW LIFE OF THE CHRISTIAN

In the ancient Christian churches, it was widely understood that the resurrected life could be anticipated and experienced even before death. Almost inevitably, ancient Christian writers, taking their cue from Paul (above all Romans 6, as we shall see in some detail), associated the beginning of this experience with the sacrament of baptism. Indeed, it was all but universally believed in the early church that baptism was absolutely necessary for a Christian to participate in the resurrected life. The scriptural anchor for this is in John 3:5: "No one can enter the kingdom of God without being born of water and Spirit." Before baptism, the candidates were locked into a covenant with the forces of evil and death, hopelessly trapped in an alliance with hell. Only baptism could liberate them from the terms of that fearsome covenant.

Today, some people think of baptism merely as the ritual occasion at which infants are given their name. But in the ancient church "christening" had a different meaning. Christening people at baptism meant, not naming them primarily, but making them into Christians and inducting them into the resurrected life. Baptism, in other words, was the cause and ritual celebration of the candidates' removal from the realm of sin and idolatry. It marked the moment at which they were transferred from the domain of Satan and death to that of God and life. It was the time at which the covenant with the powers of evil was smashed.

Everything about the baptismal ritual, as well as the intricate rituals preceding it, was designed to reinforce this message of transferal. For example, exorcism, rarely practiced today in connection with baptism, and even regarded as an exotic (if not embarrassing) relic of the church's early liturgical practice, was a staple of the rituals that occurred during the week before baptism.

In the early church, the candidates underwent exorcism in order to begin the cleansing process that would prepare them to be delivered from the kingdom of sin and to the dominion of purity. As Cyril, priest and then bishop of Jerusalem (he lived about 315–86), expressed it in one of his catechetical lectures, delivered after baptism, the candidate anointed with the oil of exorcism was now safe. That oil, he declared, was a "charm to drive away every trace of hostile influence" and could "chase away all the invisible powers of the evil one" (*Catechetical Lectures* 20.3).

Every movement of the body during the baptismal ritual was designed to reinforce the ancient Jewish notion that there were two ways, good and evil, and that the candidates were about to reject one and embrace the other. During the vigil, the candidates were asked explicitly to abjure their old ways and to renounce Satan. While renouncing Satan, the candidates faced toward the west. (In ancient Christianity, the west, the land of the setting sun, was regarded as a symbol of darkness.) Having completed their renunciation, they turned toward the east—that is, toward the land of the rising sun and therefore of light. For Christians in Africa and Europe, to face east was also, of course, to face the Holy Land, the place where all the redemptive events of salvation history had taken place.

As always, bodily movements were rich in symbolism. Here the orientation of the body, the literal change of posture, and the turning away from the Occident, the realm of paganism and the region of sensory darkness, were all meant to signify the deeper change in personal aspect and trajectory. As Cyril plainly put it in one of his catechetical lectures, the newly baptized had been "renewed from an old state to a new" (*Catechetical Lectures* 20.1). Cyril goes on to explain that the candidates put off their tunics "as an image of putting off the old man with his deeds"—again relying on a core Pauline idea. They had divested themselves of the old man, their "former way of life, [their] old self, corrupt and deluded by its lusts" (Eph 4:22). At another level, these movements were designed to mirror and reverberate with the cosmic shift in aeons that occurred when Christ rose from his grave.

West and east, death and resurrection, slavery and liberation, light and darkness, flesh and spirit, Satan and God—the entire baptismal liturgy was suffused with physical and symbolic opposites. Even in his explanation of the sacrament, the great theologian Gregory of Nyssa (who died about 385) could not help speaking in terms of these opposites: "For Thou truly, O Lord, art the pure and eternal fount of goodness, Who justly turned away from us, and in loving kindness had mercy upon us. You hated, and were reconciled; You cursed, and blessed; You banished us from Paradise, and recalled us; You stripped off the fig-tree leaves, an unseemly covering, and put upon us a costly garment; You opened the prison, and released the condemned; You sprinkled us with clean water, and cleansed us from our filthiness" (*On the Baptism of Christ*). The baptismal candidates were instructed, both before and after the liturgy, that they had lived on one side of a cosmic divide; they would now dwell, graciously, on the other side. They had put themselves in league with Satan; they would now stand in covenant with God. Their turning, their revolving was thus both a physical and spiritual revolution. They had been presented with a choice: death or life. The choice was absolutely stark. Everyone had chosen to be alienated from God; now one could be united forever to him.

Further underlining this message was the calendrical placement of the baptismal ritual. Following a period of instruction for catechumens (those who had converted to Christianity and had received instruction in Christian doctrine and life before baptism), the ritual began on the Easter vigil and was completed early on Easter Sunday. Needless to say and hardly by coincidence, this was the day commemorating the resurrection of Jesus. Again, every movement and gesture was designed to associate the candidate with Christ and to initiate the process by which the person, once dead to sin, would be raised to new life. Candidates were fully immersed in water, for example. This, of course, was a symbol of cleansing and believed to be sacramentally efficacious for forgiving sins. But there was more to it. When immersed, the candidates were covered by the elements of the earth, just as Jesus was buried in the ground. Further, they were immersed three times as a way of associating them with Jesus' three days in the tomb. As Cyril explained: "You were led to the holy pool of Divine Baptism . . . and descended three times into the water, and ascended again; here also hinting by a symbol at the three-day burial of Christ. For as our Savior passed three days and three nights in the heart of the earth, so you also in your first ascent out of the water, represented the first day of Christ in the earth, and by your descent, the night . . . " (*Catechetical Lectures* 20.4). Here, Paul's theology of baptism and incorporation into the body of Christ is clearly in the background: "Do you not know that all of us who have been baptized into Christ Jesus were baptized into his death?" (Rom 6:3). When the candidates, who had been concealed as their savior was concealed in the earth, emerged for the third time from the water, they had entered the promised land of God's salvation. The sufferings of Christ crucified in which they had shared were reversed when they were assimilated to the risen body of their Lord and Savior. Again, Paul (as well as the exodus from Egypt) lurks in the background:

> ⁴Therefore we have been buried with him by baptism into death, so that, just as Christ was raised from the dead by the glory of the Father, so we too might walk in newness of life. ⁵For if we have been united with him in a death like his, we will certainly be united with him in a resurrection like his." (Rom 6:4–5)

This scriptural passage was crucial to the development of religious instruction on baptism in the early church.

The language of liberation derives from Paul but the ritual, and the catechetical instruction that accompanied it, drew its power from that deeper background of the exodus, a moment of liberation to which early theologians of baptism habitually harkened, beginning with the apostle to the gentiles:

> ⁶We know that our old self was crucified with him so that the body of sin might be destroyed, and we might no longer be enslaved to sin. ⁷For whoever has died is freed from sin." (Rom 6:6–7).

Like Paul, ancient bishops and teachers regularly drew on the exodus in order to explain the meaning of baptism, to link it with the history of Israel, and to invest it with the deeper significances and historical depth of the classic moment of liberation in Israelite history. For example, when candidates for baptism faced west to renounce the world of Satan, they were commanded to stretch forth their hands. This, Cyril explains, was to recall Moses leading his afflicted people out of Egypt: "Then the tyrant pursued the Israelites to the sea," Cyril says. "Here the author of evil pursues the candidate to the very streams of salvation. But the tyrant of old drowned; this one disappears in the waters of salvation" (*Catechetical Lectures* 19.3).

Tertullian makes a similar observation: "The nations are set free from the world by means of water, and the devil, their old tyrant, they leave quite behind, overwhelmed in the water" (*On Baptism* 9). The great fourth-century bishop of Constantinople, Gregory of Nazianzus, sums up this tradition neatly when he observes that baptism is "the removal of slavery, the loosing of chains" (*Oration on Baptism* 40.3). The baptismal oil, he added, functioned in the same way as the blood on the Israelites' lintels and doorposts (Exod 12:22–23): it prevented the destroyer from destroying. This liberation from the realm of sin was concretely symbolized in the baptismal ritual when the candidates received tokens — milk and honey — that were again designed to serve as reminders of liberation and promise. The baptized had been liberated from the land of oppression and dwelt now in the promised land of resurrection, and everything they experienced physically — eating, drinking, moving — was intended to affect them with the memory of salvation and cosmic history, a history into which they had now been graciously integrated.

If ancient Christian writers symbolized the baptismal liberation in the story of Exodus, it was with Genesis that they attempted to evoke the nature of resurrected life in this world: "When therefore you renounce Satan, and utterly break your covenant with him, that ancient league with hell [the allusion is to Isa 28:15], there is opened to you the paradise of God, which He planted towards the East, where for his transgression our first father was banished and a symbol of this was your turning from West to East, the place of light" (Cyril, *Catechetical Lectures* 19.9). In renouncing Satan and turning toward the Orient, newly baptized Christians could now experience the resurrected life, which was like nothing so much as life in the Garden of Eden before the Fall. Gregory of Nyssa exploited the same imagery beautifully: "The time, then, has come, and bears in its course the remembrance of holy mysteries, purifying man — mysteries which purge out from soul and body even that sin which is hard to cleanse away, and which bring us back to that fairness of our first estate which God, the best of artificers, impressed upon us . . . No longer shall Adam be confounded when called by You, nor hide himself, convicted by his conscience, cowering in the thicket of Paradise. Nor shall the flaming sword encircle Paradise around, and make the entrance inaccessible to those that draw near; but all is turned to joy for us that were the heirs of sin" (*On the Baptism of Christ*).

In short, the change wrought by God at baptism was not only a cleansing and forgiveness of sin but a restoration of the graced candidate to the state of perfection, plenitude, and purity enjoyed by Adam and Eve in Eden. This, too, was an idea that received symbolic representation in the liturgy. The candidates, baptized nude as a way to represent their enslavement to sin and as a symbolic reminder of the primordial couple's shame, received a white tunic on emerging from the baptismal pool, their shame wiped away forever. They were restored to splendor of life before the Fall, life in the presence of God.

In ancient Christianity, it was expected that baptism would have real, concrete moral consequences. Put in the language of theology, an intimate connection between sacrament and code, exorcism and ethics, was simply presumed. Ancient Christian writers furnished long lists of virtues that the newly baptized person would be expected to practice. In their eyes, the moral life was supposed to reflect and reinforce the effect of the ritual action of the forgiveness of sins and cleansing of the soul.

So Gregory of Nazianzus (*Oration* 40.33) preached to the newly baptized:

> You were raised up from your bed, or rather you took up your bed, and publicly acknowledged the benefit. Do not again be thrown upon your bed by sinning, in the evil rest of a body paralyzed by its pleasures. But as you now are, so walk, mindful of the command, Behold you are made whole; sin no more lest a worse thing happen unto you if thou prove yourself bad after the blessing you have received. You have heard the loud voice, "Lazarus, come forth" as you lay in the tomb; not, however, after four days, but after many days; and you were loosed from the bonds of your shrouds. Do not again become dead, nor live with those who dwell in the tombs; nor bind yourself with the bonds of your own sins; for it is uncertain whether you will rise again from the tomb till the last and universal resurrection, which will bring every work into judgment, not to be healed, but to be judged, and to give account of all which for good or evil it has treasured up.

In Gregory's eyes, those who had emerged from the saving waters were, in a word, expected to *be* that which they had become. Raised like Lazarus from the dead, they were to live now, in the here and now, the life of the resurrected. With baptism, that new life had begun, and it would be gained in full at one's third and last birth (one's first birth was from one's mother, one's second to new life at baptism), when one rises from the ground. As Theodore, bishop of Mopsuestia (a city near Antioch) in the fifth century, explained in his third *Baptismal Homily*: "You will receive this truly when you rise again to your new birth. However, now you have faith in Christ our Lord, and while you are waiting for the resurrection you must be satisfied to accept signs and symbols of it in this wondrous sacrament. Through it, you acquire certitude of a share in the gifts to come."

THE EUCHARIST

The habits of Jesus, the New Testament gospels, and early Christian writings all strongly suggest that the Eucharist as practiced in ancient Christianity was also strongly associated with, and expected to supply the believer a foretaste of, the resurrected life. The Eucharist, in particular, was imagined as a meal, a feast, one that anticipated the eschatological banquet.

The Christian practice of the Eucharist, and the understanding of it as an anticipation of the eschatological banquet, had origins, needless to say, in Jesus' Last Supper. The deeper background to the Lord's Supper, however, are the words and images in the Hebrew Bible, particularly Isaiah 25, which helped lastingly lend it its unique meaning, historical depth, and resonance:

> [6]The LORD of Hosts will make on this mount
> For all the peoples
> A banquet of rich viands,
> A banquet of choice wines —
> Of rich viands seasoned with marrow,
> Of choice wines well refined.
> [7]And He will destroy on this mount the shroud
> That is drawn over the faces of all the peoples
> And the covering that is spread
> Over all the nations:
> [8]He will swallow up death forever. (Isa 25:6–8)

When Jesus ate his final meal with his disciples, he predicted that he would not partake of such a banquet with them again until they were gathered together in the kingdom of God (Luke 22:14–20). Here it is altogether likely that he was thinking in terms of the eschatological vision from the book of Isaiah quoted above. That is, he was thinking of the feast prepared by the Lord on Mount Zion, when death would be swallowed up forever. As his followers were steeped in scripture, they would have understood that the meal in which they partook was meant to allude to, and participate in, that glorious banquet on Mount Zion. In Isaiah, feasting, the destruction of death, and the enjoyment of everlasting life, imagined as a banquet of rich food, are intimately linked. This was a connection, in turn, reinforced by

Jesus' words and by early Christian practice and thought. Accordingly, the Eucharist had from the beginning an eschatological dimension and meaning. Partaking in the eucharistic meal was thus to experience, in part, what the resurrected life would be.

Throughout the New Testament gospels, Jesus describes the new life after resurrection as a heavenly banquet. In Luke 13, for example, he foresees that people will come "from east and west, from north and south, and will eat in the kingdom of God" (Luke 13:29). In the following chapter of Luke, Jesus talks about the "resurrection of the righteous" (Luke 14:14), and one of his auditors responds, "Blessed is anyone who will eat bread in the kingdom of God!" (Luke 14:15). Many of Jesus' parables portray the kingdom as a banquet (for example, Matt 22:1–14; 25:1–13). For his part, Paul associated eucharistic eating and drinking with the promise of Jesus' second and final coming: "For as often as you eat this bread and drink the cup, you proclaim the Lord's death until he comes" (1 Cor 11:26). The early Christian celebration of the Eucharist on Sunday, the day of Jesus' resurrection, cemented the connection between the eating and drinking of the Lord's Supper with the feasting of the messianic, paradisiacal banquet. Thus the celebration through eating bread and drinking wine in the Lord's Supper was imagined, already very early in Christian history, as a literal and metaphorical experience and taste of the future resurrected life.

Early Christian writings that speak of the Eucharist almost inevitably contain this eschatological dimension. A prime example of this is a document called the *Didaché*, which was discovered only in the late nineteenth century. Though this is the first document to refer to the Lord's Supper as "the Eucharist" (the verb *eucharistein*, "to give thanks," *is* found in 1 Cor 11:23–25), we know almost nothing about it. Purporting to be the "Teaching [*Didaché*] of the Twelve Apostles," this short writing gives brief moral, disciplinary, and ritual instruction. Our best guess is that it was written during the second half of the second century of the common era (perhaps 160–180); it seems to have been composed in Syria. What is of interest (aside from the fact that it describes a eucharistic meal that clearly has Jewish festive meals as its model) is that it, too, establishes a close connection between the Eucharist and the eschatological life:

> We thank you, our Father, for the life and knowledge which you made known to us through Jesus your Servant; to you be the glory for ever. Even as

this broken bread was scattered over the hills, and was gathered together and became one, so let your Church be gathered together from the ends of the earth into your kingdom. (*Didaché* 9:8)

Here the harvesting of the wheat, culminating in the eucharistic meal, is linked to the ingathering of all of God's faithful at the end of time. The entire document is imbued with apocalyptic fervor and the hope of eschatological completion. It looks forward explicitly to the coming of the Lord on the clouds of heaven, accompanied by his saints (*Didaché* 16:3–8). Almost every practice it recommends is intended to allude to or echo life in the World-to-Come. Here, the Eucharist is understood to be a figure or anticipation of heavenly beatitude and glory. The Didaché is focused on the future fulfillment of that of which the Eucharist furnishes a foretaste; therefore, it is surprising that the eucharistic prayers it recommends contain no allusion to Jesus' Last Supper, the institution narrative, or the words of Jesus' blessing of bread and wine. The banqueting with the risen ones is what the author had in mind.

THE LORD'S PRAYER

The Our Father was clearly central to the prayer life of early Christians, and it, too, was expected to anticipate aspects of the resurrected life. As far as we can see, there is no direct evidence that the Lord's Prayer was recited during the eucharistic liturgy. The *Didaché*, however, as well as other early Christian writings, indicate that it was so important a prayer that the baptized were expected to pray it three times a day, with special emphasis on its morning and evening recitation. It was thus a central prayer for the baptized Christian and, more than any other, a prayer that gave the Christian a glimpse and experience of the resurrected life.

No early Christian writer gave more eloquent expression to this idea than Origen (who lived about 185–254), a prolific Greek church father who wrote a long commentary, *On Prayer*, in which he writes at length on the Our Father. Origen begins with the observation that all are tyrannized by the ruler of the world—Satan. Indeed, one prays for God's kingdom to come because of the fearsomeness of this tyranny. One prays in order that God may defeat the tyrannical enemy and establish his rightful place as sovereign in the interior kingdom of each Christian. With God emplaced on his interior throne, rule and order prevails, and the well-ordered mind and soul are ready to practice righteousness. When we address God as "our Father," we pray that these conditions may prevail. In addressing "our Father," Christians wrap themselves in the paternal immortality that will be their eternal reward.

But by transferring our allegiances from the ruler of this world to God, by putting on the incorruptible holiness of the Lord, Christians begin to enjoy in this life the gifts of the resurrected life: "so that, being ruled over by God," Origen says, "*we may even now live* amid the blessings of regeneration and resurrection" (*On Prayer* 15; emphasis added). The point — it is obviously a Pauline one — is that, once baptized, Christians cannot let sin continue to rule. The ruler of this world is no longer their ruler. As Origen puts it, the Lord "alone rules over us" now; the Lord walks in us "as in a spiritual garden" — again an allusion to Eden and the restoration of primordial bliss as an image for the enjoyment of the resurrected life. Once we transfer our allegiance to God, but only then, do we enjoy in the here and now the blessings of the resurrected life, when we will be fully regenerated in body and soul.

For early Christians, then, resurrection was both a present reality and a future hope. The newly baptized, capable now of addressing God as their Lord and participating in the eucharistic meal, stood poised between the present life, still struggling with sin and sadness, and future bliss, when every blemish and tear would be wiped away, in the general resurrection, of which baptism and the life of Christian practice had given them a foretaste.

TORAH AND ETERNAL LIFE

In Chapter 5, we had occasion to observe that in Jewish tradition the metaphor of the Tree of Life remained in force; it was not thought to have lost its point with the expulsion from Eden, which denied humankind access to the tree itself. In the book of Proverbs, for example, the Tree of Life was equated with Wisdom, so that those who diligently pursue Wisdom and live their lives according to its dictates find life and contentment:

> She [Wisdom] is a tree of life to those who grasp her,
> And whoever holds on to her is happy. (Prov 3:18)

As things developed, Wisdom came to be equated, in turn, with the Torah, and the "wise" of Proverbs thus with rabbinic sages, learned in the five books of Moses and the oral tradition as well. This equation of Torah and Wisdom led naturally to an equation of the Torah with the other term, the Tree of Life. Consider the blessing that Jews recite when they have finished being called up to the public reading of the Torah. It proclaims that God has "planted within us eternal life." Like the tree, the Torah, too, is a source of eternal life; the verb "planted" may not be coincidental.

Many modern Jews think of the Torah and its practices as an ornament that beautifies or otherwise enriches their lives or as a way to connect to their ancestors or to ethnic identity. The devotion of the rabbis to Torah, however, was rooted in certain claims that are thoroughly *theological.* Contrary to a misperception common today, the "people of the book," as Muhammad was later to call the Jews (along with the Christians), did not devote themselves to the book (by which the Muslim prophet meant the scriptures) purely for intellectual or educational purposes. Rather, given the rabbis' understanding of human nature, the study and practice of Torah was a moral and theological necessity for them. In their thinking, the alternative to it (for Jews, at least) was nothing less than death, in this world and the next.

Were human nature morally neutral, equally balanced between good and evil, this dire situation might not exist. In rabbinic thinking, however, human beings are continually assaulted by a formidable innate impulse that the rabbis call the "Inclination" (*yetzer*) or the "Evil Inclination" (*yetzer hara'*). The Talmud quotes an illuminating comment of Rabbi Simon ben Laqish, a sage from the Land of Israel in the early third century C.E.:

> A man's Inclination [*yetzer*] attacks him every day and seeks to put him to death, as it is said, "The wicked watches for the righteous, / seeking to put him to death" (Ps 37:32), and were it not for the Holy One (blessed be He!), who helps him, he could not withstand it, as it is said, "The LORD will not abandon him to his power; / He will not let him be condemned in judgment." (v 33)

In this midrash, the "wicked" who is on the lookout for an opportunity to kill the righteous is not another person, as in the verses in the Psalter that serve as the prooftext. Rather, the "wicked" is a person's own nature, continually waging acts of potentially lethal aggression against him or her.

Were people to rely on their own moral character alone, they would surely perish, because their only ally would in that case also be their assailant. Fortunately, the righteous have a real ally in God, who, protecting them from the powerful enemy within, keeps them alive by enabling them to persevere in their own fragile righteousness. To put the point another way, when God "sustains the living in kindness," as the rabbinic liturgy affirms, he does so in part by protecting the living from their own propensity for conduct that results in death. Were they to rely only upon themselves, the result would be fatal.

In this theology, death is not natural, or at least not altogether so. It results, rather, from human choices, which are themselves partly the consequence of human nature, with its powerful and resilient appetite for evil. It thus makes sense that the same Rabbi Simon ben Laqish (whose theology on this is typical) deduces the following three-way equation: "Satan, the Evil Inclination, and the Angel of Death are all one and the same." The devil, in sum, kills, but his prey are anything but passive victims. Rather, they are actively complicit in their own demise, choosing the path that leads to death over its life-giving, life-extending alternative. The choice is theirs, but they make it in response to deep God-given promptings within themselves. By failing to check and counteract instincts that they never chose to have in the first place, the wicked do themselves in. Having done so, however, they can (many rabbinic texts tell us) still change a death sentence to a decree of new life, if only they choose to walk through the gates of repentance, which are, amazingly, always open to them.

Confronted with the knowledge that one carries within oneself a poison as potent as the Evil Inclination, one is quickly predisposed to inquire after the appropriate antidote, and here rabbinic thinking does not disappoint. For the rabbis saw in the Torah itself a prime remedy against the lethal enemy within. Consider the revealing wordplay in the following early midrash:

> Our rabbis taught: "Therefore impress [vesamtem] [these My words upon your very heart]" (Deut 11:18)—perfect medicine [sam tam]. Why is the Torah likened to a life-giving medicine? This can be compared to the case of a man who struck his son with a huge blow and put a compress on his wound. He said to him, "My son, so long as this compress is on your wound, eat whatever you like and drink whatever you like, and bathe in either hot or

cold water, and you needn't be afraid. But if you take it off, it will break into ulcers." Thus the Holy One (blessed be He!) said to Israel, "My son, I created the Evil Inclination; I created Torah as its antidote. If you occupy yourselves with Torah, you will not be delivered into its power, as it is said, 'Surely, if you do right, / There is uplift.' But if you do not occupy yourselves with Torah, you will be delivered into its power, as it is said, 'Sin couches at the door.' Not only that: All of its business centers on you, as it is said, 'Its urge is toward you.' But if you want, you can rule over it, as it is said, 'Yet you can be its master'" (Gen 4:7).

In this midrash, human beings first become conscious of themselves not in a state of wholeness and health, but in a gravely wounded state. They have been wounded by their very created nature and are thus victims, as it were, of their creator. Perhaps we can detect therein a tinge of resentment against God for having made human beings defective. But if so, the human case is weak, for the victims never existed without the defect, and it is only through the kindness of God that they survive and thrive. Furthermore, as the decoded parable makes clear, the wound is not physical but moral, its immediate cause being the Evil Inclination. Given how natural the wound is to the patient (for it results, as we have been at pains to point out, from a constituent element of human nature), it is too much to expect it to be eradicated, at least in this world.

Rather than questing after a final elimination of the poison within, we must, the rabbis thought, content ourselves in the here and now with long-term suppressive therapy. A prime form in which this comes is the Torah, which is a medicine so effective that patients can live healthy, normal lives — as long as they do not forget to take it. By use of Gen 4:7, the rabbis transformed the LORD's warning to Cain as he seethed with fratricidal jealousy into a commendation of Torah as an antidote to the destructive impulses the first murderer felt. Cain, of course, failed to heed the admonition and became the slave rather than the master of his own sinful urge. Israel, by contrast, has an enormous advantage that he lacked. They have the Torah, which is vastly more encompassing and vastly more substantive than any simple admonition. For Torah is a total life practice with which the people can occupy themselves communally and individually, mentally and morally. At its best, it serves to distract its practitioners from the thoughts and actions that lead to sin, to habituate them to do the good, and to fortify their will against the wound within that would otherwise break into deadly ulcers—to awaken, in short, the better angels of their nature.

In the main, the rabbis viewed the Torah as the inheritance of the Jews alone and did not think that gentiles ought to observe it. There is, in other words, no reason whatsoever that non-Jews should observe the commandments having to do with the Sabbath, the festivals, the dietary laws, circumcision, or most of the other commandments of the Torah, which Jewish tradition has long numbered as 613. Rather, their obligation is to a much smaller set of norms, known as the Seven Commandments of the Noahides—to set up a system of law and justice and to refrain from blasphemy, idolatry, sexual perversion, murder, robbery, and eating flesh from an animal that remains alive. The tradition has generally held that a gentile who observes these will have a portion in the World-to-Come. He or she does not need to convert to Judaism. The Jew, however, has no such option. He or she is obligated to follow the Torah.

Like the other modalities of good that God has put at the disposal of human beings, the Torah requires constant vigilance, indeed the moral equivalent of war in order to counter the evil within. Another statement in the name of Rabbi Simon ben Laqish puts it well:

> A person should always incite his Good Inclination [*yetzer hattov*] against his Evil Inclination [*yetzer hara'*] as it is written, "So tremble, and sin no more." If he is victorious over it, well and good. If not, let him occupy himself with Torah, as it is said, "ponder it." If he is victorious over it, well and good. If not, let him recite the *Shema*, as it is said, "on your bed." If he is victorious over it, well and good. If not, let him remind himself of the day of his death, as it is said, "and be still" (Ps 4:5).

Here the rabbi interprets the successive phrases of Ps 4:5 in terms of the assaults of the Evil Inclination upon its prey. The countervailing force of the Good Inclination may, with considerable effort, suffice to allow for the desired moral victory. But it may not, and if so, the Torah is the next weapon of choice. Should it fail as well, one must resort to the recitation of the central text of the rabbinic liturgy known (after its first word) as the *Shema*, which is recited before going to sleep (among other times) and whose second paragraph (Deut 11:13–21) focuses on reward and punishment. If even this fails, then the thought of one's own inevitable death, and the judgment that follows, is the last weapon in the arsenal of moral struggle that the rabbi develops.

As the rabbis saw it, this moral struggle is not just internal to the individual engaged in it. According to a number of rabbinic texts, the struggle against the Evil Inclination serves the larger purpose of contributing to the ultimate victory of God over human evil. Here, as often in rabbinic thought, the two worlds, This World (*ha-'olam hazzeh*) and the World-to-Come (*ha-'olam ha-ba'*), to use the rabbis' own terminology, are inextricably connected; the rabbinic focus on ethical action in This World bespeaks anything but indifference toward the World-to-Come. One indication of this is the way the rabbis can describe certain practices as evidence that the person performing them is a member of the World-to-Come. For example, one text affirms, "Anyone who studies *halakhot* [Jewish laws] every day is assured that he is a member of the World-to-Come." Another tells us that Psalm 92, whose first verse prescribes it "for the sabbath day," is sung on that day because it is "a song for the Future Age, for the day that will be completely Sabbath and rest in eternal life." The implication is that the observance of the Sabbath provides a foretaste of the World-to-Come. Both of these passages came into prayer books, where they are found to this day, and thus became widely known even among Jews without much rabbinic learning.

Such passages are usually understood as commendations of the practices in question in the hope that Jews will observe them, and that they surely are. But there are other ways to commend a practice, and to limit the meaning of such statements to that one function is to miss the fact that they also serve to characterize the World-to-Come, that is, the nature of life after redemption. The following midrash builds beautifully on prophetic promises of the redemption—indeed, the re-creation—of human beings to make the connection of life before redemption and afterward:

> Israel said to the Holy One (blessed be He!), "Master of the Universe, You know the power of the Evil Inclination, how formidable it is!" The Holy One (blessed be He!) said to them, "Chip away [*saqqelu*] at it a little in this world, and I will remove it from you in the future," as it said, "Build up, build up the highway, / Remove the rocks [*saqqelu me'even*]!" (Isa 62:10). Similarly, it says, "Build up, build up a highway! / Clear a road! / Remove all obstacles /

From the road of My people!" (Isa 57:14). In the World-to-Come, I will uproot it from you: "I will remove the heart of stone (*'even*) from your body and
give [you a heart of flesh]" (Ezek 36:26).

The last verse cited comes from the oracle we considered in Chapter 8 in
which the prophet Ezekiel speaks of God's future repatriation and restoration of Israel. For Ezekiel, however, human nature is so incorrigibly evil
that there are no grounds to imagine human beings in the state of righteousness that such a restoration requires. Without such righteousness, the
sins that resulted in exile would immediately manifest themselves anew,
and the restoration, far from being permanent, as the prophet intends,
would be exceedingly short-lived. The answer is nothing short of a re-creation of human beings, in which God replaces their stony hearts with
fleshy ones, that is, hearts that are sensitive and obedient to the divine will,
and it is this that God promises to do in Ezekiel's oracle. The image of removing stones in Ezek 36:26, in turn, recalls the oracles of restoration in
Isaiah, which repeatedly speak of the urgency of raising up a highway by
clearing out the rocks that obstruct the march of the redeemed back to
Zion (Isa 57:14; 62:10). Finally, putting the oracles in the books of Ezekiel
and Isaiah together, we must infer that the "obstacles" to be removed from
the road of the redeemed are not only literal rocks, but metaphorical ones
as well, namely, the moral character of the would-be redeemed themselves, a character marked by the formidable power of the Evil Inclination.
The practical counsel of this sophisticated and complex little midrash is
that the people of Israel should chip away at those rocks best they can in
this world. They should engage in what we earlier termed "long-term suppressive therapy" so that God in his grace may remove the Evil Inclination
altogether, endowing them in the World-to-Come with a nature free of the
appetite for sin so prominent in This World. Moral victories are possible—
indeed, individuals can even train themselves to face a lessened degree of
temptation—in the here and now. Human righteousness is not solely a
consequence of divine grace; those who would be righteous must do their
own part. But the final victory, the one that allows for a life without inces-
sant moral struggle, requires the intervention of the creator to uproot the
Evil Inclination that he implanted within us in the beginning.

   The Jewish theology that we have been developing here is one that
avoids two familiar extremes. One is the position that says people can build

the perfect world on their own, as if the flawed, indeed wounded nature of the builders themselves were not an impediment to that utopian goal. The other extreme is the position that maintains that redemption is solely a matter of God's gracious intervention and there is nothing human beings can do to bring the higher world any closer. The theology that rejects these two extremes views life in the here and now as a set of tasks whose completion depends on, and will surely come through, God's act of re-creating human beings with a higher nature than they now have.

The notion of a re-creation of human beings to render them fit for life in the World-to-Come naturally calls to mind the resurrection of the dead. For, as we saw in Chapter 8, resurrection, too, is in the nature of a new creation. The logic of resurrection as a form of restoration and purification requires, in fact, that the new individuals rise from the dead without the tell-tale infirmities, moral or bodily, that defined their mortal lives. But here a serious problem presents itself. If the new individuals lack the physical characteristics they had in their lifetimes, surely the suspicion will arise that they are not the same individuals at all, that a sleight of hand and not the hand of God accounts for their putative return to life. To this problem, too, reports the Talmud, Rabbi Simon ben Laqish had an answer: "They shall rise with their defects and then be healed." Later, Rava, a Babylonian sage of the fourth century C.E., made use of a familiar verse to make the same point:

> I deal death and give life;
> I wounded and I will heal. (Deut 32:39)

He reconciled the seeming contradiction thus:

> The Holy One (blessed be He!) said: What I killed I will bring to life, and then what I wounded I will heal.

In other words, people will first be resurrected with their infirmities and then healed of them. Just as it would make no sense to enter the World-to-Come with the same flawed moral nature, so it would make no sense to enter it with the same flawed, mortal nature that defines the physical human beings in This World.

In Rava's two stages of resurrection, we see the paradox of the whole idea of resurrection as it has developed. On the one hand, were the dead to come back already healed and transformed, they would no longer be the same people—the same inextricable combination of body and soul—that they were in this life. On the other hand, were they to come back with their same defective, mortal bodies and morally ambiguous souls, they would be glaringly unfit for the eternal life in the World-to-Come for which they are to be resurrected. The schema of two stages—first resurrection, then healing—navigates the paradox brilliantly. It both preserves the continuity of personal identity and subjects the risen dead to a process of re-creation that renders them fit for life after death—a process and a state that are discontinuous with ordinary existence and barely imaginable by those who have not yet undergone them.

RESURRECTION AT SINAI

We have seen that according to the rabbis, observance of the commandments in the Torah is the major conduit by which Jews might come to resurrection and the life of the World-to-Come. The idea that Mosaic revelation presented the people Israel with the choice of life or death was already ancient, however, by the time of the rabbis. "See, I set before you this day life and prosperity, death and adversity," Moses is reported to have admonished Israel just before he died (Deut 30:15), equating life to obedience to the LORD's commandments and laws, and death to defection to other gods. It is significant that some rabbinic texts present these dynamics of life and death as enacted already on Mount Sinai, and not simply spoken of there: the Israelites experience first death, then resurrection even as the Torah is being revealed to them:

> Rabbi Joshua ben Levi said: At every utterance that went out from the mouth of the Holy One (blessed be He!), the souls of Israel went out [of them], as it is said, "My life went away when he spoke" (Song 5:6). Inasmuch as their souls went out [of them] at the first utterance, how did they accept the second utterance? He brought down the dew with which he will resurrect the dead and resurrected them, as it is said, "You released a bountiful rain, O God; / when Your inheritance languished, You sustained it" (Ps 68:10).

What caused Israel to die with each successive revelation in the Decalogue? The prooftext from the Song of Songs suggests one answer: the sheer emotional intensity of hearing God's voice, of standing so close to the ultimate source of all that is, caused Israel to swoon like a lover in the presence of her beloved. But the dual metaphor of medicine and poison that we have seen suggests another possibility (by no means mutually exclusive) — that the Torah itself, as Moses' address in Deut 30:15–20 already asserted, has within it potentials both for life and for death, depending on Israel's response to its injunctions. Indeed, on the same page of the Talmud in which we find Rabbi Joshua ben Levi's midrash, we also find this comment about the Torah by Rava: "To those who go to the right side of it, it is a life-giving medicine [*samma' dechayyei*]. To those who go to the left side of it, it is a deadly poison [*samma' demuta'*]." This, in turn, is simply another way of saying that if the wounded son (to revert to a midrash we cited earlier) keeps the compress on his injury, he thrives, but if he takes it off, he becomes gravely ill. The Torah offers no unconditional guarantee to any individual; it only presents the choice of two paths, one leading to life and one to death, and urges Israel, in Moses' words, to "Choose life" (Deut 30:19). In Rabbi Joshua ben Levi's midrash about Israel's death on Sinai, God's preference for life is so overwhelming that God pre-enacts the eschatological resurrection then and there, with the selfsame agent (the dew) with which he will revive the deceased of all generations at the end of days. At Sinai are both life and death, but at Sinai, too, the last word lies with life.

An augmented version of this same midrash appears in the *Pirké de-Rabbi Eliezer*, an early medieval collection:

> God spoke all these words, saying: "I am the LORD your God who brought you . . ." (Exod 20:1–2). The first sound went forth, and the heavens and earth quaked before it, the seas and rivers fled, the mountains and hills tottered, all the trees bent over, and the dead in Sheol came to life and stood up on their feet, as it is said, "[I make this covenant, with its sanctions, not with you alone, but both] with those who are standing here with us this day [before the LORD our God and with those who are not with us here this day]." All those who are destined to be created stood there with them on Mount Sinai, as it is said, "and with those who are not with us here this day" (Deut 29:13–14). And the Israelites who were living fell on their faces and died. A second sound went forth, and they came to life, stood up on their feet, and said to Moses, "Moses our master, if we are able to hear the voice of the Holy One (blessed be He!), we shall die the way we just did, as it is said, 'My life went away when he spoke'" (Song 5:6).

Here, an artful interpretation of Deut 29:13–14 weaves together even more tightly the two moments, the Sinaitic and the eschatological, or, if you will, revelation and resurrection. Not only does Israel experience death and resurrection on Sinai, but also those long deceased come back to life, to receive the Torah offered only after their deaths. Indeed, extending the Deuteronomic emphasis on the unending validity of God's covenant with the Jewish people, this midrash places at Sinai even generations yet to be, as all Israel — the dead, the living, and the unborn alike — face the supreme moment of revelation as one. The Sinaitic moment anticipates the Day of Judgment, just as the commandments of the Torah connect the Jew in the here and now to the World-to-Come.

CHRISTIANS AND JEWS — AGAIN

The theologies and practices of Judaism and Christianity are not only different but even, in some ways, mutually exclusive, and in drawing the parallels that we have, it has not been our intention to imply otherwise. Jewish-Christian dialogue is authentic only to the extent that it includes comparison as well as contrast, an examination and frank discussion of both the commonalities and the points of difference. One outstanding difference relates to the identity of the community that is defined as the people of God. In Christian theology, that community is the church, the mystical body of Christ, to use the classical theological language. Christians differ among themselves, of course, as to which church most fully manifests the body of Christ, but rarely about the theological and practical importance of the church itself. In Judaism, although God is the father of everyone, not just the Jews, his covenant is still and forever with the people Israel. As we saw in Chapter 2, this difference between Christianity and Judaism is not the difference between universalism and particularism, but one between two forms of particularism, both of which make, each in its own way, universal claims.

Another outstanding difference relates to the issue of the form of life that God requires of the particular community, offering it a foretaste of the post-resurrection reality. The life of Christian discipleship and the life of Torah observance are not the same thing, obviously. Baptism, the Eucharist, and the Our Father are not the same thing as observance of the Sabbath and study of the Torah, for example, though they play analogous roles in pro-

viding the respective communities an anticipation in the present of the redeemed life of the future. The parallels lie not only in the function these
distinctive practices play and in the moral norms of the two communities
but also in the role that religious practice plays in the spiritual drama of the
self in the two religions. The Christians who at baptism renounce Satan
and commit themselves to a life free of Satan's power have more than a little in common with the Jews who, faced with the insidious power of the
Evil Inclination, turn to Torah in the hope of overcoming the temptations
it presents. And the Jews who experience a foretaste of the World-to-Come
in the weekly Sabbath or in the daily study of Jewish laws have a striking
parallel in the Christians for whom the Eucharist is a precious mode of
participation in the resurrected life.

Earlier in this chapter, we saw that Torah came to be equated with the
Wisdom that Proverbs associates with the Tree of Life and thus, understood in the context of late antiquity, with the conduit to eternal life as well.
On the Christian side, we can productively compare—but also contrast—
the apostle Paul, for whom not the Jewish Torah but Jesus is "the wisdom
of God" (1 Cor 1:24). And it is Jesus whom Paul believes to have reversed
the death sentence of Eden, ushering in the unmerited gift of eternal life
(Rom 5:12–21). For all the obvious differences between Torah and gospel,
the traditions focused on them find in them the basis for the reversal of the
death sentence on human beings. Contrary to what one often hears, the
difference between Judaism and Christianity, as they took shape in late antiquity, is not a difference between a this-worldly and an otherworldly religion, for both traditions affirm both worlds and take them with utmost se-
riousness. It is rather a difference about what constitutes God's highest
revelation of the Wisdom that defines the way faithful members of each
community should live even now and that, according to the classical form
of each tradition, will surely result in the resurrection of the dead and the
gift of eternal life.

NOTES

CHAPTER 1: CHRISTIAN HOPE AND ITS JEWISH ROOTS

Our use of the term "wise" in Dan 12:3 departs from the NJPS, for reasons that will become clear in Chap. 10. For a thorough introduction to restoration eschatology, see E. P. Sanders, *Jesus and Judaism* (Philadelphia: Fortress, 1985), which profoundly shaped our thinking on the relation of Jesus to Jewish apocalyptic eschatology. Sanders' thoughts on the relationship of the twelve tribes and Jesus' twelve apostles may be found in this book, pp. 95–106. John Collins provides a fine introduction to Jewish apocalyptic thought and literature in *The Apocalyptic Imagination: An Introduction to Jewish Apocalyptic Literature* (Grand Rapids, Mich.: William B. Eerdmans, 1998). For a sociological analysis of this literature, see Paul D. Hanson, *The Dawn of Apocalyptic: the Historical and Sociological Roots of Jewish Apocalyptic Eschatology* (Philadelphia: Fortress, 1979). A very readable survey of this literature and of Second Temple Judaism may be found in Paula Fredriksen, *From Jesus to Christ* (2nd ed.; New Haven, Conn., and London: Yale University Press, 2000), Part II, 65–93. Those interested in the works of Josephus might start with some of the seven volumes of his *Jewish Antiquities* (Loeb Classical Library; Cambridge, Mass.: Harvard University Press, 1930–65), or his account of the Jewish-Roman war, *The Jewish War*, 2 vols. (Loeb Classical Library; Cambridge, Mass.: Harvard University Press, 1926). Readers interested in the Dead Sea Scrolls discovered at Qumran should see Florentino García Martínez, *Qumran and Apocalyptic: Studies on the Aramaic Texts from Qumran*. Studies on the Texts of the Desert of Judah, vol. 9 (Leiden and New York: E. J. Brill, 1992). The text from the *War Rule* quoted here was translated by Geza Vermes in *The Complete Dead Sea Scrolls in English* (rev. ed.; London: Penguin, 2004), 185. Albert Schweitzer's path-breaking book on Jesus, warmly recommended, is *The Quest of the Historical Jesus: A Critical Study of Its Progress from Reimarus to Wrede* (London: A. and C. Black Ltd.,

1926). For a very fine short analysis of the quests for the historical Jesus, see Mark Allan Powell, *Jesus as a Figure in History: How Modern Historians View the Man from Galilee* (Louisville, Ky.: Westminster John Knox Press, 1998). For Jesus in his historical context, we have found the recent work of Dale Allison extremely helpful. See his *Jesus of Nazareth: Millenarian Prophet* (Philadelphia: Fortress, 1998). Allison persuasively debates Marcus Borg, John Dominic Crossan, and Stephen Patterson on whether or not Jesus should be understood in apocalyptic terms in *The Apocalyptic Jesus: A Debate* (Santa Rosa, Calif.: Polebridge Press, 2001). Allison's observation that Jesus' chief goal, as "the last prophet in the cosmic drama," was "to prepare his people for the eschatological finale" appears on p. 29 of this book. (For similar observations, see *Jesus of Nazareth: Millenarian Prophet*, 68–69). This book also has the merit of providing brief summaries of the positions of other leading figures in the debate on the historical Jesus. E. P. Sanders has a fine, short book on the historical Jesus as an eschatological prophet: *The Historical Figure of Jesus* (London: Penguin, 1993). The observations on the centrality of the Temple to Jesus and Palestinian Judaism may be found in this book, pp. 255–56. (We have left the quotations of Isa 56:7 and Jer 7:11 in Mark 11:17 as they appear in the NRSV). Another short, readable introduction to the historical Jesus, whose title says it all, is Bart D. Ehrman, *Jesus: Apocalyptic Prophet of the New Millennium* (New York and Oxford: Oxford University Press, 1999). The book of Enoch is translated in R. H. Charles, *The Apocrypha and Pseudepigrapha of the Old Testament* (Oxford: Clarendon Press, 1998; originally published 1913). The quote from 1 Enoch 90 is taken from this edition. Reflections on the "transphysical" nature of Jesus' body may be found *passim* in N. T. Wright, *The Resurrection of the Son of God* (Philadelphia: Fortress, 2003). His observation on Jesus' resurrection as "the proleptic fulfillment of Israel's great hope" may be found in this book, p. 587.

CHAPTER 2: THE FIRST FRUITS OF THOSE WHO HAVE DIED

The quote from N. T. Wright regarding Paul's doctrine of the resurrection and its resemblance to that of the Pharisees may be found in *The Resurrection of the Son of God*, 215. For George A. Lindbeck's use of the term "Israel-like" body to describe the early church, see "Confession and Community: An Israel-Like View of the Church," *The Christian Century* 107: 16 (1990): 492–96; and Lindbeck, "Ecumenical Imperatives for the Twenty-First Century," *Currents in Theology and Mission* 20 (1993): 363–64. The quotes from E. P. Sanders in this chapter are from *Paul and Palestinian Judaism* (Minneapolis: Fortress, 1977). The quote on the distinction between those outside and inside the covenant may be found on p. 257; that on the compatibility for Paul of salvation by grace and reward for deeds on p. 516; that on the destruction of those who are apart from Christ and the salvation of those who participate in his body on p. 473; that on the corporate and participatory nature of Paul's soteriology on pp. 502 and 508; that on the need to give up "righteousness by faith" as a clue to Paul's thought on p. 438; and on Christ's death as effecting a change in lordship on pp. 466 and 500.

We have quoted Isa 59:20–21 from the NRSV in this chapter in order to capture Paul's understanding of it in Rom 11:25–27. The quotes from Troy Martin on the class, ethnic, and gender distinctions of Gal 3:28 may be found in "The Covenant of Circumcision [Genesis 17:9–14] and the Situational Antitheses in Galatians 3:28," *Journal of Biblical Literature* 122 (2003): 111–25, 122, 124. The importance of the expression of being "in Christ," stressed by Schweitzer, may be found in *The Mysticism of Paul the Apostle* (New York: Macmillan, 1955), 125. His observation on what takes place during baptism may be found in the same volume, p. 19. The quote from Dale Martin on a segment of the Corinthian community questioning the idea that human bodies can survive after death may be found in *The Corinthian Body* (New Haven, Conn.: Yale University Press), 122. The quote from Martin on what parts of the human body are capable of being raised may be found in the same book, p. 128.

CHAPTER 3: A JOURNEY TO SHEOL (AND BACK)

The quotations from Johannes Pedersen are taken from *Israel: Its Life and Culture* (*South Florida Studies in the History of Judaism* 28; Atlanta, Ga.: Scholars Press, 1991; originally published 1926–40), 461, 470. The observation on 1 Kgs 2:6 is found in John Gray, *I and II Kings* (2nd ed.; London: SCM, 1970), 102. The translations from Akkadian are those of Ephraim A. Speiser in *Ancient Near Eastern Texts Relating to the Old Testament*, ed. James B. Pritchard (3rd ed.: Princeton, N.J.: Princeton University Press, 1969), 98–99, 107. The summary judgment about the gloominess of the Mesopotamian netherworld comes from Jerrold S. Cooper, "The Fate of Mankind: Death and Afterlife in Ancient Mesopotamia," in *Death and Afterlife: Perspectives of World Religions*, ed. Hiroshi Obayashi (New York: Greenwood Press, 1992), 27. On Sheol, see Philip S. Johnston, *Shades of Sheol: Death and Afterlife in the Old Testament* (Downers Grove, Ill.: Intervarsity, 2002), 69–124. The quotation about the feeling of the endangered that they are already in Sheol is taken from Nicholas J. Tromp, *Primitive Conceptions of Death and the Netherworld in the Old Testament* (*Biblica et orientalia* 21; Rome: Pontifical Biblical Institute, 1969), 36. Other citations from Tromp can be found on pp. 36, 37, and 39. In our translation of 2 Sam 22:11, we read "he flew" for "he was seen" with several ancient versions and with Ps 18:11 for reasons of sense; the two Hebrew words differ in only one consonant, r/d (the two can look exceedingly similar in some periods). On creation as an act of rescue from the death-dealing waters, see Jon D. Levenson, *Creation and the Persistence of Evil: The Jewish Drama of Divine Omnipotence* (2nd ed., Princeton, N.J.: Princeton University Press, 1994). On the cult of the dead, see Theodore J. Lewis, *Cults of the Dead in Ancient Israel and Ugarit* (*Harvard Semitic Monographs* 39; Atlanta, Ga.: Scholars Press, 1989); Karel van der Toorn, *Family Religion in Babylonia, Syria and Israel* (Leiden: Brill, 1996), 206–35; and Johnston, *Shades*, 150–95. A more skeptical view can be found in Brian B. Schmidt, *Israel's Beneficent Dead: Ancestor Cult and Necromancy in Ancient Israelite Religion and Tradition* (*Forschungen zum Alten Testament* 11; Tübingen: J. C. B. Mohr [Paul Siebeck], 1994). On Deut 26:14 as approving food offerings to the dead, see, for example, Herbert Chanan Brichto, "Kin, Cult, Land and Afterlife: A Biblical Complex," *Hebrew Union College Annual* 45 (1973): 29; Elizabeth Bloch-Smith, *Judahite Burial Practices and Beliefs about the Dead* (*Journal for the Study of the Old Testament* Supplement Series [JSOTSS] 123; Sheffield, U.K.: Sheffield Academic Press, 1992), 126; and Rachel S. Hallote, *Death, Burial, and Afterlife in the Biblical World: How the Israelites and their Neighbors Treated the Dead* (Chicago: Ivan R. Dee, 2001), 62. The citations from Hallote are found in *Death*, 36–37, and 65. In Isa 29:3, we read *kedavid* for *kaddur* with the Greek, unlike the NJPS. In v 5, we read *zedayik* for *zarayik*, with the Dead Sea Scrolls. The citations from van der Toorn are drawn from *Family Religion*, 230. On the rendezvous with the deceased father in the Greco-Roman world, see *Odyssey* 11:150–224 and *Aeneid* 6:680–83, 756–885. Abraham's near sacrifice of Isaac is explored in Jon D. Levenson, *The Death and Resurrection of the Beloved Son: The Transformation of Child Sacrifice in Judaism and Christianity* (New Haven, Conn., and London: Yale University Press, 1993), esp. 3–31, 111–42. A good argument in favor of connecting the proscription of the cult of the dead with Hezekiah can be found in B. Halpern, "Jerusalem and the Lineages in the Seventh Century BCE: Kinship and the Rise of Individual Moral Liability," in *Law and Ideology in Monarchic Israel* (JSOTSS 124; ed. Baruch Halpern and Deborah Hobson; Sheffield, U.K.: Sheffield Academic Press, 1991), 71–74.

CHAPTER 4: WHO GOES TO SHEOL — AND WHO DOES NOT

The quotation from Johnston is taken from *Shades*, 72. Those from Rosenberg can be found in "The Concept of Sheol within the Context of Ancient Near Eastern Beliefs," a dissertation in the Department of Near Eastern Languages and Civilizations, Harvard University (1981), 71, 163, 71, 85. The citation from the Talmud can be found on *b. Ber.* 57b. A good discussion of the distribution of "he slept/he lay with his fathers" as opposed to "he died" can be found in Johnston, *Shades*, 34–35. The observation by James L. Kugel can be found in "Wisdom and the Anthological Temper," *Prooftexts* 17 (1997): 14–15. This translation of Prov 10:7 departs from the NJPS, which, by rendering *livrakha* "is invoked in blessing," provides more specificity than the words themselves allow, and whose rendering of *shem* as "fame" seems doubtful, for reasons that will be-

come evident later. The distinction between a "bad" death and a "good" death is suc-
cinctly made in Lloyd R. Bailey Sr., *Biblical Perspectives on Death* (*Overtures to Biblical Theology*; Philadelphia: Fortress, 1979), 48–52.

<h2 style="text-align:center">CHAPTER 5: HEAVEN ON EARTH</h2>

In Ezek 28:12, we read *chotam tavnit*. Lawrence E. Stager's article is "Jerusalem and
the Garden of Eden," *Eretz-Israel* 26 (1999): 184–94. The passages cited are found on
pp. 183–86. On the religious meaning of the Zion traditions, see Jon D. Levenson,
Sinai and Zion: An Entry into the Jewish Bible (pbk. ed.; San Francisco: Harper-
Collins, 1987), 89–184. In Ps 36:7, we have altered the NJPS "high mountains" to
"mountains of El" in order to capture the likely mythological resonance of the phrase.
In Ezek 47:7, read *'el-hammayim* with the Greek for *'el-hayyamma*. In verse 10, read
ya'amdu. On the connection of Eden/Temple with life, see Gary A. Anderson, *The
Genesis of Perfection: Adam and Eve in Jewish and Christian Imagination* (Louisville,
Ky., and Leiden: Westminster John Knox, 2001), esp. pp. 46–52. The midrash about
Adam and the destruction of the Temple is *Gen. Rab.* 21:8. The quotation about the
Mesopotamian Enmeduranna is taken from E. A. Speiser, *Genesis* (Anchor Bible 1;
Garden City, N.Y.: Doubleday, 1964), 43. The quotations from Rashi and ibn Ezra are
found in their comments on Gen 5:24. The translation from Jubilees is by O. S. Win-
termute in *The Old Testament Pseudepigrapha*, ed. James H. Charlesworth (Garden
City, N.Y.: Doubleday, 1985), 2:62. In Ps 73:24, we have changed "led me toward
honor" (NJPS) to "will receive me with glory" for reasons that become apparent in the
ensuing discussion. God's teaching Torah to little children who have died appears in *b.
Abod. Zara* 3b.

<h2 style="text-align:center">CHAPTER 6: HOW BIRTH REVERSES DEATH</h2>

The quote from Hans Walter Wolff is found in his *Anthropology of the Old Testament* (Philadelphia: Fortress, 1974), 20. Aubrey Johnson's quote is taken from *The Vitality of the Individual in the Thought of Ancient Israel* (Cardiff: University of Wales
Press, 1949), 66. Those of Robert Di Vito are drawn from "Old Testament Anthropology and the Construction of Personal Identity," *Catholic Biblical Quarterly* 61 (1999):
220, 221, 223. The comment of Rabbi David Kimchi appears in his commentary to Gen
22:1. For rabbinic observations on *karet*, see Rashi to Gen 17:14 and to *b. Shab.* 25b.
Donald J. Wold's comment can be found in "The *Kareth* Penalty in P: Rationale and
Cases," ed. Paul J. Achtemeier (SBL Seminar Papers 1979, Vol. 1; Missoula, Mont.:
Scholars Press, 1979), 15. Our translation of Prov 10:7 departs from the NJPS, which, by
rendering *livrakhah* as "is invoked in blessing," provides more specificity than the

words themselves allow, and whose rendering of *shem* as "fame" seems doubtful, for reasons that should be evident from the discussion. William McKane's observation appears in *Proverbs: A New Approach* (Philadelphia: Westminster Press, 1970), 422–23.

CHAPTER 7: THE DEATH AND RESURRECTION OF THE PROMISED SON

For the translation of *'ednah* as "fertility" in Gen 18:12 (as opposed to the NJPS "enjoyment"), see Jonas Greenfield, "A Touch of Eden," in *Al Kanfei Yonah*, ed. Shalom Paul et al., 2:750–55. We have changed the NJPS translation "at the time that life is due" in verse 14 simply to "next year." On this translation of the elusive phrase *ka'et chayyah*, see Mordechai Cogan and Hayim Tadmor, *II Kings* (Anchor Bible 11; Garden City, N.Y.: Doubleday, 1988), 57. The observation about "entrance" or "doorway" in Genesis 18 and 2 Kings 4 is taken from Robert L. Cohn, *2 Kings* (Berit Olam; Collegeville, Minn.: Liturgical Press, 2000), 29. On the binding of Isaac in Genesis 22, see Levenson, *Death*, 125–42; on its counterpart in Genesis 21, pp. 125–42; and on the role of Judah's losses in the Joseph story, pp. 157–64.

CHAPTER 8: REVIVAL IN TWO MODES

In Isa 54:2, the translation "extend" reads *hattu* in place of *yattu* with several ancient versions. The quotations from John F. Kutsko are taken from his book *Between Heaven and Earth: Divine Presence and Absence in the Book of Ezekiel* (*Biblical and Judaic Studies from the University of California, San Diego* 7; Winona Lake, Ind.: Eisenbrauns, 2000), 133–37. The rabbinic connection between creation and resurrection is made on *b. Sanh.* 91a, and the quotation from Rabbi Eliezer appears on *b. Sanh.* 92b.

CHAPTER 9: "I DEAL DEATH AND GIVE LIFE"

The quotation from Lloyd R. Bailey Sr. can found in his *Biblical Perspectives*, 38. We have borrowed the helpful term "biological cessation" from p. 39 of the same book. The Talmudic passage cited is on *b. Sanh.* 91b. Aubrey Johnson's observation comes from *The Vitality*, 94. "Fattened" in 1 Sam 2:5 departs from the NJPS for reasons nicely laid out in P. Kyle McCarter, *I Samuel* (Anchor Bible 8; Garden City, N.Y.: Doubleday, 1980), 72.

CHAPTER 10: THE GREAT AWAKENING

We depart from the NJPS in rendering *maskilim* in Daniel 11–12 as "wise" rather than "knowledgeable." The Talmudic expression "Sleep is one-sixtieth of death" can be found on *b. Ber.* 57b. In Isa 52:14, we read *'alayv* with the Syriac and Targum. *Yazzeh* in verse 15 is very unclear and here translated *ad sensum* and in accordance with the Greek. Rav's characterization of the World-to-Come is found on *b. Ber. 17a.* The words of George W. E. Nickelsburg Jr. are found in his *Resurrection, Immortality, and Eternal Life in Intertestamental Judaism* (Harvard Theological Studies 26; Cambridge, Mass.: Harvard University Press, 1972), 19. The translations from 1 Enoch are those of Ephraim Isaac in *The Old Testament Pseudepigrapha,* ed. James H. Charlesworth (Garden City, N.Y.: Doubleday, 1983), 1:24. Isa 26:19 presents several challenges to the translator. On our translation "as a corpse," see Philip C. Schmitz, "The Grammar of Resurrection in Isaiah 26:19a–c," *Journal of Biblical Literature* 122 (2003): 145–49. In Isa 26:19, the term may have the more usual meaning, "lights." The translation of the last line departs from the NJPS, which reads, "You make the land of the shades come to life," apparently on the grounds that the Hebrew verb *hippil* has the meaning "to drop young" and thus carries with it a connotation of new life. The more usual translation "to make something fall" seems more in order, with "dew" as the understood object. Brevard S. Childs' observation about Isaiah 26 can be found in his *Isaiah* (Old Testament Library; Louisville, Ky.: Westminster John Knox, 2001), 189. John Day's development of the connections between these verses in Isaiah and the book of Hosea can be found in his *[Yнwн] and the Gods and Goddesses of Canaan* (JSOTSS 265; Sheffield, U.K.: Sheffield Academic Press, 2000), 116–27. His comment on the difference between Zoroastrian and Jewish notions of resurrection is found in his article "The Development of Belief in Life after Death in Ancient Israel," in *After the Exile,* ed. John Barton and David J. Reimer (Macon, Ga.: Mercer University Press, 1996), 242. Michael Barré's comment on death and life can be found in his article "New Light on the Interpretation of Hosea VI 2," *Vetus Testamentum* 28 (1978): 137–38. Our translation of Hos 6:2 departs from the NJPS rendering of the first and last verbs as "make whole" and "be whole," respectively, a rendering that seems to have been dictated by a dubious interpretation of the verse as having nothing to do with resurrection. We render *lephanayv* as "in His presence," though the NJPS translation "by His favor" is surely also possible. Frank Moore Cross' remarks on the Divine Warrior are taken from his book *Canaanite Myth and Hebrew Epic* (Cambridge: Harvard University Press, 1973), 162–63. Our discussion of Isaiah 34–35 is indebted to Cross' treatment on pp. 17–74, 164–74. Note that Cross associates Isaiah 34–35 with the work of Second Isaiah (chaps. 40–55). Leonard J. Greenspoon's observation is taken from his study of "The Origins of the Idea of Resurrection," in *Traditions in Transformation,* ed. Baruch Halpern and Jon D. Levenson (Winona Lake, Ind.: Eisenbrauns, 1981), 280.

CHAPTER 11: THE LEAST KNOWN TEACHING IN JUDAISM

In our translation of Gevurot, "You make the wind blow and the rain fall" appears in parentheses because it is recited only during the rainy season in the Land of Israel (roughly October to April). The parable of the two watchmen is found in *b. Sanh.* 91a—b. We have altered the NJPS translation of Ps 50:4 so as to bring out the point of the parable. The prayer upon waking is found in *b. Ber.* 60b (the wording in most prayer books today is slightly different). The mishnah that defines belief in the resurrection of the dead as a requirement is *Sanh.* 10:1. "He denied the resurrection of the dead . . ." is found on *b. Sanh.* 90a. "Then Moses sang [*shar*]" comes from *Mekilta de-Rabbi Ishmael*, Shirta' 1. The Talmudic exegeses of Num 18:28 and Exod 6:4 are found on *b. Sanh.* 90b. Maimonides' interpretation of the Talmudic expression that the righteous "enjoy the radiance of the Divine Presence" appears in his *Mishneh Torah, Hilkhot Teshuvah* 8:2. His response to his critics can be found in *Moses Maimonides' Treatise on Resurrection*, ed. Fred Rosner (New York: KTAV, 1982), and Abraham Halkin and David Hartman, *Crisis and Leadership* (Philadelphia: Jewish Publication Society of America, 1985), 209–92. The passages we have quoted come from pp. 35 and 33, respectively, in Rosner. On the controversy surrounding Maimonides' thinking on resurrection, see Daniel Jeremy Silver, "The Resurrection Debate," in *Moses Maimonides'* (ed. Rosner), 71–102, reprinted from D. J. Silver, *Maimonidean Criticism and the Maimonidean Controversy, 1180–1240* (Leiden: Brill, 1965); Louis Jacobs, *Principles of the Jewish Faith* (New York: Basic Books, 1964), 399–408; and Marc B. Shapiro, *The Limits of Orthodox Theology* (Portland, Ore.: Littmann Library of Jewish Classics, 2004), 149–56. The three modern options for dealing with unpalatable doctrines in the prayer book are quoted from Neil Gillman, *The Death of Death: Resurrection and Immortality in Jewish Thought* (Woodstock, Vt.: Jewish Lights, 1997), 193. His quoted remarks on Geiger, Einhorn, and the *Gates of Prayer* are found on pp. 198–201. "Only the body has died" is taken from *The Union Prayerbook for Jewish Worship* (New York: Central Conference of American Rabbis, 1961), 72. The translation "Thou preservest all" can be found on p. 124 of the same edition. "We pray . . . for love through which we may all blossom into persons who have gained power over our own lives" and "Praised be the God whose gift is life" are taken from *The Gates of Prayer: The New Union Prayer Book* (New York: Central Conference of American Rabbis, 5735/1975), 255–56. Gillman's quote about the translation practices of the *Sabbath and Festival Prayer Book* (New York: The Rabbinical Assembly of America and the United Synagogue of America, 1946) can be found on p. 206 of *The Death of Death*. His reference there is to the introduction by Rabbi Robert Gordis to *Sabbath and Festival Prayer Book*, viii—ix. His remark about *Siddur Sim Shalom* is on p. 207 of *The Death of Death*. The translation "Master of [or over] life and death" can be found, for example, in *Siddur Sim*

Shalom: For Shabbat and Festivals (New York: The Rabbinical Assembly and the
United Synagogue for Conservative Judaism, 1998), 35a.

CHAPTER 12: WHAT WAS WRONG WITH THE GNOSTIC GOSPEL?

The quotations from Tertullian are from his *De resurrectione*, ed. J. G. Ph. Borleffs,
in *Corpus Christianorum* 2 (Turnhout: Brepols, 1954), pp. 921–1012. The quotations
from Irenaeus, and those reported of Basilides and Valentinus, are all from Irenaeus,
Contre les heresies, ed. A. Rousseau, L. Doutreleau, and C. A. Mercier, in *Sources chré-
tiennes*, 10 vols., nos. 100, 152–53, 210–11, 263–64, 293–94 (Paris: Éditions du Cerf,
1963–2002). Generally, we have relied on translations from the *Ante-Nicene Christian
Library*, checking them against the original Latin of Tertullian and the Latin in which
Irenaeus survives in the two editions cited. The quotation from Celsus is found in Origen, *Contra Celsum*, ed. Henry Chadwick (New York: Cambridge University Press,
1980), 274. The quote from the *Gospel of Philip* 73.1–3 and from *The Treatise on Resurrection* may be found in *The Nag Hammadi Library in English*, ed. James M. Robin-
son (New York: Harper and Row, 1977), 153 and 56, respectively.

Some have argued that, in order to understand why the orthodox view of the bodily
resurrection won out, we need to understand how it functioned politically in the early
Christian community. In the first chapter of her book *The Gnostic Gospels* (New York:
Vintage, 1979), Elaine Pagels has argued that the doctrine served to legitimate the authority of those bishops who claimed to be in succession to the apostles. Looking at the
doctrine not in terms of its religious content but its function, she concludes that bodily
resurrection was intended to undergird the power of the emerging, male orthodox hierarchy. See also Ulrich Wilckens, *Resurrection* (Edinburgh: St. Andrews, 1977), and
John Gager, "Body Symbols and Social Reality: Resurrection, Incarnation and Asceti-
cism in Early Christianity," *Religion* 12 (1982), 345–64, both of which develop this
theme.

The quotes from Caroline Walker Bynum challenging this thesis may be found in
her *The Resurrection of the Body in Western Christianity* (New York: Columbia University Press, 1995), 109–13, esp. p. 110. Calling Bynum's observations "too kind," Jan N.
Bremmer has pointed out that the argument that resurrection was a "displaced dis-
course about status and hierarchy in the church" suffers from several fatal defects. He
observes, most importantly, that "very little" is supplied "in the way of argument." The
few texts that are adduced focus, crucially, "on the importance of the resurrection to
the early Christian movement." See his *The Rise and Fall of the Afterlife* (New York:
Routledge, 2002), esp. 51–53.

CHAPTER 13: THE REDEEMED LIFE—IN THE HERE AND NOW

The comments from Cyril of Jerusalem's *Catechetical Lectures* and Gregory of Nazianzus' *Oration on Baptism* may be found in vol. 7 of the *Ante-Nicene Fathers Series*, series 2, ed. Philip Schaff (New York: Christian Literature Publishing Co., 1892), 283, 284 (two quotations), 279, 282, 300, and 372. The comments from Gregory of Nyssa's *On the Baptism of Christ* may be found in vol. 5 of the *Ante-Nicene Fathers Series*, series 2, pp. 708 and 717. The quotation from Tertullian's *On Baptism* may be found in vol. 3 of the *Ante-Nicene Fathers Series*, ed. Philip Schaff (New York: Christian Literature Publishing Co., 1885), p. 673. The quotation from Theodore of Mopsuestia may be found in his *Homélies Catéchétiques*, ed. and trans. R. Tonneau and R. Devreesse (Vatican City: Apostolic Library, 1949), 408–09. The quotation from the *Didaché* may be found in *Early Christian Fathers*, ed. Cyril C. Richardson (New York: Collier, 1970), 175. The comment from *On Prayer* may be found in *Origen: An Exhortation to Martyrdom, Prayer and Selected Works*, ed. Rowan Greer (New York: Paulist Press, 1979), 132–33. We have departed from the NJPS translation of Isa 28:8 in the direction of greater literalism in order to bring out the connection to feasting.

The first comment by Rabbi Simon ben Laqish is found on *b. Suk.* 52b; the second, about the identity of Satan, the Evil Inclination, and the Angel of Death, appears on *b. B. Bat.* 16a;, and the third, on inciting the Good Inclination, on *b. Ber.* 5a. In the last of these, we have rendered the last verb in accordance with the alternative translation in the NJPS note in order to bring out the association with death that the midrash makes. The list of the seven commandments incumbent on gentiles is found on *b. Sanh.* 56a. The midrash comparing the Torah to a life-giving medicine is found on *b. Qidd.* 30b. The statement about studying *halakhot* appears on *b. Meg.* 28b. The association of Psalm 92 with the Future Age appears in *m. Tam.* 7:4, and the midrash about chipping away at the Evil Inclination, in *Num. Rab.* 15:16. Rava's comment on Deut 32:39 and the objection voiced by Rabbi Shimon ben Laqish that it answers appear on *b. Sanh.* 91b. Rabbi Joshua ben Levi's midrash about resurrection on Sinai and Rava's on the Torah as medicine or poison are found on *b. Shab.* 88b. We have changed the biblical quotes in Rabbi Joshua ben Levi's midrash from the NJPS version in order to facilitate the understanding of the midrash. The midrash about resurrection on Sinai in the *Pirké de-Rabbi Eliezer* is taken from chapter 41 of that work. On the problems with the familiar modern idea that Judaism teaches that human beings are fundamentally good, see Joel S. Kaminsky, "Paradise Regained: Rabbinic Reflections on Israel at Sinai," in *Jews, Christians, and the Theology of the Hebrew Scriptures*, ed. Alice Ogden Bellis and Joel S. Kaminsky (Society of Biblical Literature Symposium Series 8; Atlanta, Ga.: Society of Biblical Literature, 2000), 15–43.

INDEX OF PRIMARY SOURCES

HEBREW BIBLE

Genesis

1:2	53	12:2–3	125
1:6–7	51	12:7	211
1:9–10	51	12:7–8	64
2–3	88	12:10–20	62
2:7	84, 229	13:14–17	125
2:10–14	85	13:16	135
2:15	84	15	110
2:21	175	15:1–2	112
2:25–3:24	169	15:1–6	63, 125
3	84, 91	15:12	175
3:19	204	16	125
3:22–24	82, 89, 97	16:1–2	125
4:1–16	127, 181	16:9–11	125
4:4–5	181	17	110
4:7	249	17–18	125
4:10	181	17:4	112
4:12	181	17:17	125, 137
4:14	181	17:20	74
4:15	181	18:1–15	122
4:25	114	18:1–18	122
5:21–24	101, 168	18:10	123, 124
5:24	105	18:12	122, 125
6:1–4	169	18:13–14	123
12:1–7	135	18:14	123
12:2	74	18:25	70
		20	62

Genesis (*continued*)

21	125
21:9–14	125
21:16–17	125–26
21:18	74
21:18–19	126
21:33	64
22:1–19	64, 115, 122, 125
22:11–12	112
22:11	124
22:15	124
22:19	125
25:1–18	74
25:4	60
25:8	69, 71, 111, 159
25:20	137
25:20–21	63
25:21–23	135
25:26b	137
26:1–5	62
26:6–11	62
27:1–45	63
27:45	127
28:1–4	107–8
28:3–4	74
28:18–19	64
29:21–30	64
29:31	63, 138
30:1–2	63
30:1–8	137
30:22–24	137
32:13	135
35:28–29	63
37:18–28	53, 151
37:31–35	114
37:33–35	107
37:35	76, 139
37:36	53
38:6–11	127
38:9	114
39:20	53
41:14	53
42:13	139
42:32	139
42:36–38	127
43:1–14	127
45:26–27	115
48:5–7	115
48:11	74
50:2–3	64
50:23	74

Exodus

1:8–22	53, 128, 151
1:21	80
3:6	16, 211
3:15–16	16
6:4	211
6:6–8	150
6:9	151
6:24	60
12:22–23	240
13:11–13	64
13:17–14:31	53
14:21	51
14:21–23	9, 99
14:26	51
15:1a	208, 210, 211
15:10	51
15:12	47, 51
15:26	206
20:1–2	255
20:5	166
21:12	181
22:28–29	64
28:17–20	84
31:6	60
32:9–14	75
32:32–33	173
34:19–20	64

Leviticus

7:16–18	64
18:5	158
18:18	64
19:31	56, 65

20:2–5	64
20:27	56, 65
21:1–4	19
26	160

Numbers

1:12	60
2:22	60
16:30	47
16:32–34	47
18:28	210, 211
19	91
23:10	109
27:3–4	117
27:5–8	117
27:20	63
35:9–34	92
36:1–12	117

Deuteronomy

5:9	166
8:3	130
11:13–21	250
11:18	248
12:1–27	64
12:29–31	64
18:9–14	56, 57, 65
19:1–13	92
21:17	99–100
25:5–10	114, 117
25:6	117–18
26:12–14	55–56
26:14	64
28	160
29:13–14	255–56
30:15–20	255
30:19	169, 255
30:19–20	157
31:9–13	75
31:16	72
32:39	161, 162–63, 164, 191, 253
34	74
34:1	75

34:5–6	64
34:6	72
34:7	69

Joshua

1:6–8	75
3:9–4:24	99
12:22	60
17:2	60

Judges

13:2	63
16:30	109

1 Samuel

1:1–8	138
1:4–11	63
1:19b–20	138
2:1–10	67–68, 162
2:4–5	162
2:6	162–63, 164, 191
2:7–9	162
7:5–14	138
28:3	58, 65
28:3–25	57–59
28:4–7	58
28:13	61
28:15	58
28:19	58

2 Samuel

7:8–16	110
13	156
14:7	156
14:14	156, 163
18:18	64, 118
22:5–6	49, 51
22:8–19	50
22:17–18	51

1 Kings

1:32–40	86
2:5	43

1 Kings (*continued*)

2:6	43
2:9	104
5:7	164
5:13	84
5:15	164
12:1–24	63
17:1	100
17:17–24	168
17:24	164
18:3	181
18:20–40	182
21:3	181
21:27–29	182

2 Kings

2:1–12	98–100
2:6–12	168
4:1–7	126–28, 144
4:8	126
4:8–9	121
4:8–11	122
4:8–37	121–27, 131, 154–55, 163, 168
4:9	124
4:13–18	121
4:14	122
4:15	123–4
4:16	123
4:17	123
4:19	126
4:19–20	122
4:21	122
4:22–30	122
4:28	123, 154
4:31	122, 175
4:31–32	72
4:32–37	122
4:36	126
4:37	125
4:38	129
4:38–41	128–29
4:42–44	129–30
9:30–37	182

13:20–21	168
18:1–8	65
21:11–15	166
22:1–2	65
23:19–25	65
24:3–4	166

Isaiah

4:3	173–74
8:5–8	86
11:4	8
11:11–12	13–14
14:3–21	69
22:13	25
24–27	186–89, 196, 198
25:6–8	243
25:8	187, 196, 198
26:13–14	186, 187
26:17–18	187
26:19	6, 186, 188, 189, 196, 198
26:20–21	187
27:2–6	190
27:8	190
28:15	241
29:3–5	57
34–35	195–96
35:1–2	195
35:5	209
35:5–6	13
35:5–7	195
35:6	209
35:8–10	195
38:1–3	159
38:10	159
38:16–20	159
40:5	232
43:1–8	133–34
44:1–5	134–35, 136
44:2	135
44:3	135
48:17–19	135
48:19	135
49:14–26	142

50:1–3	143–44
51:3	98
52:13–15	177
52:13–53:12	177, 181, 188, 197
53:7–9	177
53:10	177
53:11	178, 197
54:1–10	136–38
54:4–6	144
54:6	144
56:5	118
56:7	17
57:14	251–52
58:8	209
59:20–21	33
60:5	209
60:13	18
60:21	206–7
61:1–3	12
62:10	251–52
66:22–24	179

Jeremiah

7:11	17
17:5–8	193–94
30:5–7	173
31:13	209
31:15	107, 139
31:15–17	139
33:15	202
51:39	175
51:57	175

Ezekiel

18	166–68
18:2	166
18:4	166
18:5–9	166
18:10–13	166
18:14–19	166
18:20	166
18:21–23	167
18:23	168

18:24	167
18:28	168
20	151–52
28:11–19	81–83
32:17–32	69, 72
34:23	108
36:24–28	149–50
36:26	252
36:33–36	98
37 38	227–29
37:1–8	149
37:1–10	151
37:1–14	146–55, 169, 188
37:5	228–29
37:6	148
37:9–10	148
37:11	150
37:12–14	148, 150
37:13–14	154
40–48	88
47:1–12	87–88, 90

Hosea

1–2	139–40
2:9	140
5–6	190
5:14	191
6:2	20, 26, 190
6:5	191
13–14	189–92
13:14	189
13:15	189
14:2–9	190, 198
14:5–6	189

Jonah

2:1	20, 96
2:3–8	49
2:3–10	95–96
2:11	50
4:3	101

Micah

5:1–5	138

Zechariah

9:9	16

Malachi

3:23–24	100

Psalms

1	194
3:6	175
4:5	250
6:6	96
9:8	52
9:14–15	51–52
15	92–93
16:10	71
18:5–7	96
23:4	53
23:5–6	93
30:4	163
36:6–11	86–87
36:10	89
37:32–33	247
49:6–13	169
49:15–16	102–3, 104, 105
50:4	205
61:2–5	48
68:10	254
69:29	173
73:19	105
73:23–28	103–4, 105
84:5	93, 94
84:11–13	93
88:2–10	45–46
88:4	54
88:5–6	54
88:7	54
88:19	54
89:20–38	110
89:49	73
90:12	159
92	251
92:13–16	85, 89
96:11–13	192
96:13	199
103:3–4	164
107:10–22	52–53
115:17	94
125:1–2	93
126:2	209
128	120
133	89–91
145:20	185

Proverbs

3:1–2	158–59, 168
3:13–18	158–59, 168, 176
3:18	82, 246–47
4:20–22	158–59
10:7	77, 117
15:24	176
30:15–16	111–12

Job

1	183
1:2	113
1:13–19	112
3	112
7:7–10	44–45
10:8	149
10:9	149
10:11	149
14:12	175
23:2–7	183
42:11–17	78
42:13	113
42:13–15	183
42:16	74, 81
42:17	69, 111, 159

Song of Songs (Song of Solomon, Canticles)

5:6	254, 255

Ruth

1:11–13	63
1:12–13	113

1:19b — 21   113, 114
4:11–12   113
4:16–17   113
4:16–22   138
4:17   113

Lamentations
1:1   141
3:16   97

Qohelet (Ecclesiastes)
9:2   69, 79, 182–83
11:9 –12:8   183

Daniel
2:44   176
7:13   28
10:16   171
11:21–31   180
11:32   173, 180
11:32–35   172
11:36–37   172
11:45   172
12:1   173, 185
12:1–3   171–181, 185–89, 196–200,
                    201, 203, 206
12:2   28, 79, 106, 131, 152, 153,
                    74, 175, 178, 180
12:2–3   6
12:3   177, 178, 197

1 Chronicles
5:30   60

APOCRYPHA

Tobit
14:5   19

Wisdom of Joshua ben Sira
(Ecclesiasticus)
11:26–28   184
50:23–24   184
50:25–26   184

2 Maccabees
7:23   229

OTHER SECOND TEMPLE JEWISH
LITERATURE

1 Enoch
22   174
22:3–4   185
90:28–29   18

Jubilees
4:22–25   102

War Rule   8

NEW TESTAMENT

Matthew
5:3–10   12
8:11–12   14
10:23   13, 28
10:28   20
10:31   230
11:4–6   13
11:18–19   11
12:41   20
17:11   19
19:28   19
21:1–8   16–17
21:12–17   17
22:1–14   244
22:31–32   211
25:1–13   244
28:9   21, 22

Mark
6:14   11
6:15   11
8:31   20
9:1   13
9:12   19
9:31   20

Mark (*continued*)

10:33–34	20
11:15–18	17
12:18–27	16
12:26–27	211
13: 29	13
13:30	13
16:6	20

Luke

3:9	10
3:17	10
7:11–17	11
11:32	20
12:4	20
13:28–29	14
13:29	244
14:12–14	20
14:14	244
14:15	244
15:11–32	14–16
19:11	19
19:38	17
19:45–48	17
20:37	211
22:14–20	243
22:16	21
22:18	21
24:30	21

John

2:13–22	17
3:5	237
11:1–44	22
20:19	22
20:24–28	22
20:24–29	221

Acts of the Apostles

1:6	19
2:22	29
2:24	20
2:36	29

3:12	29
4:10	29
5:35	29
21:38	9
23:8	208

Romans

1:16	34
2:12	33
4:16	31
5:12–21	82, 257
6	237
6:3	239
6:3–8	38
6:4	30, 39
6:4–5	240
6:6–7	240
8:1	39
8:17	25
8:21	34
8:29	37
11:1	32
11:22	34
11:23–25	244
11:25–27	33
11:26	244
12:3–8	35
12:4	36
12:11–12	29
13:12	29

1 Corinthians

1:24	257
3:16–17	37
6:9	33
6:19	232
7:1–16	35
7:25–40	35
7:29	29
8:11	33
10:6	33
10:11	29
11:2–16	35

11:19	227
11:28–31	35
12:12–13	34–35
12:13	38
15:1–2	34
15:3	25
15:4	26
15:6–8	26
15:9	24
15:14	2, 234
15:19	25
15:20	21, 24, 39, 175
15:22	35
15:23	27
15:32	25
15:35	40
15:40	40
15:42–43	40
15:44	41, 178
15:49	41
15:50	40, 232
15:54	40, 41, 233
15:55	41

2 Corinthians

2:15	33
4:3	33
5:17	37

Galatians

1:13	24
2:19–20	37
3:26	37–38
3:28	35
3:29	38
4:28	32
5:21	34

Ephesians

4:22	238
5:14	29

Philippians

1:6	29

3:5	26
3:10–11	36
3:18–19	33
3:20	39
3:21	41, 233
4:5	29

1 Thessalonians

4:13	28
4:16–17	28
5:2	28
5:6	28

1 John

3:2	233

RABBINIC LITERATURE

b. Avodah Zarah

3b	106

b. Bava Batra

16a	248

b. Berakhot

5a	250
17a	178
57b	72, 175
60b	205

Genesis Rabbah

21:8	96–98

Rabbi Abraham ibn Ezra's Commentary on the Torah

to Gen 5:24	101

b. Megillah

28b	251

Mekhilta de-Rabbi Ishmael

Shirta 1	208–9

Mishneh Torah, Hilkhot Teshuvah
(Maimonides)
8:2   213–14

Numbers Rabbah
15:16   251–52

Pirké de-Rabbi Eliezer
41   255–56

*Rabbi David Kimchi's Commentary
on the Torah*
to Gen 22:1   112

Rashi's Commentary on the Torah
to Gen 5:24   101

Targum Onkelos
Gen 5:24   102

b. Qiddushin
30b   248–49

m. Sanhedrin
10:1   206–7

b. Sanhedrin
56a   268
90a   207
90b   210–11
91a   149
91a–91b   204–5
91b   161, 253–54
92b   153

b. Shabbat
88b   254–55

b. Sukkah
52b   247

m. Tamid
7:4   251

Treatise on Resurrection
(Maimonides)   214–15

CLASSICAL CHRISTIAN
LITERATURE

Adversus Haereses (Irenaeus)
1.1.11   223
1.1.11–12   223
1.19.3   223
3   233
5.3.2   230
5.7.1   232
5.9.1   232
5.15.1–2   229

Apostles' Creed 2

Baptismal Homilies
(Theodore of Mopsuestia)
3   242

Catechetical Lectures (Cyril of
Jerusalem)
19.3   240
19.9   241
20.1   238
20.3   238
20.4   239

Contra Celsum (Origen)
5.14   226

Didaché
9:8   244–45
16:3–8   245

De resurrectione (Tertullian)
1   226
3   230
4   231, 234
7   232
11   229, 230

12	231
13	230
14–17	232
18	231
20	228
22	228
23–24	233
29–30	228
30	228
34	233
55	232

Gospel of Phillip   223

Nicene Creed   2
On Baptism (Tertullian)

9	240

On Prayer (Origen)

15	246

On the Baptism of Christ (Gregory of Nissa)   238–39, 241

Oration on Baptism (Tertullian)

40.3	240
40.33	242

The Treatise on Resurrection (Nag Hammadi text)   223

General Index

Aaron, 47, 90, 210–11
Abba Saul, 206–7
Abraham: and birth of Isaac, 123, 125; blessing of/promise to, 107–8, 110, 113, 132, 135, 150, 211–12; death of, 62–64, 66, 69–75, 78, 111, 159; in Paul's thought, 31–33. *See also* aqedah/binding of Isaac
Absalom, 64, 118, 156
Adam: creation of, 229; in Ezekiel, 84; and Garden of Eden narrative, 82, 88, 96–98, 116, 204, 241; in Paul's thought, 31, 35, 41, 82; and Seth, 114
Aeneid, 62
aeons, shift in, 36, 38–39, 238
Akiva, Rabbi, 206–7
Allison, Dale, 10, 13
Amidah, 201–3, 215
Antiochus IV, 180, 185, 188, 199
Apocalypse of Abraham, 7–8
Apocalyptic, 6–10, 14, 19–21, 27–29, 41, 131, 165, 176, 197–200
apocalyptic prophet, 9–17
apocalyptic sign, 9, 21
Apostles' Creed, 2–4
aqedah/binding of Isaac, 115, 122, 124–25

Baal, 62, 182, 198
Babylonia: empire of, 83, 175, 199; and exile of Israel, 5, 132, 146, 166, 189; Land of, 84, 148, 253
Bailey, Lloyd R., Sr., 157
Baptism, 10, 30, 31, 32, 35–39, 41
Barré, Michael, 190
Baruch, Second Book of, 7
Basilides, 223, 225
Baur, Ferdinand Christian, 30–32
Beatitudes, 12
Benjamin, 114, 127
body: church as, 30, 31–32, 34–36, 38–39, 239, 256; and death, 91, 102; and Jesus, 21–22, 222, 224–25, 240; and judgment, 204–5; and resurrection, 39–41, 109, 178, 206, 215–16, 232–34. *See also* soul: and body
Bynum, Caroline Walker, 234

Caligula, 9
Catechumen, 239–40
Celsus, 226
change in lordships (or sonships), 37–38
Chanukkah, 180
childlessness (infertility): and death, 74, 111–13, 116, 118, 121–28, 130, 146, 191; and matriarchs, 63, 67, 137, 169
children: and death, 106, 112–13, 115, 117, 160; of God, 12, 25, 233; as memorial, 74,

76–77, 118; of men, 102; of the promise, 32, 37; role in society, 107; and Zion, 132–53

Childs, Brevard S., 186

christening, 237

cities of refuge, 92

Cohn, Robert L., 123

Conservative Judaism, 218

Cross, Frank Moore, 192

cult of the dead, 55–56

Cyril of Jerusalem, 237–41

David, King, 8, 43, 57, 59, 65, 66, 67, 108, 110, 114, 118, 138, 156, 157, 202

Day, John, 189–90, 199

Dead Sea Scrolls, 8, 29, 30

Decalogue, 166, 254–55

Didaché, 244–45

Divine Presence, 178, 214

Divine Warrior, 143, 192–96, 200

Di Vito, Robert, 109–10

docetic, 222, 223

Doubting Thomas, 22, 221

Easter, 1, 35, 239

Eden, Garden of, 76–77, 80, 81–102, 241, 246, 257

"Egyptian, the," 9

Einhorn, David, 216

El, 86

Eliezer, Rabbi, 153

Elijah, 19, 37, 98–101, 103–5, 129, 163–64, 168–69, 182

Elisha, 98–100, 121–22, 125–29, 144, 163–64, 168–69, 191. *See also* Shunammite woman

Enoch, 101–5, 168, 185

eschatological banquet, 14, 243

eternal life: Christian hope for, 42, 237, 257; in Hebrew Bible, 68, 79, 91, 106, 131, 152–53, 171, 176, 178–80, 197; in Judaism, 82, 216, 237, 246–54, 257. *See also* Divine Warrior

Eucharist, 243–46, 256–57

Eve, 116, 127, 241

Evil Inclination, 247–53, 257

exclusivism, 30, 34

Exodus, 9, 134, 150–51, 209, 227, 240–41

Exorcism, 237–38, 242

Ezra, Abraham ibn, 101

Ezekiel, 83–84, 101, 108, 146–55, 160, 166–69, 186, 227–29, 252

first fruits, 21, 24–25, 27, 175

Gates of Prayer, 217

Gehinnom, 76, 81, 174

Geiger, Abraham, 215–16

Gevurot, 201–4, 215–20

Gilgamesh, 43–44

Gilman, Neil, 215–18

Gnostic, 222–34

Gospel of Judas, 222

Gospel of Thomas, 221–22

grave: and cult of the dead, 60, 63–64; and death, 43, 45–48, 53, 71–72, 76, 121, 159, 204; resurrection from, xii, 1, 90, 157, 217, 238

Greenspoon, Leonard J., 194

Gregory of Nazianzus, 240, 242

Gregory of Nyssa, 238–39, 241

Hagar, 125

Halakhah, 215

Hallote, Rachel S., 56

Hannah, 63, 138, 140

heaven: Christian concept of, 6, 74, 76–77, 80, 81–82, 94, 119; kingdom of, 12, 14, 39, 41, 176; place from which Jesus descends, 27–28

heavenly banquet, 244

hell, 76, 81, 237, 241

Hezekiah, King, 65, 159

illness, 46–47, 145, 159, 163, 190, 202

immortality: nature of, 40, 101, 106, 109,

immortality (*continued*)
116, 233, 246; and relationship to resurrection, xii, 105, 153, 178, 204, 206; and
the Temple, 85, 89–91, 94–95, 97, 98,
104. *See also* soul: immortality or transmigration of
incorporation, 38, 56, 239
indwelling, 37
Irenaeus, 226–27, 228–29, 230, 231–34
Isaac, 32, 62–63, 66, 74, 107, 112–13, 115. *See
also* Abraham: and birth of Isaac;
aqedah/binding of Isaac
Isaianic Apocalypse, 186–88, 189–90, 198
Ishmael, 74, 113, 125–26
Ishtar, 60
Islam, 168, 213
Israel: church as, 29–30; House of, 160,
210; kingdom of, 132, 164; Land of, 84,
97, 98, 147, 150, 153, 199, 210, 247; people
of, 27, 31, 33, 47, 53, 55–59, 66, 70, 74,
75, 80, 90, 118, 120, 128–33, 139, 140, 146,
147, 149, 153, 165, 172, 177, 188, 191, 197,
199, 202, 224, 249, 252, 254–56; prophets
of, 19; religion and society in ancient,
61–65, 107–10, 115, 116, 132, 136, 148, 150,
152, 157, 160, 170, 175–76, 192, 199, 200,
209, 235; restoration of, 8–9, 12–16, 18–
21, 23, 25, 26, 28, 138, 143, 146, 151, 153–
57, 184, 186, 198, 228, 252; suffering of,
143, 144, 151

Jacob/Israel, 63–64, 66, 74–77, 107, 114–
16, 127, 134–36, 138–39
Jerusalem: destruction of, 97, 132; and "the
Egyptian," 9; restoration of, 5, 8, 19; siege
of, 56; as temple city, 80, 84–86, 90
Jesus of Nazareth: as apocalyptic prophet,
9–17; death of, 1; resurrection of, xii, 2–
4, 20–23, 24–27, 35–39, 219, 239; return
of, 27–29. *See also* messiah/messianic
king: Jesus as; Temple: and Jesus
Jezebel, 181

Joab, 43, 156
Job: children of, 74, 77–78, 80, 81, 111–13,
116, 134, 183; death of, 69, 71, 73, 111, 159;
restoration of, 183
Johnson, Aubrey, 109, 162
Johnston, Philip, 70
John the Baptizer, 8–10, 13
Jonah, 20, 26, 49, 96, 101
Joseph, 53, 74–78, 114–15, 127, 138–39, 151
Josephus, 7, 9, 11
Joshua, 9, 63, 99
Joshua ben Levi, Rabbi, 254–55
Josiah, King, 65
Judah: biblical character, 114, 116, 127; land
of, 14, 84, 86, 90, 108, 113, 132, 166, 228
Judah the Galilean, 9, 11
Judah the Patriarch, Rabbi, 208–10, 211
judgment: day of last, 20–21, 68, 79, 102,
105, 131, 152–53, 185, 188, 194, 256; divine,
7–8, 27, 52, 167, 181–82, 186–87, 204–5,
216, 242, 247; oracle of, 152

Kimchi, David, 112
Kohanim, 91, 210
Korah, 47, 117
Kugel, James L., 77
Kutsko, John F., 148–49

Last Supper, 243–45
Lazarus, 22, 242
Levirate marriage, 117–18
liberation, 12–13, 26, 39, 53, 91, 209–10, 223,
238–41
Lindbeck, George, 31
Lord's Prayer, 245–46
Luther, 36,

Maimonides, 213–15, 218–19
Manasseh, 167
Marcion, 223–24, 225
Martin, Dale B., 39–40
Martin, Troy W., 35–36

McKane, William, 117
messiah/messianic king: expectation of, 5, 8, 202, 214, 224; Jesus as, 3, 27, 29, 32, 35
midrash, 96–98, 208, 212, 248–49, 251–52, 255–56
mikveh, 10
Moses: death of, 64, 66, 69, 71–75, 78; and golden calf, 173; oracles to, 150–51; and Sinai, 254–55; and splitting of the Sea of Reeds, 99, 208, 10, 212, 240. See also Korah; Zelophehad
Mot, 103
mysticism, 37

Naaman, 164
Naboth, 181–83
Naomi, 63, 113–14, 116, 134, 138
Nag Hammadi, 222, 223
Name, 59–61, 64, 77, 80, 117–20, 156–57, 211–12
nature: and death, 41, 71, 124, 163, 165, 226; and prophets, 99, 123, 131; reason and, 230; restoration of, 8, 27, 34, 140, 146, 198. See also Divine Warrior
necromancy, 56–58, 62, 65, 70
Nicene Creed, 2
Nickelsburg, George W. E., 180–81

Odyssey, 62

participation, 36–39, 41, 56, 65, 197, 257
particularism, 30, 34, 256
Paul: and Baptism, 237, 240; and Eucharist, 244; and Resurrection, 2, 21–42, 175, 178, 221, 227, 232–34, 257. See also Adam: in Paul's thought
Pedersen, Johannes, 42, 43, 45
Pentateuch, xii, 16, 64, 115, 124, 150, 151
Pharaoh, 47, 53, 69, 128, 139, 151
Pharisees, 3, 16, 26–27, 32, 207–8
pit, 45–47, 49, 52–54, 71, 78, 95–96, 104, 159

Plato, 213
Prodigal son, 14–15

Qumran, 8, 33–34

Rachel, 137–40
Rashi, 101
Rav, 178
Rava, 253, 255
Rebecca, 127, 137
Reform Judaism, 215–16
Rehoboam, 63
restoration eschatology, 5, 7–8, 10, 13, 29
Rome, 4–5, 24, 30, 224, 226
Rosenberg, Ruth, 70–71, 77

Sabbath, 1, 118, 152, 179, 201, 250–51, 257
Sabbath and Festival Prayer Book, 218
sacrament, 237–39, 242
Sadducees, 3, 16, 183, 207–8, 212, 232
Samson, 63, 109
Samuel, 57–60, 64, 67, 138
Sanders, E. P., 5, 10, 13–14, 17–18, 19, 34, 36, 37
Satan, 237–41, 245, 248, 257
Saul, King, 57–59, 62, 64, 65
School of Rabbi Ishmael, 210, 211
Schweitzer, Albert, 9–10, 36–38
Second Isaiah, 132–36, 139–40, 143, 144, 149, 153
Seleucid, 180, 199
Seven Commandments of the Noahides, 250
Shekhinah. See Divine Presence
Shema, 250
Shemoneh Esreh. See Amidah
Sheol: deliverance from, 189, 191; and infertility, 111; nature of, 42–68, 75–80; and resurrection, 162–63, 169, 174, 255; and the Temple, 81, 94–96, 102–6, 120; who goes to, 69–75, 105–6, 119, 197

Shunammite woman, 72, 123–26, 128–29, 131, 134, 154–55, 164, 175–76
Siddur Sim Shalom, 218
Simai, Rabbi, 211–12
Simeon, 114, 127
Simon ben Laqish, Rabbi, 247–48, 250
sleep: and inactivity, 106, 171; and judgment, 197, 250; as metaphor for death, 6, 28, 72, 174–76, 201–5, 231
Solomon, 43, 63, 84–85
soul: and body, xii, 3, 109, 232, 233, 236, 241, 246, 254; cleansing of, 242; and Enoch, 102; and Gnosticism, 223, 228, 233; immortality or transmigration of, xii, 3, 41, 94, 105, 108, 120, 178, 206, 216, 230; as individual self, 119; and *nephesh*, 108–10, 176; and Platonic philosophy, 213–14; rabbinic conception of, 175, 204–6, 219
Stager, Lawrence E., 84–86
suffering servant, 177

Targum Onkelos, 102
Tefillah. See Amidah
Temple: and Caligula, 9; desecration of, 171, 180; destruction of, 132, 166, 175; as Garden of Eden, 81–106, 119, 120; and God's presence, 37; and Jesus, 17–20; personification of, 140–41; as place of devotion, 49, 80, 172, 209, 210; rebuilding of, 2, 5, 7, 8
ten tribes, restoration of, 5, 13–14, 20
Tertullian, 226–28, 229–34, 240
Testament of Moses, 7
Theodore of Mopsuestia, 242
Theudas, 9, 11

Thomas Community, 221–22
Tish'ah Be'Av, 97
Toorn, Karel van der, 60–61
Torah: as gift of God, 4; and legalism, 30; life of, 1, 75, 180, 237, 248–51, 256–57; liturgical division of, 124; Oral, 208; and resurrection, 161, 184, 206–12, 254–56; teaching of, 106; and Wisdom, 82, 247
Tree of Life, 82, 88–89, 97, 158, 194, 246–47, 257
Tromp, Nicholas J., 48, 54

Union Prayer Book, 216–17
universalism, 30, 207, 256

Valentinus, 223, 225

War Rule, 8
widowhood, 137, 144–45
Wisdom, 82, 158, 246–47, 257
"the wise," 171–73, 176–78, 180, 197, 247
wise woman of Tekoa, 156–57, 163
Wold, Donald J., 112
Wolff, Hans Walter, 109
World-to-Come, 89, 94, 106, 178, 206–7, 213–14, 250–54, 256–57
Wright, N. T., 21, 22, 26

Zelophehad, 117–18
Zion: Mount, 53, 90–91, 93, 243; personification of, 17, 51–52, 97–98, 140–45; place of, 12, 33, 120, 195, 252; theology of, 86, 90
Zoroastrianism, 147, 175, 199